D0745999

the truce

the truce

Lessons from an L.A. Gang War

Karen Umemoto

Cornell University Press
Ithaca and London

Copyright © 2006 by Cornell University

All rights reserved. Except for brief quotations in a review, this book, or parts thereof, must not be reproduced in any form without permission in writing from the publisher. For information, address Cornell University Press, Sage House, 512 East State Street, Ithaca, New York 14850.

First published 2006 by Cornell University Press
First printing, Cornell Paperbacks, 2006

Printed in the United States of America

Design by Scott Levine

Library of Congress Cataloging-in-Publication Data

Umemoto, Karen.
    The truce : lessons from an L.A. gang war / Karen
    Umemoto.
        p. cm.
    Includes bibliographical references and index.
    ISBN-13: 978-0-8014-4372-5 (cloth : alk. paper)
    ISBN-10: 0-8014-4372-5 (cloth : alk. paper)
    ISBN-13: 978-0-8014-7305-0 (pbk. : alk. paper)
    ISBN-10: 0-8014-7305-5 (pbk. : alk. paper)
    1. Gangs—California— Los Angeles.   2. Ethnic conflict
    —California—Los Angeles.   3. Venice (Los Angeles, Calif.)
    —Race relations.   4. Los Angeles (Calif.)—Race relations.
    I. Title.
    HV6439.U7L777   2006
    364.106′60979494—dc22   2006001821

Cornell University Press strives to use environmentally responsible suppliers and materials to the fullest extent possible in the publishing of its books. Such materials include vegetable-based, low-VOC inks and acid-free papers that are recycled, totally chlorine-free, or partly composed of nonwood fibers. For further information, visit our website at www.cornellpress.cornell.edu.

Cloth printing   10 9 8 7 6 5 4 3 2 1
Paperback printing   10 9 8 7 6 5 4 3 2 1

This is dedicated to those who have lost their lives and loved ones, in the hopes that tragic conflicts such as these will one day cease.

Contents

Tables, Figures, and Maps

Preface

Most of my formative years were spent alongside major Los Angeles freeway intersections. In a place like Los Angeles, freeways are the "railroad tracks" that separate neighborhoods from one another. Driving under the freeway underpass was often like passing through a gateway into another world. I grew up in Gardena, which at the time was one of the most racially and ethnically diverse cities in the country. To the south lay what was then the middle-class white suburb of Torrance. To the north and east were the then-predominantly African American communities of Watts and Compton. To the west were the predominantly white and middle-class coastal cities of Hermosa and Manhattan Beach. Gardena was what I called a "buffer zone" community separating the predominately white suburbs from communities of color.

If you grow up in a place like Gardena, you become well aware from a young age that people live very different lives, speak different languages, use different slang, practice different faiths and rituals, enjoy different standards of living, and have access to different privileges. You learn to "code switch," as they say in the field of bilingual education. But instead of switching from one language to another, you occasionally switch cultural and experiential world views. Even as a third-generation Japanese American raised in Los Angeles public schools, I would find my voice going up a whole octave and my head lowering about a foot immediately after walking onto the grounds of my grandmother's church. In other situations, I would not know how to really switch or wouldn't feel the need to, but I would know that words and actions did not mean the same thing to all people present. I was acutely aware of the differences in past experiences that could lead to radically different interpretations of the same phenomena and of the difficulty in explaining across world views.

Perhaps that's why I related strongly to the chorus on Warren G's hit rap album: "You don't see what I see, everyday as Warren G. You don't hear what

I hear, it's so hard to live through these years." Sometimes you wouldn't even try to explain yourself to someone, feeling overwhelmed with everything they would need to know in order to understand.

When I started interviewing people for my dissertation research on the racialized gang conflict in Venice, one of the first things that struck me was the vastly different stories about what was going on there. I did not know how I would be able to reconcile these different accounts to separate myth from fact. Upon reflection, it soon occurred to me that that was in fact the story—that there were different views of the same phenomena, which made it much more difficult to find an effective solution. The coexistence of "multiple realities" is the current reality of U.S. society, especially in such diverse cities as Los Angeles, especially as it had been through my childhood years.

For policymakers and residents alike, reconciling conflicting realities in the policymaking arena is perhaps one of the greatest challenges of the twenty-first century. This became even more apparent to me in the aftermath of the Los Angeles Police Department trial involving the beating of Rodney King and in the O. J. Simpson trial, as I witnessed the potential of such events to fragment society even further. On one hand, the generous media attention given to these two events produced a public forum for debate much in line with our notions of deliberative democracy. Yet due to the differences in perceptions and judgments based on the differences in beliefs and life experiences of viewers and participants, the chasms created by these jury decisions were enormous. In aired debates following the juries' decisions, we learned more about how different we are but little about the nature of our differences.

As the global village continues to shrink, our ability to traverse points of view becomes more critical. This is not an easy task, as I've learned from my own life experiences and from writing this book. To capture the many vantage points and to understand the interplay between them is almost impossible to do in a way that does justice to all voices. Mine is a modest attempt in this endeavor. I know full well that there will likely be disagreement with the depictions and characterizations of groups and their positions in the case of the gang conflict in Venice and Mar Vista, for no two people saw things the same way. I only hope that this effort and the framework I have tried to provide can help us become more aware of knowing what we do not know and what we need to understand in order to find collaborative solutions to the problems we face. I hope that this book contributes to overcoming the larger challenge we face—the challenge of creating more inclusive, democratic, and consensual decision-making processes in a world of multiple publics.

Acknowledgments

There are many people to whom I am indebted. First of all, I would like to acknowledge all the members of my family who supported me during my years of schooling through the completion of this book, especially my mother, whose unwavering support has been a source of strength, together with the spiritual guidance of my late aunt, May Niiyama, and my late grandmother, Fumi Niiyama. Much of this journey has benefited from the support and companionship of my husband, Brian, who deserves a diploma of his own for bearing with me, providing assistance both tangible and intangible. I am also indebted to his parents, my mother- and father-in-law, who have provided for me like their own daughter.

I am also grateful to my dissertation advisers, Martin Rein, Mel King, and Mary Waters, who provided thoughtful guidance during my years in the doctoral program, when most of the research for this book was conducted. Also contributing to my growth and understanding were my friends from a dissertation writing group, including Regina Freer, (the late) Hae Won Park, Curtiss Rooks, Edward Park, Tarry Hum, and Kristi Woods. There are other friends who have supported me in so many ways; while there are too many to name individually, I would like to give special thanks to Julie Noh, who made sure I enjoyed life all the while.

I would also like to acknowledge the many colleagues who have helped me over the years. In particular, Don Nakanishi and Paul Ong have served as mentors and advisers for well over two decades since my days as a graduate student at UCLA. More recently, I could not have completed the project without the support of my colleagues at the University of Hawai'i. Kem Lowry and the faculty at the Department of Urban and Regional Planning have been most supportive since my arrival, and I am thankful to them for allowing me the time and resources I had to devote to my research. The staff in the department, including Irene Takata, Susan Chow, Jodi Nakamura, and Allison Tai, went beyond the call of duty to help me, especially during a period of disability. I would especially like to thank Dana Singer for all of the things that she has done to keep my life and work in order. I am also fortunate to have friends and colleagues, Jon Okamura and Angela Oh, who along with Brian carefully read through the manuscript and offered helpful suggestions. I would also like to acknowledge Ron Wakabayashi and Robin Toma, who provided not only feedback to many formative ideas but also provided me with opportunities to work on issues and problems in the area of human relations and racial tension in Los Angeles. And right up to the last stages of book preparation, Krisna Suryanata was always patient and supportive, as a true friend would be.

I would also like to acknowledge the American Council of Learned Societies for the fellowship support in the fall of 2001, which allowed me to extend the scope of the preliminary study. The production of this book has been made possible under the tutelage of editors at Cornell University Press. I would like to thank Sheri Englund for her initial encouragement and shepherding of the manuscript as well as Peter Wissoker for providing guidance toward its completion. Also, Ho Nguyen of the Santa Monica Historical Society Museum was instrumental in locating the photos reproduced in this book from the Outlook Newspaper collection of their archives.

Last and most important, this book would not have been possible without the generosity of the many individuals living and working in Culver City, Mar Vista, and Venice who took the time to share their stories with me. I am especially grateful to Flora Chavez, Pearl White, and Melvyn Hayward Sr., who first encouraged me to learn about Oakwood—its history and its personalities, its virtues as well as its problems. They, along with many, many others, gave of their time, knowledge, and feelings about the events that were taking place at the time. Since most preferred to remain anonymous, I will not mention names here. It is my hope that I have treated their stories with integrity.

the truce

Chapter 1

Urban Conflict in Multicultural Cities

I heard that there had been some shootings and some Hispanics had been killed by some African Americans. And then vice versa. I didn't think so much of that initially, but then it seemed to trigger another shooting. And then it was happening during broad daylight. And then it happened in front of Venice High School. And then I realized that this was escalating and the people's fears were escalating, and then the anger was escalating. And I said, "You know. We could have our very own race war right, right here in our backyard."

—Father Beruman
St. Clements Church
Venice, California

As we enter a new millennium, racial conflict in the United States is a much more complex phenomenon than at any time in our history. This is due to the increasing diversity of our population, the multiple realities that differences of perception create, the multiple identities that individuals embrace, and the crosscutting cleavages created by factors such as class, ancestry, religion, gender, and ideology even among racially or ethnically homogeneous groups. Furthermore, not only do contemporary conflicts often involve more than two contesting parties, they also involve multiple issues and travel along shifting trajectories within which the centrality of race can ebb and flow. Small, localized conflicts can expand in scope, leading to wider conflict, division, and animosity among a broader population. Conflicts among non-white groups in the United States are commonly nested within larger conflicts and configurations of power involving both whites and nonwhites. As other scholars have recently noted, the more static, bi-polar, class-bound race relations paradigms that dominated the scholarly discourse over most of the past century are no longer adequate to explain the ever-shifting dynamics of contemporary urban social conflict.[1]

This book examines racialized gang conflict in order to illuminate the complexities of contemporary urban conflicts in multicultural environments and shows why processes of racial polarization often accompany such clashes. The episode of Los Angeles gang conflict covered in this book took place just minutes from the famed Venice boardwalk in a neighborhood known as Oakwood. It is one of the oldest neighborhoods in the region and one of the more racially integrated, with African American, Latino, European American, Asian American, and Native American families living side by side. Architecturally, Oakwood is equally diverse, with hundred-year-old bungalows situated alongside new condominiums—a sign of the gradual gentrification of the historic beachfront community. Fourteen HUD-subsidized apartment buildings are also scattered through the one-square-mile neighborhood of approximately 10,000 residents. The diversity of architectural styles also reflects the vast differences in income and wealth among neighbors who, though living in close proximity, lead lifestyles worlds apart.

Over a ten-month period in 1993–94, this neighborhood on the coastal edge of Los Angeles was the center of what was commonly referred to as a "gang war" that began in the nearby neighborhood of Mar Vista. The warfare left seventeen African American and Latino residents dead and over fifty injured. Most incidents occurred within a one-mile radius of its epicenter. Among the victims were gang members, individuals who were mistaken for gang members, former gang affiliates, youths targeted because of some physical feature, and bystanders unintentionally caught in the line of fire. Less than a third of those killed were actual members of the gangs themselves. For months, the Oakwood section of Venice looked like an abandoned town. Few ventured onto the sidewalks even in the middle of the day. The playground and park were deserted. Residents barricaded their porch windows with old furniture and wooden doors. Some bedded their children down in their bathtubs for protection through the night. The silence that plagued the neighborhood was uncharacteristic of this residential community, which normally bustled with life.

The gang war involved three different gangs: the Culver City Boys, the Venice-13 (the V-13), and the Venice Shoreline Crips (the Shoreline). Demographically, the Culver City Boys and the V-13 were comprised of Latino male youths and young adults. Most of them were U.S.-born but some were immigrants with ancestral ties mainly going back to Mexico, but a few members were of other ethnic backgrounds, including from Southeast Asia. The Shoreline was comprised of African American male youths and young adults, with a few exceptions including youths of mixed Latino-black racial ancestry. The gang war began as a battle between members of the Culver City Boys and members of the Shoreline Crips based in the housing development over turf and over the drug trade in the Mar Vista Gardens public housing project. It later shifted to the nearby Oakwood neighborhood of Venice, where tensions between individual members of the V-13 and the Shoreline Crips had also begun. Both locations were home to a high concentration of low-income residents surrounded by middle- and upper-income residential tracts. As such, they had become "drive-thru" drug distribution points attracting customers from Santa Monica to the north and Marina del Rey to the south, providing gang members an economic niche in an underground economy. While the initial fighting in the Mar Vista Gardens housing project was sparked by competition in the drug trade, the battle lines were also drawn in defense of honor and reputation.

Retaliatory Rounds of Violence and Escalation

Several months into the fighting, many in the Mar Vista and Oakwood neighborhoods feared the advent of racial targeting, particularly as it became evident that many of the victims had no direct gang affiliation. It was suspected that several African American victims known not to be gang members were killed by Latino gang members, and it was suspected that several older Latino men who were not gang-affiliated were killed by African American gang members or affiliates. In late November 1993, the headlines of the local daily *Outlook* and its free weekly, the *Venice-Marina News,* proclaimed, "Deadly Venice Gang War Turns to Race War." In characterizing the violence, the *Venice-Marina News* article read, "In the beginning, it appeared gang members were targeted, but in recent weeks targets were apparently chosen because of their race."[2] Controversy arose as to whether or not it was accurate to describe the conflict as a "race war." Public proclamations during the dispute that it was becoming a "race war" tended, if anything, to drive it in that direction.

Tensions along racial cleavages grew as the racially charged violence claimed more victims. African American and Latino residents who had freely interacted over many generations were suddenly faced with mounting animosities generated by the gang conflict. Some of the fear and frustration took the form of anger and resentment directed indiscriminately toward people identified with the "other" racial group. Social polarization throughout many segments of the neighborhood made it increasingly difficult to create meaningful dialogue across color lines, even among those who had felt themselves immune to racial bias. In the Oakwood section of Venice, where the battle became concentrated, racial divisions grew in a neighborhood that had been primarily divided along class and other cleavages resulting from the ongoing process of neighborhood gentrification.

The events that transpired changed the attitudes and relations in the community for years to follow. These types of episodes in a community's history can shape social relations and become part of the collective memories of residents who experience those times. Social bonds that were once strong can become severed or strained, at least for a significant period. Precious goods such as trust, loyalty, camaraderie, and community pride can be altered. Racial tensions that arose from the gang war affected both gang members and non–gang members alike. A year after the eventual truce was struck, one resident shared her recollections of the impact of the conflict on friends who were in different gangs and who had grown up together:

> All V-13s and Shorelines, they all went to school together, they hung out together, they even watched each other's backs, with all the other rival gangs. When V-13 and Culver City Boys [were fighting] and all those guys were comin' into Venice to shoot the V-13s, then the Shorelines was helpin' them. And the same for the Shorelines when the other gangs were comin' in to shoot the Shorelines, the V-13s was helpin' them. You know, that's just how close these kids were with each other. They spent nights over each other's house. They do everything, all the time together. . . .
>
> You know, even to this point, things haven't gotten back to where they're supposed to be. We don't have that. Venice will probably never, ever be the way it used to be. You know, I mean, too much has happened. Too many lives have been lost. Too much blood has been shed.[3]

Even seniors in the community shared stories describing some of their peers who expressed racial animosities in ways that were uncharacteristic for them. Youths in the schools that were not directly involved in the "war" confronted new definitions of manhood, as they openly asked, "Is that what it means to be a man?" Some engaged in their own scuffles on campus grounds as tensions filled the air.

While divisions grew, there were also many who worked across the racial divide in attempts to secure peace. Some risked their safety and reputation to communicate to those whom their peers viewed as being on the "other side" of the conflict, some openly and others more discreetly. Crisscrossing lines of alliances and divisions surrounding the racialized gang conflict were nested in a longer history marked by efforts to maintain Oakwood as one of the last affordable coastal neighborhoods in the region. Longtime civil rights activists continued their efforts to create bridges across racial divides, as they had during that earlier era. During the gang war, for example, well-known community advocate Pearl White tried to help affected families find the resources they needed:

> We worked with lawyers for both sides and a lot of people didn't even know that. I got lawyers for the Mexicans and the blacks. . . . So, I always had a positive relation with both groups.[4]

This is one of many examples of individuals extending their hands across color lines in efforts to help one another and reach for peace.

Meanwhile, the incessant violence drove numerous families to leave the neighborhood. This fueled suspicions among many longtime community advocates that the violence was part of a conspiracy between the police and real estate speculators, who would benefit from the exodus of low-income residents and the completion of the gentrification process. Others interpreted the problem differently. Differences in interpretations of events and interventions complicated the already intricate social dynamics and confounded efforts to intervene.

This book pays particular attention to a crucial feature of conflict among diverse constituencies: the existence of "multiple realities" or differences between groups and individuals in how they see the world around them and experience life events. These differences in life experiences and positionalities affect both the social dynamics of conflict and the responses to various efforts to address the problem. The beachfront neighborhood of Venice serves as an instructive microcosm for the study of this form of social conflict, as this westernmost edge of the Los Angeles metropolis has captured a wide swathe of demographic and socioeconomic diversity that presages that of many other neighborhoods across the nation. This book explains how race can ebb and flow as one of several salient boundaries of division and distinction in a conflict and how race can become the central and most salient boundary along which social divisions are drawn in a community that previously may have been defined primarily (though certainly not exclusively) along other sets of boundaries. And most importantly, it examines the arsenal of policy and programmatic tools used to address the problem of gang violence and the results of such interventions.

The central concern of this book is the relatively quick process through which rather harmonious social relations across racial boundaries are overcome by racial tensions and distancing, which set in place a more fractured pattern of race relations. One of the most disturbing and ominous characteristics of this gang war was the way in which the conflict escalated in intensity and expanded in scope, leading to the eventual distancing and racial polarization across many segments of the community at large among two historically disenfranchised populations—African Americans and Latinos. The book reveals the various macro-forces and micro-social processes that pulled in the direction of racial polarization as well as cooperation as it examines the ebb and flow of race as a salient social boundary along which tensions rose and later subsided.

I suggest that in order to understand the complexity of contemporary racial and ethnic conflict, we do best by studying its "morphology." I refer to the "morphology of conflict" as an analytical approach that examines the transformation of conflict over time. This includes the ebb and flow of racial and other lines of division in the evolution of conflict as well as the substance and forms of contestation as they alter over the course of interaction. It focuses on the ways in which people construct and contest the meaning of acts and events that are situated in a historical context and grounded in certain empirical realities of time and place. This approach seeks to examine *interests and actions* as well as *interpretations of meanings and motives* between or among participants and observers.[5] This allows us to understand the process of meaning-making as it shapes the scope and trajectory of conflict. It enables us to understand how actions, decisions, and events can take on racially charged meanings that can lead to antagonism and polarization as conflicts gain greater symbolism. It also enables us to understand how racial animosities and divisions may ebb under certain conditions. It is my hope that an approach that takes account of the role of meaning and social identity can lead us to more effective solutions in our attempts to intervene in conflicts so that we can minimize the reification of racial divisions and unnecessary hardships felt by all of the affected parties. The understanding we gain may enable us to design better policies and practices that can transform conflicted situations into opportunities to work toward more collaborative solutions to social problems we mutually face.

Race and Social Conflict in the New Millennium

This book, covering a fairly extreme case of racialized gang conflict, offers a close examination of four important aspects of urban conflict in post–civil rights America. First, it demonstrates *the contested nature of conflict itself.* For the way that individuals define a conflict, the divisions that emerge based on the varying definitions of a conflict, and the course of action that groups decide to take given their respective interpretations of a situation are important features of conflict under constant deliberation. In this case, the primary social cleavage shifted from individuals to families and from there to gangs, later edging toward a racial divide, before it eventually notched back down to gang boundaries over the evolution of the conflict. Each shift represented a redefinition of the problem and a realignment of groups based on the shifting salience of identity group boundaries in relation to the problem as it was redefined. Individuals and groups engage in verbal or discursive as well as physical acts to define the problem as they perceive it in order to pursue specific goals. The outcomes of these contests shape the trajectory of conflicts as well as their scope and intensity.

Second, the book illustrates *the ebb and flow of race as an axis of division relative to other identity boundaries* along which conflicts could potentially travel. The treatment of the case highlights the fact that race as a social construction, while a central identity for many urban residents, is one of multiple identities that individuals may deem important and that may serve as a line of cleavage. Other identities based on dimensions of difference such as gender, gang affiliation, residential neighborhood, home ownership, income level, religion, sexual orientation, occupation, civic organization, citizenship, and language indeed coexist, though with varying relevance, salience, and interdependence, and overlap in relationship to race. Examining the shifting lines of cleavage and the process of racialization allows us to avoid viewing race or any identity boundary as a static or sole boundary defining group formation in urban spaces characterized by increasing dimensions of difference.

Third, the book reveals *the role of contemporary institutions in the reproduction or realignment of racial divisions.* In the case of gang-related conflict, I examine the dominant role that law enforcement and criminal justice institutions play in the interface between government and community residents in distressed urban neighborhoods. This dominance amplifies the role that these institutions play (along with the mass media) in influencing race relations. The book illustrates how institutions shape intergroup relations in at least three ways: (a) through the construction of racial meanings embedded in and affecting the design of policies and practices; (b) in real or perceived differentiation of practices toward various racial groups; and (c) by structuring interactions between groups, as in the practice of racial segregation in prisons.

Fourth, the book highlights *the nested relationship between two roughly defined types of conflict: intra-class, inter-minority conflict* and *inter-class, minority-white conflict.* In multiracial neighborhoods, there are different types of conflict over different issues among different groups of people, all occurring simultaneously. At one moment, class can trump race as the salient identity boundary along which conflicts occur, but this line of division can shift as race becomes a relatively more salient line of division. The book illustrates the nested relationship of inter-minority group conflict within a setting marked by conflict between higher-income white residents and low-income nonwhite residents, as wealthier newcomers who were mainly white displaced lower-income families, most of whom were African American and Latino. The tensions surrounding neighborhood gentrification not only served as a backdrop for the racialized gang war, it also directly affected the interpretive narratives of the war itself. The conflicts surrounding gentrification also established alliances and networks that were later activated during the gang conflict.

Of course, conflict in itself is not necessarily always negative; a great deal of social progress has been a direct outcome of conflict. In fact, some of the social conflicts in the 1980s and 1990s that occurred in large metropolitan cities could be viewed as manifestations of community-based efforts among historically disenfranchised groups to seek social justice, much like the social struggles during the civil rights movement of the 1960s (Kim 2000). This book, however, is concerned with racial conflicts that are not necessarily driven by a broad or explicit social justice agenda. It looks at conflicts arising at the neighborhood level that hinder the long-term well-being of communities that would benefit from collaboration toward larger goals of democracy, economic opportunity, and political inclusion. In particular, my concern is focused on racial conflicts that occur between equally disenfranchised communities and populations, which lead to further social distancing, antagonism, and political and economic marginalization.

Significance of the Gang War

One of the most serious forms of urban racial conflict falls among youths in disenfranchised neighborhoods. Many cases involve youth gangs, whether white supremacist–oriented youth gangs or traditional street gangs (Pinderhughes 1997). This problem has become particularly acute in California, where racially organized prison gangs in state correctional facilities have clashed in persistent and highly publicized race riots. During the 1980s and 1990s, Los Angeles was particularly affected by racial conflicts involving gang-affiliated youths. Areas of Los Angeles County, for example, including Azusa, Hawaiian Gardens, Watts, Harbor Gateway, Sunland, Palmdale, and Lancaster, have been sites of repeated racially motivated hate crimes involving youths and youth gangs (Umemoto 1999). Repeated rounds of racial violence have led to racial polarization and broader racial tensions in these neighborhoods. These conflicts and the simmering racial animosities that surround them continually challenge the will and ingenuity of the public officials, law enforcement agencies, community and human relations organizations, and other institutions that are called upon to respond, not to mention the residents themselves.

The Mar Vista and Venice "gang wars" of 1993–94 marked the peak period of gang violence in the history of Los Angeles County and in the recent history of the United States.[6] Gang violence reached epidemic proportions in many urban centers of the United States in the mid-1990s. Los Angeles County was referred to as the "capitol" of gang violence, registering 803 gang-related homicides in 1992, peaking at 807 in 1995.[7] Gang-related violence had become more serious due to several factors, including easy access to lethal firearms, the use of violence to protect underground economic activities, the effects of consumer culture feeding materialism, aspects of youth culture glorifying violence, the effects of imprisonment on street and prison gangs, and the limited opportunities that many marginalized youths experience (Hagedorn 1998). Gangs had also grown in size, which had a major influence on "street subculture" and activities spanning the social and recreational to the cultural and economic. Especially vulnerable to gang involvement were adolescent young men who had experienced personal or family trauma, marginalization, or victimization and who were in search of social support, protection, camaraderie, and fulfillment of a definition of manhood they did not find elsewhere (Vigil 1988, 2003). Studies have shown that the most aggressive acts of violence are disproportionately committed by males between the ages of 14 and 18 years as they face the uncertainties and challenges of adolescence (Hirschi and Gottfredson 1983; Gottfredson and Hirschi 1990; Zimring 1996).

The causes and nature of urban gang violence are extremely complex. Scholars and practitioners have offered varying explanations. Vigil (2003) described two of the more dominant views in the literature. One explains the problem as emanating from a "subculture of violence" where the values and norms of the street embrace aggressive, violent behavior. From this perspective, violent behavior is part of gang life and is often required in order to maintain the respect of peers and avoid losing one's honor and reputation (Cohen and Short 1958; Miller 1958; Cloward and Ohlin 1960; Wolfgang and Ferracuti 1967; Horowitz 1983). Others see violence less as a cultural phenomenon than as an outgrowth of the "routine activities" that gang members engage in, such as hanging out with delinquent peers in high-crime neighborhoods with little supervision from capable guardians. According to this view, the day-to-day circumstances increase the probability of becoming involved in violent encounters and criminal activity (Felson and Cohen 1980; Felson 1987; Kennedy and Baron 1993). Vigil argues that neither alone is sufficient to explain youth participation in gang violence and suggests a more holistic, interactive model he refers to as a "multiple marginality" approach that includes these concepts but also integrates macro-processes such as the economic structures of opportunity (or lack thereof) as well as micro-social processes such as social dynamics within groups that encourage risky behavior. According to Vigil, "Gang violence necessitates examining many factors, such as neighborhood effects, poverty, culture conflict and sociocultural marginalization, and social control, among other gang dynamics" (230).

When gang members engage in violent acts, especially those that involve rival gangs, retaliation often occurs. A succession of retaliatory acts can lead to the intensification and severity of violence. The scope of the target population that is victimized in the escalating conflict can expand. Decker (1996) describes this process as one of "contagion," borrowing the term from Loftin (1984). Contagion occurs when there is a spatial concentration of assaultive violence, reciprocal violence, and escalations in assaultive violence. The escalating spiral is also energized when gangs resort to more sophisticated weapons and when they are able to recruit others to join the fray, appealing to their need for self-defense and mutual protection in the midst of battle. In the course of conflict, bonds of unity within each respective gang can strengthen, often deepening loyalties and the commitment to avenge harm done to any one member.

The outbreak of gang violence in Venice conforms to this description of contagion. However, this case had an added dimension in that the scope of violence extended along racial boundaries beyond gang boundaries. The interracial nature of the gang conflict was significant in that it indicated a momentary shift in the character of regional gang conflict. Historically, gang conflict had been intra-racial, that is, between gangs that were mainly homogeneous in racial composition. There were only sporadic gang fights between African American, Latino, Asian, and white gangs through most of the 1980s. A change had begun to occur during the late 1980s and early 1990s that also coincided with economic and demographic shifts discussed further in the following chapter. It was during this period that city officials and gang intervention organizations in Los Angeles began reporting an increase in interracial gang conflict on the streets, though they were not completely absent before then.[8] Interracial gang violence on the streets also mirrored the increase in interracial violence among California inmates within the correctional system. Numerous race riots in the prison system erupted, particularly in the late 1980s and early 1990s (Morain 1996). Outbreaks of racial violence led to the institution of segregation within many of the state's prisons, a practice that was ruled unconstitutional by the U.S. Supreme Court over a decade later.

Venice's role in the larger economy brought wider scrutiny to the gang war among a range of public officials and government agencies than to gang violence elsewhere in the city. The Venice boardwalk was a major visitor destination and played a critical role in the regional tourism economy. Tourism had already been crippled by the civil unrest of 1992 following the acquittal of Los Angeles police officers in the beating of Rodney King. Business leaders and elected officials saw the protection of the Venice boardwalk, deemed the second most frequented tourist destination in the region, as critical to the rebound of the region. While gang violence throughout the region heralded the resources of many government agencies, this particular conflict in Venice attracted even greater attention, with an onslaught of resources from local, state, and federal agencies. The ability of government agencies and communities to control the spread of interracial gang violence would serve as an indication of the preparedness of the city to address the larger social problem of racial tensions among youths that was emerging in other forms as well, such as racial confrontations in the public schools.

The public attention given to this outbreak was not only a result of its location in Venice. It was also due to the fact that the image of Venice in the regional landscape was evoked to give the war greater symbolic meaning. Gang violence had persisted in lower-income minority communities such as the MacArthur Park district, South Central, San Pedro, Long Beach, and East Los Angeles in years past. But the eruption of similar problems in Venice struck a chord among a wider segment of middle-class residents who viewed Venice as somehow immune to such problems historically restricted to the "inner city."[9] Venice was a place many throughout the region viewed as representing the essence and character of Los Angeles. Writer and professor Kevin Starr described the angst that gripped the Westside's broad middle class, as he explained in a *Los Angeles Times* opinion piece: "What began as a power struggle over crack-cocaine sales has escalated into something that should send a chill down the spine of every Angeleno: The Venice killings threaten the identity of Los Angeles as a city." The "fear and terror would do violence to the very nature of Los Angeles," and what was underway was "a struggle for the soul of Los Angeles itself" (Starr 1994).

The racialized gang conflict presented a new challenge for the law enforcement agencies, community organizations, and concerned individuals who responded to the problem. A number of recent events had sown divisions along racial cleavages: conflict over the proliferation of liquor stores in South Central in which the media featured African American residents and Korean merchants as protagonists, the Los Angeles Police Department officers' beating of motorist Rodney King and the subsequent verdict and outbreak of mass civil unrest, public discourse over the principles and implementation of affirmative action, and heated debates over immigration policy and multilingualism, among others. This was taking place in a period of increased globalization, persistent economic recession, and shrinking public coffers, all of which intensified competition for jobs and services. The rise of "identity politics" in the form of voter registration and electoral campaigns also raised issues of rights and representation in a competitive arena among communities historically underrepresented in public office. The interracial character of the gang war tended to overlap with other arenas of social tension, making it difficult to isolate the effects of the war and the effects of official interventions in response to it from the larger map of social discord.

A full suite of law enforcement agencies took action in response to the war. They included the Los Angeles Police Department (LAPD), the Office of the City Attorney, the Office of the County Attorney, the County Probation Department, the State Office of Corrections, the Federal Bureau of Investigation (FBI), and the Federal Bureau of Alcohol, Tobacco, and Firearms (ATF). The most visible law enforcement presence among them was the LAPD, which conducted several major operations in an effort to suppress the violence.

Non–law enforcement government agencies and officials also came to the scene: City Councilwoman Ruth Galanter and her staff, several state legislative aides, U.S. Department of Justice community relations officers, and the staff of the Los Angeles City and Los Angeles County Human Relations Commissions as well as the City Recreation and Parks Department. Among residents and community-based organizations, there were many groups and individuals that worked to find a path toward peace. Church leaders, several former and active gang members, community activists, gang prevention workers, and others pursued various strategies to nudge the warring gangs toward a truce.

After ten months of violence and many frustrated attempts to quell it, a gang truce was struck between two of the three gangs involved. This brought a temporary period of relative peace. This period of events lasting through the summer of 1994 did not settle the conflict with the third gang, nor could it undo the lost lives and injuries that had taken an immeasurable toll on families. Nor was the road to truce an easy one. Continued community and government efforts were made to maintain peace. There were many social relationships left to rebuild. Many sources of conflict like economic competition and tensions in the prisons still remained. So too did many of the socioeconomic and political conditions that had contributed to the problem, such as poverty, unemployment, housing and job discrimination, and the proliferation of firearms. These persistent problems continue to raise skepticism over the efficacy of the policies and practices intended to achieve more lasting solutions to the problem of youth violence and racial tension.

Research Methodology

Ethnographic community case studies are useful in examining the dialectical and iterative processes that are involved in identity formation and the creation of social institutions while being attentive to group interaction and differences in interpretation. As Pinderhughes (1997) writes,

> Communities are the locations and institutions where racial ideologies crystallize. Racial beliefs are community constructions, and racial actions are community activities. . . . The community is the nexus where the societal forces combine with the individual factors to influence ethnic and racial attitudes and behavior. (8)

The advantages of city- and community-level case studies are underscored by Bollens (1998), who argues that cities are not "simple reflectors of larger societal tensions and dynamics, but rather as capable through their physical and political qualities to exert independent effects on ethnic tensions, conflict and violence" (189). Most significantly, there seems to be an emerging approach in recent case studies that I call "grounded interpretation," in which scholars pay attention to the interpretation of voices, texts, and physical acts and gestures in the study of intergroup dynamics, while remaining mindful of the physical and material realities within which and toward which people make meaning of life events (Waters 1992; Freer 1994; Umemoto 1994; Park 1995; Pinderhughes 1997; Romer et al. 1997; Bollens 1998; Kim 2000).

This work is based on two years of ethnographic research, mainly conducted during and immediately following the gang war that subsided in 1994. Much of the ethnographic research was conducted through participant observation, as I found myself joining activities organized by community organizations working to address the problem. As I became more familiar with the surrounding dynamics, I began to interview various individuals who could provide their interpretation of what was happening from different vantage points. Interview data were gathered through formal semi-structured discussions with residents, ministers, political representatives, gang intervention workers, gang members, police officers, district attorneys, business leaders, and leaders of community organizations. These formal interviews of one to three hours each were conducted with fifty-eight individuals. I also used archival sources such as newspaper articles, historical books, and various types of government records to gather information about the community and the events that had taken place.

The examination of "multiple realities" or different epistemic lenses did not begin until I had conducted a number of interviews, after I found that no two people had seen the events the same way. That the first cross section of interviewees had such different interpretations of the major events in the unfolding drama prompted a rethinking of the original study. The basic question changed from "What was happening here?" to "How can we best understand what is happening here?" Once in the field, I soon found myself adjusting my approach to the research, focusing not only on understanding what may have factually taken place but also on understanding how different groups and individuals experienced and interpreted what had taken place—what happened and why from their particular vantage point and lens.

One way in which I examined group differences was through the study of "frames." Frames can be defined as socially constructed lenses through which individuals or groups view the world.[10] The study of frames was useful in identifying differing points of view. Frames can be used to sort out the selection of facts, the establishment of truths, the definition of self and other, and the lenses through which interpretations are made and acted upon (Gamson and Modigliani 1989; Schön and Rein 1994).[11]

I began field research in October 1993, approximately one month into the war after reading news accounts in the local weekly about incidents in the Mar Vista Gardens public housing development (incidents leading up to the war had taken place in Oakwood earlier that year and in Mar Vista Gardens over the previous year). I started attending meetings attended by residents and community organizations actively seeking avenues to reclaim peace and working to provide gang members alternatives to that lifestyle. Joining these and other efforts—peace marches, community gatherings, meetings with government agencies—allowed me to understand better the sentiments and viewpoints of the various groups and individuals who were working for a peaceful outcome, and it allowed me to reciprocate in some way for the generosity with which so many individuals shared their thoughts and feelings. In interviewing individuals across the social, demographic, occupational, organizational, and political spectrum, I tried to capture the breadth of roles, experiences, interest groups, and identities surrounding the conflict. Though I certainly did not capture them all, the sample includes the main viewpoints and positions made publicly explicit in the period under study.[12]

My own personal background and experiences shaped my own lens and vantage point. I was born and raised in Los Angeles and lived in different parts of the city and county over the years, including the South Bay, Boyle Heights, and the Westside. I spent most of my childhood in Gardena, which is located south of Watts and west of Compton and was one of the most racially diverse neighborhoods in the region, much like Venice. I am a product of the Los Angeles public school system as well as the California state university system. I lived in Culver City at the time of the study, not too far from the housing project where the conflict initially broke out. As a third-generation Japanese American female, I was offered some degree of "neutrality," being identified not as Caucasian, Latino, African American, or male in the racialized and gendered context of the situation. At the same time, I was always aware that my lack of shared background also posed limitations as to what I was able to share or understand. Awareness of these limitations helped to temper programmed inclinations to analyze situations based on a priori assumptions or settle on judgments based on my own positionality. That said, I am sure I will discover omissions and errors I have made with the assistance of those who read this book.

What I present here is a narrative that pieces together stories told to me and my own observations, along with "facts" collected from a variety of sources. They are sifted through my own framework of analysis in an attempt to capture the interplay between multiple realities simultaneously lived. In doing so, I hope to underscore the need to understand the world from many different vantage points in order to find better solutions and to avoid unintended consequences of our actions. I begin with an explanation of this framework followed by an orientation to Venice, California, told to uncover the historic foundations from which social differences and disparate lenses of interpretation had arisen. I describe the conditions out of which the gang war emerged and proceed to chronicle its escalation. It is significant to note here that there were two very different approaches among law enforcement and related public agencies that spearheaded attempts to quell the violence. I detail these two approaches in separate chapters. At the close, I reflect upon the lessons we can draw from this tragic episode for those of us concerned about youth and gang violence generally as well as policy makers and institutions that are routinely called upon to respond. The good news is that we can do better. This book is part of the ongoing dialogue as to how.

Chapter 2

Understanding the Morphology of Conflict

Like other types of violent conflict, gang conflict goes through stages of escalation and decline. Violence can spread, involving more and more people and intensifying in frequency and force. Conversely, conflicts can ease, as the scope of participation narrows and the level of intensity lessens. Also, conflict can spread along one trajectory over another, along ethnic or racial lines over class or geographic boundaries, for example. How can we better understand the escalation or decline of violence and the reasons they take the specific trajectories they do? In the case of simmering tensions on the western edge of Los Angeles, what were the factors that led to the widening of the scope of conflict, which began as spats between individuals and then eventually expanded to involve families and then whole gangs? How did the conflict become racialized, polarizing many in the community along color lines in this place where people of many different backgrounds had built strong social and family bonds over several generations? And how was a path to a truce paved, at least for two of the three gangs involved?

There are many studies of gang violence and of racial and ethnic conflict in the United States that have explored the causes and dynamics of conflict. Here, we focus specifically on the evolutionary course of conflict over an episode's duration and the reasons that conflicts take the particular form and trajectory they do, given alternative paths a conflict may potentially travel. While a single case is not enough to capture the breadth of variation in the types of gang rivalries that occur or the varied circumstances under which gang conflicts erupt, a closer examination of the evolution of a gang war can reveal the macro-environments and micro-processes that shape the form and direction of conflict as well as the points at which interventions can either aggravate or ameliorate intergroup tensions.

In order to capture the dynamism and complexity of contemporary racial conflict, I find it useful to conceptualize conflict in terms of its "morphology."

The morphology of conflict refers to the numerous transformations in a conflict's *perceived substance, lines of division,* and *characteristics.* The analogy of "morphing" is useful to describe the incremental, iterative, and seemingly seamless transformation of conflict from one defined along one salient set of group boundaries and points of contestation to a revised set of boundaries and issues. The notion encourages a more subtle observation of the forces that pull people apart and those that bring them together, including tensions that exist within seemingly stable groups. As an interdisciplinary framework, the morphology of conflict pays attention to both macro-forces, such as poverty or legal structures, and micro-processes, such as interpersonal relations, that can contribute to group formation and intergroup dynamics. Most important, it incorporates the study of multiple interpretations—different ways of looking at the world—that mediate group interaction and often complicate the problem at hand.

This approach to the study of racial conflict emphasizes the ways in which conflicts can acquire different meanings to different people and how those meanings can change over time. Aggressive or defensive actions may be taken "for the sake of the family," "in the name of the gang," "to uphold the race," or "for the benefit of the community." The meanings attached to actions can serve as explanatory justifications or as causes to mobilize others in support of one's efforts. Regardless of the call, others can read actions in ways not intended. Depending on the meaning that is given to actions and depending on how actions are "read" by others, they can either lead to greater escalation or de-escalation. Meanings given to words or actions shape the trajectory of division, whether along racial or other potential cleavages. As a primary line of division, race or any other identity marker for that reason can ebb and flow, as loyalties may also be pulled along other related but distinct social boundaries such as class, gender, or gang—the boundaries of which are to varying degrees intertwined with others.

This approach is consistent with recent scholarship on racial or ethnic conflict in the United States, which can be characterized by the following features: (1) a recognition of the multiracial and multi-ethnic character of race relations; (2) an emphasis on situational conflict with a focus on neighborhood and community-based case studies; (3) an attempt to integrate social, cultural, interpretive, and structural explanations of racial and ethnic conflict; (4) increased attention to discursive processes and the construction of racial meanings; and (5) a wider recognition of multiple realities based on the different lenses and meanings assigned to group experiences. This approach also follows other studies that recognize that incidents of conflict often coexist alongside acts of cooperation and that webs of tension pull people apart at the same time as they draw others closer together. In a study of ethnic and racial conflict and violence in New York City, for example, Pinderhughes (1997) examined cases of violence among various youth groups to explore how structural factors, historical context, political and social interplays, and attitudes and behavior all converged at the community level to produce racial tension as well as tolerance.

This book chronicles the morphology of a gang conflict and looks more specifically at its "racialization" and its later "deracialization." "Racialization" refers to the elevation of racial meanings that may come to dominate the interpretations and perceptions of a controversy. It includes the attribution or emphasis of race as a defining feature in the expression of motives, interests, and rationales for actions by various participants.[1] This often results in a widening divide along racially defined boundaries relative to other potential lines of cleavage, such as class or gender, that can extend beyond the parties directly involved in a controversy, in this case gangs. By branding rationales, motives, and interests with "racial" labels, contestants as well as observers can begin to view other groups through a color-contrasted lens. Race can eventually become the characteristic feature of a conflict in the public eye, regardless of the more complicated set of issues at the crux of the dispute.

There have been many conflicts in the United States that have been branded as "racial" despite the existence of much more intricate details. Claire Kim (2000), for example, illustrated how the tensions between a group of Korean grocers and African American residents in New York City were framed in public discourse as a "Black-Korean conflict" when the organizers of the protests, who were mainly but not exclusively African and African American, were struggling to portray their actions *not* as anti-Korean but as part of a larger set of activities and a broader movement for economic and social justice. But the actions of various actors, including media and political aspirers, attached racially charged, symbolic meanings to the conflict, which raised the stakes along racial boundaries and led to heightened racial tensions. Oppositional identities grew along racial trajectories, overshadowing other lines of division and discouraging the ties of solidarity that did exist across racial divides. While this controversy had the potential to incite division along other social boundaries such as class or political stance, the political and media discourse or "framing" tended to simplify the complex bundle of issues as mainly one of racial competition and resentment, thereby undermining, at least in this instance, the social justice goals that activists were seeking.

A chronicle of the gang conflict in Los Angeles illuminates how race as a constructed identity can be mobilized in conflicts and how racial boundaries can come to overshadow coexisting and closely related axes of division, such as that of class, gang, or family. When this happens, adversaries can attribute motives or interests to whole racial groups rather than to a more specific group or subset, such as a gang or family, and actions that may once have been limited to that smaller group may begin to spill over to a larger one. Distinctions between individuals or families can fade, as color lines become the prominent marker between friend and foe, leading to the victimization of many people who have no relation to any of the gangs originally party to the conflict. Conversely, it shows how race can be downplayed as a feature of conflict so that issues and alignments can be rearticulated in efforts to de-escalate a conflict by narrowing its scope.

By examining the morphology of conflict, we can find more meaningful answers to questions such as: How do groups construct oppositional identities in which racial boundaries become most salient? How do changing definitions of the problem affect group formation and their alignments? How do differences among groups in the interpretation of words and actions complicate conflicts? How do individuals and institutions assign racial meanings to motives and actions in conflict? What techniques of power do individuals and institutions use to aid or abet such trajectories of conflict? And how can residents and public and private sector agencies intervene in such a way that does not exacerbate racial antagonisms but rather helps reduce them?

The Metaphor of Morphing

The metaphor of "morphing" is borrowed from visual arts technology used in popular media to transform live action images of figures or objects seamlessly from one "look" to another. The term was coined with the 1992 debut of Michael Jackson's music video "Black or White" and became a popular term to describe the special effects now commonly used in popular films in which characters transform from one figure to another. When morphing one image into another, caricaturing is used to systematically distort an image away from an existing image and toward a second image of a similar type of object. Important features of the existing image are aligned with the following image. The existing image then warps into a common set of features in the following image. In the act of warping, pixels that fall between the key points used to align two images are interpolated and animation techniques are used to move from one image to the next (Rhodes, Brennan, and Carey 1987; Maruo and Kubovy 1992; Benson and Perrett 1993). Morphing is a technique used to transform images in a way that is seemingly natural and uninterrupted. Determining a close correspondence between the existing image and a following image is important to maintain a level of continuity, hence believability, in the minds of viewers.

In applying the metaphor of media morphing to the problem of social conflict, the transformation of subjects or scenes is analogous to the transformation in the boundaries and substance of conflict. That is, a conflict can "morph" from one focal issue to another and from one set of stakeholders to a new configuration of groups. The process of "warping" is analogous to the process of interpretation. Real events or actions take place, which are then subject to interpretation. The process of interpretation shapes the way the events or actions are seen. The interpretive process links a series of events together in narrative explanation, which not only gives meaning to past events but also sets the stage to view the next series of events.

Conflict morphing takes place both in real time as well as retrospectively, just as caricaturing can alter the look of a succeeding image even as it creates connections over a series of historical snapshots. Treatments of past images can affect the trajectory of future events by defining the scope of possibilities that are considered for the future, based on a particular interpretation of what has taken place thus far. In other words, there is a mutually influential relationship between events and interpretations of them. Past events are woven together in interpretive narratives (often contested and debated) that shape how actors see, experience, and act upon the next event or series of events, and so forth.[2]

The idea of morphing is based on the underlying premise that the construction of social meaning takes place *in step with* the changing experiences of actors themselves. Experience, interpretation, and action constitute an intertwined social process in which one feeds upon another in blended iteration. In the social interplay of events, the interpretative process is often socially contested and openly debated, steeped in the tangle of individual and group interests, values, motives, goals, and aspirations. Especially when there are distinct cultural groups, there are often differences in epistemologies or "ways of knowing" that designate what can be known, whose knowledge commands legitimacy, what constitutes evidence, and what are acceptable responses given what becomes known. This takes place within a historical context based on past events as well as recollections of that past.

When one image morphs into the next, the second image cannot stray too far from the first in order to preserve a sense of continuity in the scene of change. Similarly, interpretations of events among individuals cannot stray too far from the perceived realities that one may experience or witness in an event. However, one can promote an interpretation that can certainly embellish, distort, change, or "spin" the perceived meanings of actions as the actors intended them. Compelling stories can gracefully tie together events and persuade groups to embrace a set of causal explanations and strategies for joint action. In conflict-ridden settings, spun narratives can give events an added momentum that can guide a conflict along a tracked trajectory. Alternatively, actions can lead to totally unanticipated consequences due to misinterpretations of intentions or misplaced behavioral assumptions, which either reinforce or change its trajectory.

This approach shares a set of basic premises initially outlined by symbolic interaction theorists (Blumer 1969). The first premise is that individuals act toward things based on the meanings that those things have to them. Second, the meaning of things is derived or emerges from social interaction between networks or groups of individuals. And third, it is through an interpretative process that meanings are constructed as one deals with the things that one encounters. The formation of joint action is a social process based upon interpretations of a problem or situation. As Herbert Blumer (1969) stated:

A network or an institution does not function automatically because of some inner dynamics or system requirements; it functions because people at different points do something, and *what they do is a result of how they define the situation in which they are called on to act.* (emphasis added)

He also emphasized that any "new form of joint actions always emerges out of and is connected with a context of previous joint action" (20). In this sense, interpretations are always situation-specific and nested within an accumulation of historical referents.

This is not to say that "material" interests such as control over territory and resources do not play a significant role in intergroup tensions. Indeed, there is a wealth of literature identifying sources of conflict throughout history that can be described in material and even quantifiable terms. In accounts of racial conflict during earlier periods of North American history, for example, conflict was explained in terms of oppression and resistance of racial groups; conflict was an outgrowth of the struggle for domination by white elites on the one hand and against slavery, colonial conquest, and other forms of oppression by minorities and laborers on the other (Blauner 1972; Hechter 1975). To explain divisions among minority groups themselves, neo-Marxists identified representatives of ruling-class interests who fanned divisions among workers of different ethnic backgrounds for the purpose of perpetuating racial or ethnic division in the interest of capital accumulation and worker exploitation (Baran and Sweezy 1966; Blauner 1972). The racial segmentation of workers within the labor market and racial segmentation among business owners has also set conditions for the outbreak of intergroup conflict (Bonacich 1980). These and other explanations of materially based motives and sources of conflict remain plausible ingredients in the mix of contributing factors to episodes of violence.

Nor does a morphology of conflict lose "rationality" to the fictionalizing power of discourse in the calculus of conflict. There are many studies that have examined the calculations that groups make in choosing a course of action in conflict settings. For example, ethnic and racial conflicts often arise from deliberate social and political mobilization accompanied by intensified competition between groups (Nagel and Olzak 1982; Nielson 1985). Barth (1956, 1969) proposed that conflict can arise in cases of competition between ethnic groups over the same valued resources, particularly when rival groups are in an equally powerful position to overcome the other and do not choose to voluntarily accommodate the other group. Olzak (1992) has studied this phenomenon in the United States, noting that groups often come into conflict when they find themselves competing in the same economic niches.[3]

Morphology of conflict does not delimit the possible factors that may contribute to violence, in this case gang violence. It is, however, mindful of the limitations to explanations of racial and ethnic conflict that focus too narrowly on material or "tangible" bases of conflict. There are also limitations to the assumption that people act to advance their material self-interest in a deliberate and consistent manner without equal consideration of a host of other social, cultural, and psychological factors.[4] Potential adversaries in competitive relationships, for example, may not always pursue a course of conflict, either out of fear generated by a particular perception of outcomes or out of a view of the existing distribution of resources as legitimate (Coser 1968) or for reasons attributable to cultural norms and practices.[5] While competition over resources or opportunities is often at the center of conflict, competition theories alone do not explain why those who find themselves in conflict are often not those in direct competitive relations. Also, it is often that case that groups mobilize along ethnic or racial cleavages despite the knowledge that only a select few within that group may directly benefit from victory in a competitive battle. And while some conflicts begin over competition for resources and opportunities, those "goods" may not remain the point of contention over time, as other types of issues become defined as more important (Coleman 1957).

I encourage an approach that considers these and other "tangible" objects of contestation, including territorial control and economic activity, as contributing variables in the explanation of violent conflict, but I also argue that the meaning of these objects and the surrounding events is mediated by the situated and historically conditioned lenses through which groups interpret the world around them. In looking at the morphology of conflict, we can pay attention to the way that objects of contestation are framed, the nature of appeals to group mobilization, the attribution of motives to the actions of others, and the interpretive dimension to intergroup conflict more generally. This approach hones in on the iterative process through which actual circumstances, actions, and events *fuse together in a narrative logic* that can be understood, in part, by studying the public discourse concerning their meaning. Interpretations of circumstances, events, and actions cannot stray too far from acknowledged "facts" about them, but through discursive practices, their meanings can certainly be embellished, distorted, and sometimes completely changed from their intended meaning or original representation.

In this way, the meaning of conflicts can change in the eyes of different groups. When this happens, the constellation and alignment of groups surrounding the problem can also change. In the case of racialized gang conflicts, physical and discursive acts can reinforce, increase, or minimize the relative salience of race as an identity boundary among other social boundaries. This can take place through the embellishment or, conversely, the negation of racial meanings. Race can easily remain a central social construct due, in part, to the historic use of race as a marker in the differentiation of rights and privileges as well as the persistence of race in the pattern of social stratification. Yet its salience varies for individuals and across situations. "Morphing," as an analytical tool, allows us to understand the relative ebb and flow of race as a salient identity boundary among multiple identity boundaries that coexist among individuals and across groups. More importantly, it can reveal opportunities to intervene effectively in simmering problems by revealing the crisscrossing lines of alliances and divisions and by more precisely tracking the evolution of issues throughout a controversy.

The Situational Salience of Identities and the Formation of Publics

There are two key interrelated ideas associated with the concept of "morphing." One is the "salience" of identity boundaries, and the other is a retooled notion of "publics." Divisions and alliances can be defined along one or more sets of identity boundaries that are *salient* in a given situation, whether these boundaries are based on class, race, gender, or any other set of differentiating markers. I refer to these groups defined along given bundles of salient identity boundaries as *publics*. Publics do not always correspond to formal organizational boundaries; they are much more fluid and more difficult to identify. But their identification is an important part of understanding *inter*group as well as *intra*group dynamics. Individuals who comprise a public based on a bundle of salient identities in a given situation tend to share a similar lens of interpretation in that situation. Interpretations of actions and events are shared and contested among people across many publics. Depending on which interpretations take hold among different individuals and how those interpretations affect the relative salience and meaning of the multiple identities each individual may possess, the *constitution* and *constellation* of publics, including their relation to one another, may shift over time.

In the case of the gang war, for example, most of the initial skirmishes in Venice began as individual tiffs. They were not read as gang conflicts in that moment. Gang membership was not the salient identity boundary in the initial confrontations between individuals, even though those individuals may have had gang affiliations. In fact, there were deliberate efforts to contain the conflict to those individuals, with explicit clarification that the conflict was not between the affiliated gangs. Thus, the conflicts were treated as individual issues to be resolved accordingly. But at a certain point in time, the ensuing conflicts began to be read as affronts to the families of those individuals and eventually to the entire gang with which they were affiliated. Gang identities became increasingly salient, and groups became mobilized accordingly. These types of realignments in the constitution and constellation of publics according to salient identity boundaries are directly related to individual and group actions as well as the contests over their interpretation.

The Situational Salience of Identities

In cases of conflict, constructions of the "self" and "other" or "*us* versus *them*" are oppositionally posed. And what "self" and "other" actually signify can evolve over time. Tajfel (1981) defined social identity as "that part of individuals' self concept which derives from knowledge of their membership in a social group (or groups) together with the value and emotional significance attached to that membership" (255). Each individual has multiple groups that he or she identifies with. Some of the more salient identity boundaries in U.S. society have been race, ethnicity, class, gender, household role, sexual orientation, political ideology, socioeconomic status, and religion. Other social identities revolve around organizational affiliation, military status, occupation, property ownership, birthplace, and civic association, to name a few.

We can think of social identities as "situational identities," similar to the concept of situational *ethnicity* coined by anthropologists.[6] The basic premise of situational ethnicity is that particular contexts may determine which of a person's identities or loyalties are appropriate or relevant at any given time (Paden 1970). Like situational ethnicity, the more generic concept of situational *identity* can be similarly understood. That is, an individual might identify with one set of individuals in one situation but might identify with a different set in another situation. While group formation may not always be so fluid, the idea of situational identities keeps us mindful of the possibilities for group reformation as well as of the types of tensions that may exist within established groups.

Identity formation is shaped by *structural* as well as *cognitive* factors (Okamura 1981). Structural factors include political, economic, and social norms and institutions that restrain or privilege different groups (Omi and Winant 1986). The relevance of race and other group boundaries varies, in part, by the degree to which these norms and institutions serve to structure social relations according to those categories. The *cognitive* dimension of situational identity refers to individuals' *perception* of a given situation and the *relevance* of any number of identity markers in that situation, despite the meanings and constraints codified by institutions. These two aspects of situational identity note the distinction between the degree to which identity is imposed by forces external to a group of individuals and the degree to which its construction originates from within such a group, though the two aspects cannot be separated.[7] In the words of Thomas Eriksen (1993), ethnic identities "are wedged between situational selection and imperatives imposed from without" (57).

Identities and sub-identities that form specific links between oneself and other individuals can vary not only in *salience* but also in *centrality* and *interdependence* (Hofman 1988). *Salience* refers to the relevance of an identity in a given situation and its propensity to "switch on" (Turner 1982). Prolonged salience enhances its *centrality* across many different situations. *Interdependence* refers to the relationship between various identities and whether they are consonant, dissonant, or indifferent. In any given situation, any set of identities assumed by an individual can become more salient than others. For each individual, some identities hold greater centrality and remain salient across many different types of situations. The level and links of interdependence among one's various identities affect the types and relative strength of affinities that an individual has to different groups simultaneously.

This has important implications, one of which is that the salience, centrality, and interdependence of one's identities affects the level of commitment that one feels toward a particular group. Hofman (1988) notes that when conflicts occur, "individuals are willingly committed to such a conflict only to the extent that relevant subidentities are engaged. . . . Sometimes, commitment is situationally specific [and] what looks like inconsistency, or even insincerity, is a consequence of situational salience and multifaceted identity" (94).

For many in the United States, racial identification maintains a relatively high degree of centrality for several reasons. First, the colonial history of the United States has placed race at the center of its development as a nation. The conquest of Native American lands; the enslavement of Africans; the conquest of the Southwest Territory from Mexico; the annexation of Alaska, Puerto Rico, Hawai'i, and several other Pacific island nations; and the importation of contract labor from Asia were key to the establishment of the United States and imprinted the centrality of race. This period continued into the mid-twentieth century, during which racially and ethnically explicit laws and restrictions were strictly enforced. Legalized segregation, anti-miscegenation laws, restrictive voting requirements, alien land laws, discriminatory housing covenants, and other measures formally prohibited people of color from places and opportunities and denied them their basic civil rights. Many of these laws were not overturned until the civil rights movement pressed passage of legislation, including the Civil Rights Act and Voting Rights Act, both passed in 1965.[8] And despite some progress, inequalities in power, wealth, and opportunity persist into the twenty-first century.

In addition, racial subordination has often resulted in the development of what Ogbu (1990) has called "oppositional identities" among subordinated groups. Racially defined groups within a social hierarchy may form identities in direct opposition to the norms, values, and lifestyles of those identified as responsible for their subjugation. The extent to which economic, political, and social inequalities persist does continue to modulate their centrality in the continuing process of racial formation (Omi and Winant 1986 and 1994).

Second, the centrality of race persists because of its construction as a physically defined category, with skin color and other phenotypic markers as primary defining characteristics. This has two implications. First, discriminating judgments are often made "at first sight" in social encounters. And second, ascription into a racial category tends to be a permanent one for most people, though it is more difficult to "pigeonhole" those of mixed racial ancestry. The system of racial categorization in the United States has historically abided by the "one drop" rule, which holds that an individual belongs to a racial group of color if one possesses any fraction of nonwhite blood in one's lineage. This system of categorization is changing due to increasing rates of intermarriage. Nevertheless, the centrality of race as an identity group marker is enhanced by the fact that racial group categories, as with gender, are more visibly identifiable (or at least many behave as if they are) and are more permanently assigned boundaries as compared to education, occupation, or other categorical distinctions.

There is a high degree of interdependence between gang and racial boundaries in most U.S. cities. This is especially so in places where gangs are racially (or ethnically) homogeneous and racial images or meanings are central to a gang's self-image as a group. Certainly, racial boundaries and gang boundaries are not altogether congruent, since racial boundaries extend beyond the membership of a gang. But to the degree that racial and gang identities are salient and intertwined, interracial gang conflict can be potentially more volatile than those occurring between gangs of the same racial group or between racially heterogeneous gangs. In racially homogenous gangs in interracial gang conflict, race is more easily evoked to recruit others for battle or to justify the selection of targets as participants lean more heavily on racial meanings in the construction of conflict. Instead of rallying cries "for the sake of our *gang*," the participants can adjust their calls as being "for the sake of our *people*." The scope and substance of conflict can broaden quite dramatically due to the close interdependence of identity boundaries and the marginalized condition of many urban communities of color in the United States where gangs have developed as an integrated part of neighborhood networks and social life.

The Definition of "Publics"

The morphology of racial conflict is also predicated on the notion of "publics" as a focal unit of analysis. I use the term "publics" to refer to those groups that share a common bundle or set of salient identity boundaries in a given situation. Defined in this way, publics are not static entities, nor are they necessarily formal organizations. They are situated groups of individuals who share salient identity boundaries and, I argue, a similar lens of understanding through which they interpret events or actions in that situation.

Publics, in this sense, transcend formal organizational group boundaries (though they may often concur with them in instances where the salient identity group boundaries coincide with that of an organization's membership). It is useful to distinguish publics from formal organizations in the study of conflict, since alliances and potential alliances may shift along identity boundaries, which do not overlap with organizational boundaries and which may not be detected if one is focused solely on organizational behavior. It is also useful to distinguish publics from traditionally defined interest groups, as publics defined along salient social identities may not necessarily share the same "material" interests.[9] While many studies of social conflict use organizations or interest groups as the main unit of analysis, a sole focus on these may lead one to overlook important social dynamics, particularly in situations involving racial polarization where publics may mobilize despite organizational ties or "tangible" interests. When an individual contemplates an action, considerations such as a sense of shared fate, collective memory, or feelings of kinship with another may override purely organizational or economic considerations. And in many cases, the tangible and the intangible aspects of group concerns are inseparable, even though they may be expressed in one form rather than the other.

There is often a great deal of ambivalence tied to group actions, and an identity-based definition of publics simultaneously accentuates the tensions that exist within groups as well as the pull of crosscutting ties across groups. These fractures and bridges can be harnessed in peacemaking and -building efforts. Traditionally, individuals are identified with groups, as with conservatives or liberals, developers or renters, capital or labor. While these categories may comprise some of the more salient group boundaries in our society, they do not necessarily capture the complexity of human preferences, the changing meanings of these categories and the ambivalence that people may feel navigating multiple allegiances. Individuals do not always align with the same groups across a spectrum of issues. Nor do individuals find affinity with one group in all situations. Similarly, a position that a group may take might not represent the viewpoint of all its members. The notion of publics allows us to study the behavior of individuals as members of multiple groups.

If we pay too little attention to internal differences within groups, we may overlook important nuances in human behavior. For example, a group of neighbors who uniformly oppose police abuse against youths may differ with one another in their views on criminal justice policies. As activities move from advocating for police accountability to working with local patrol units to police their neighborhood, the constellation of publics may very well shift. Race may be the more salient group boundary in one situation, while property ownership may be the more salient boundary in another, leading to the involvement of homeowners across a spectrum of racial backgrounds. No one boundary is necessarily exclusive of another, and differences along racial boundaries may arise in the newly reconstituted group.[10]

Most importantly, publics defined as such provide a way to capture the different epistemic lenses through which diverse populations see and interpret events. Making distinctions between publics may be the most prudent way to distinguish interpretive lenses—lenses that mediate the attachment of meaning to actions, events, categories, and symbols.[11] For it is in the process of identity formation that one situates oneself in relation to phenomena and imparts particular meaning to those events; the interpretation may or may not lead one to reposition oneself in the schematic of identities. While I agree with those who argue that historical experiences shape identity formation and the cultural lenses through which groups interpret their world,[12] I would add that history and identity formation are also interwoven and interpretive processes themselves. In other words, situationally salient social identities reveal the positionality of individuals as they cluster as publics in non-Euclidian space, each with a distinct interpretive lens poised upon or within a phenomenon.

Complications in the "Multiple Realities" of Conflict

The idea of multiple publics and distinct frames of interpretation create the basis for recognizing "multiple realities" as experienced by different groups. Stuart Hall and his colleagues (1978) put it well when he stated, "because we occupy the same society and belong to roughly the same 'culture,' it is assumed that there is, basically, only *one* perspective on events. . . . This view denies any major structural discrepancies between different groups, or between the very different maps of meaning in a society" (55). This phenomenon can become more pronounced in social conflicts, especially racial conflicts.[13] As Mary Waters (1992) notes, racial incidents "can be seen from different perspectives, each of which is equally legitimate and real to the particular groups of participants" (58). "Multiple realities" coexist in the same time and place and therefore lead to skewed interactions, understood only through the eyes of each beholder. Mach (1993) refers to these interpretive frames as "cognitive models," which are built of symbolic forms and "organize people's experience and express relations between groups" (1993, x).

Not only do differences in interpretive frames among contestants complicate conflict, but policy interventions are also based on frames that often differ from those of the conflicting parties, adding further complications to the problem. Shön and Rein (1994) warn that discordant frames can lead to intractable controversies over the appropriateness of a given set of policies to address a given problem. They define policy frames as structures of belief, perception, and appreciation—a way of making categorizations, assessments, distinctions—upon which policy positions rest. Parties to policy controversies see issues, policies, and policy situations in different and conflicting ways that embody different systems of belief and related prescriptions for action, often crystallized in generative metaphors. These frames determine what counts as a fact and how one makes the normative leap from facts to prescriptions for action. Frames are usually tacit, which means they are exempt from conscious attention and reasoning.[14] When differences over the appropriateness of policy interventions become intractable, those controversies themselves can undermine the type of public learning that is necessary to evaluate and adjust policy interventions such that they respond to the situation more effectively.

Thus, we can generally define frames as the lenses through which meanings are encoded and decoded; these lenses filter what information is seen as relevant, what meanings they impart, and how the information fits into a broader analytical narrative of events in life. The process of encoding and decoding takes many forms, from direct communication of symbols, actions, or texts between individuals or through the mass media (Hall 1980).[15] Words and actions are embedded with meanings that are socially constructed and take meaning from both their historical and immediate context (Bennett and Woollacott 1987). Because of the very fact that multiple publics do not see the world in the same way, there is great room for ambiguity or misinterpretation in meaning, as each public encodes and decodes symbols and actions through its respective lens. Groups may impute meanings to others' actions in ways in which the "other" did not impart, especially where there may be more limited interaction and lack of overlap in interpretive frames. When actions on the part of one public are not read in the way in which that group intended their meaning to be conveyed, unintended consequences abound. This problem has been referred to as "distortions" in discourse (Hall 1973, 1980). This dissonance can exacerbate conflict, often leading to unnecessary escalation of intergroup tensions. Not only do conflicting parties suffer from these distortions, but those agencies and individuals who get involved to fix the problem encounter these same complications.

The complications that "multiple realities" pose to those trying to quell conflict is analogous to a group of people all working on the same Rubik's Cube puzzle.[16] Imagine a group of people huddled around a single Rubik's Cube, all trying to solve it at once. Imagine further that each person is stuck in his or her place, with each person's view limited to a particular position around the cube, as the cube itself is also fixed in place. Each person around the cube has a unique vantage point and, therefore, is not able to see what is on the other side of the cube at any given moment in time. If there is no communication or cooperation between players, each one will likely twist the cube from their sole vantage point, each working at cross-purposes with the others. While one person twists and turns the cube with the supposition that they are making progress, another person from a different vantage point might see those same moves as an affront or a step in the wrong direction. As a result, they may engage in struggle with one another, counteracting the moves of other players and causing reactions that may be counterproductive to solving the shared problem.

Gaining a well-rounded understanding of a problem is based in large part on the ability of individuals to traverse many publics or communicate effectively across many different boundaries. I refer to individuals that deftly do this as "transpublics," able to understand a problem from many different vantage points. While such transpublics may find themselves in uneasy positions between conflicting groups, they may also be the only ones with perspectives broad enough to mediate differences effectively. Since they may share overlapping identities with more than one public, they are often able to articulate contrasting frames across group boundaries. They can translate images, meanings, and concerns between publics with whose vantage points they are familiar. They can find common ground between them. Or, to continue the metaphor, they can advise one public how a twist of the cube may affect a group positioned on the other side of it, and vice versa. They can reshape public opinion by speaking to a cross section of hearts and minds because they have a better sense of what different groups see and feel.

Multiple Publics, Techniques of Power, and the State

Publics employ various techniques of power in order to influence public perceptions and public opinion; to influence the behavior of decision-makers; to shape the norms, values, and institutions of society; and to harness human or institutional resources of the public and private sectors.[17] In the case of the gang war, groups employed the wide array of techniques at their disposal. These included state-granted privileges and sanctions, physical force, rumors, organizational sanctions, monetary incentives, threats, mass media announcements, informal modes of persuasion, and codes of secrecy, among others.

Not all publics, of course, have the same degree of leverage in twisting the cube or altering the gaze of others. There are vast inequalities in their access to various techniques of power. Critical to this is the ability of publics, including formal organizations and agencies, to produce "truth" and knowledge. As Foucault (1980) put it, "we are subjected to the production of truth through power and we cannot exercise power except through the production of truth" (93). Power and the concept of power are inseparable; they imply one another directly. In promoting their rendition of the "truth," individuals and groups battle to define the nature of problems as well as the prescriptions to remedy them. In situations of conflict or controversy, discourses include whatever techniques of power are considered legitimate by whichever groups are able to use them. In regard to state-controlled techniques of power, the establishment of "truths" and "facts" help to set the "acceptable" limits for the use of force as well as the general approach to problem-solving.

Conversely, the domain of knowledge gives the physical enforcement of social controls their meaning. Incarceration is effective as a form of punishment only to the extent to which it carries that intended meaning to those imprisoned. If, for example, imprisonment becomes an initiation ritual, part of a rite of passage into a prison fraternity, it will be unlikely to have the effect intended by the keepers of the criminal justice system. While the architecture of the prison was meant to discipline the body, prisoners may use the walls of the prison and the technology within it to discipline its inhabitants in their own way. While the incarceration of gang members is touted as a means of isolating gang members from the rest of society, prison gangs use the bounds of prisons to enforce discipline on fellow inmates to a higher degree than is possible on the streets. Based on the likelihood that gang members will eventually spend some time in prison, prison gangs have become a formidable force on the street. Power does not lie in the hands of those in charge of a secured facility as much as it is exerted in the production of meaning, as correctional officers and prisoners alike work within the physical and organizational structure of the prison to control the behavior of others in and outside its walls.

Government institutions, by virtue of their legitimate standing as well as by their technological and organizational resources, wield unique techniques of power that have a strong bearing on the tenor of race relations.[18] We can observe three major ways in which state institutions shape racial formation and race relations: (1) by giving sanction to structural constraints that discriminate along ethnic or racial boundaries; (2) by participating as an independent actor in the production of racial and ethnic meanings; and (3) by taking actions that increase or decrease the salience of racial group boundaries in specific group encounters. Let me briefly explain each of these influences, as they underscore the potential effects of government intervention in situations of ethnic and racial conflict.

First, government actions and policies have a great deal to do with the structure of race and social relations in the United States *by imposing or consenting to structural constraints that discriminate along ethnic or racial boundaries.* Government policies and state actions are racial in that they have differential impacts on racial groups, propagate certain ideas about the meaning of race, and tend (in more cases than not) to support the socioeconomic status quo as well as normative culture. State powers can be used to mediate the distribution and redistribution of wealth and capital within a society. Institutions can affect patterns of residential settlement, educational attainment, and other factors affecting racial group interaction and mobility through taxation, education, housing, employment, transportation, banking, and a myriad of other policies. State actions historically have played a dual role—creating both more and less socioeconomic and political stratification. While the mid–twentieth century saw a period of economic growth and prosperity that opened up new opportunities for communities of color in the United States, the late 1970s marked the start of a decline in those advancements and a retrenchment in racial stratification (Goldsmith and Blakely 1992; Melendez 1993; Ong 1994; Oliver and Shapiro 1995) that has reinforced racial identities, particularly among the most marginalized.

Second, government institutions affect race relations *in the cultural production of racial and ethnic meanings.* Racial meanings are implicit in the institutions, policies, supporting conditions, and rules that govern our society (Omi and Winant 1994), and the formation of racial meanings through political struggle has been the focus of numerous studies (see Carmines and Stimson 1989; Dominguez 1986; Edsall and Edsall 1991, Omi and Winant 1994). Stuart Hall and his colleagues (1978), for example, illustrated the role of state institutions in the process of racial formation, describing how government institutions, with the cooperation of the media, played an active role in marginalizing the black population in British society. Institutions defined situations, selected targets, initiated campaigns, selectively signified their actions to the public at large, and legitimated their actions through their accounts of situations. The social construction of racial meanings and their association with the meaning of place had great bearing on the way in which groups viewed themselves and each other and on the extent and types of interactions that individuals pursued.

And third, government actions can shape race relations by *taking actions that increase or decrease the salience of racial group boundaries in specific group encounters*. Government intervention can deepen racial group divisions as well as encourage cross-racial cooperation. This role of state intervention in intergroup conflict has been discussed extensively by scholars of international ethnic relations. Horowitz (1985), for example, observed that when government institutions are perceived to favor one group over another, the disfavored group often redoubles its efforts to gain recognition and redemption, resulting in intensified conflict. The desire for group worth and legitimacy can explain why conflicts are sometimes intensified by actions on the part of the state, in its role as grand arbiter of precious psychological goods (see also Esman 1990 and Ryan 1990) in addition to its role as enabler of material opportunities. Such tensions can also be further exacerbated through political mobilization, where political entrepreneurs or advocates can rally ethnic groups in the call for various rights. Similar findings have been made in psychological studies of intergroup behavior where favoritism exhibited on the part of authority figures brewed antagonisms between competing groups (Brewer and Kramer 1985). In the case at hand, government actions perceived as favoring one group over another had significant consequences.

In sum, group boundaries and substantive issues at the center of conflict are seldom static. And interpretations of a conflict situation are seldom uniform. This is especially true in places where there is great diversity in cultural influences, socioeconomic well-being, lifestyle, group history, and epistemology (ways of knowing). These conditions pose great challenges to social scientists and practitioners concerned with the study or practice of mediation and peaceful resolution of conflict. Looking closely at a conflict's morphology from multiple vantage points can be very illuminating and could help minimize unintended consequences of attempted interventions. The key to successful intervention in the future may be the role of "transpublics" who can read a conflict's morphology to find more effective and sustainable paths toward peace. As a society, we are a long way from being able to observe the fluidity and complexity of events surrounding us from the shoes of others very different from ourselves. This articulation of the morphology of conflict is my attempt to help us do that in a more thoughtful manner. Now, back to the case at hand.

Chapter 3

The Geography of Multiple Publics in Venice

As one drives through the Oakwood section of Venice, where much of the gang war was centered, one sees a neighborhood of contrasts. Century-old bungalows sit nestled behind trimmed lawns alongside techno-industrial-style condos in the rapidly changing seaside community. The real estate boom of the 1980s spurred market-driven gentrification, which encroached upon the last remaining tracts of low-income housing along the southern California coastline. The economic recession at the end of that decade, however, halted the gentrification process midstream. Longtime residents hang on to their way of life, while many newcomers and speculators wait patiently for the next boom cycle to complete the transformation process.

Unlike most neighborhoods situated along the path of metropolitan sprawl, Venice has become home to a wide spectrum of the population, mirroring much of the racial and cultural diversity that exists throughout the city. Suburbanization that would otherwise have rolled through Venice abruptly ended at this Pacific shoreline community. Population groups, which in other neighborhoods have moved progressively outwards from the central city due to suburban migration, have collected in this westernmost edge of Los Angeles. Since it is one of the oldest neighborhoods in the region, the suburban sprawl that filled the landscape from downtown to the beach simply brought a long and steady increase in population. Instead of continued westward "flight," Venice became increasingly diverse.

Ironically, the uniqueness of Venice lends it a universal quality. Its place in history and the historic structures of place make it an ideal site for a study of the social dynamics in an economically and socially diverse multicultural setting. Families tracing their ancestral roots back to preindustrial Mesoamerica reside next to newly arrived transplants. Rich, poor, old, young, immigrant, native-born, African-American, Latino, white, Asian, and Native American share the same space. Cleavages and bonds run along and across numerous boundaries of race, gender, sexuality, income, wealth, generation, language, popular culture, religion, civic association, ideology, family structure, and age. Much of the history of Venice has been shaped by the struggle of different groups to define its use. And with contemporary changes in demographic composition and changes in economic conditions within a global economy, groups continue to define themselves in relation to the creation and use of space, the definition of place, and territorial influence over both.

Excavating Maps of Meaning

The project of unearthing maps of meaning hidden in the social histories of a community can be a valuable step toward understanding the dynamics of social conflict in the present. Social conflicts involve individual identities, group mobilization, and interpretive narratives that are embedded in a community's past. Social identities may be pliable, group formation fluid, and interpretations varied, but all are rooted in the historical experiences of the individual actors who carry in their minds maps of meaning, with which they make sense of the world around them.[1] These maps shape interpretations and are themselves continually reshaped. A historical understanding of a community is useful since it is through knowledge of historical patterns of social organization that maps of meaning are made concrete (Jackson 1995).

Neighborhood histories offer insights into the way in which identities are constructed, interests are defined, groups are congealed, and meanings are contested as maps of meaning are geographically expressed and spatially constituted (Gregory and Urry 1985; Soja 1987; Jackson 1995). Social histories are important because interpretive "spins" in any discursive contest depend on the *traction* they have with an understanding of the past. The persuasiveness of one group's interpretation of a current event is partially based on its continuity with what that group understands to have happened in the past. The particularities of specific communities are telling, as meaning-making occurs in a context that is largely bounded by place and space. Interpretations of an event in a specific time and place are built upon a prior foundation of meanings (lived or learned), just as the contests over meanings are mediated by the social identities to which they are tied and to which they appeal.

For the purpose of understanding contemporary social dynamics, we excavate those strands of history that shed light on the events surrounding the gang war and truce. Historical records reveal the many changes and social struggles through which identities have been shaped and through which meanings have been affixed. Historical legacies, identity, and culture are inextricably tied, not only among themselves but also to the present. Peter Jackson (1995) wrote:

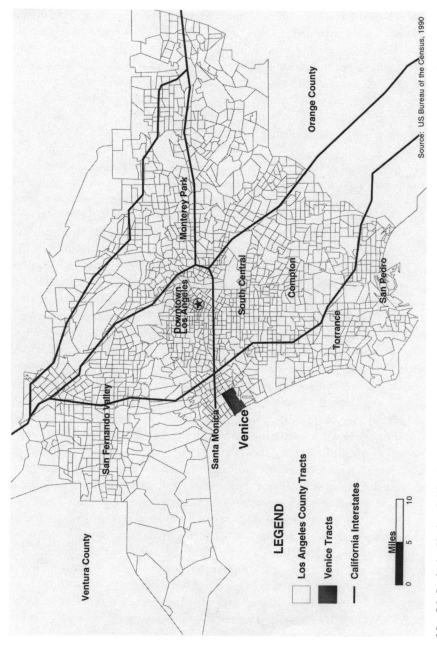

Source: US Bureau of the Census, 1990

Map 3.1 Study site: Venice, California

History is conceived of not as the simple passage of time, but as a dynamic process in which cultures are actively forged by real men and women. Similarly, geography is conceived of not as a featureless landscape on which events simply unfold, but as a series of spatial structures which provide a dynamic context for the processes and practices that give shape and form to culture. (48)

Thus, it is at this nexus of history and geography that we may find clues about the codification of social meanings specific to a time and place. Without some historical understanding of spatial structures and processes at the level of the neighborhood, albeit within the broader regional and global context, it is difficult to understand the bases upon which claims were made and actions were taken in the later period.

Constructing historical narratives that attempt to link understandings of the present with events of the past is an admittedly slippery prospect. The primary purpose here is not to reconstruct the histories that were recited at the time of the study but to explore historical records to understand *the meaning of historical referents* that were made and *how they might resonate* in the contemporary discourse. This requires us to pinpoint those historical moments that may serve as touchstones for present-day actors who experienced that episode in 1993–94. The difficulty lies in the fact that historical memory is a moving object, adapting to fit the needs of the immediate time and place. When one hears a historical account, there is no certainty as to the biases and completeness of the historical record. Nor is there any certainty as to the degree to which contemporary accounts of history resemble any historical documents or artifacts that remain. This is particularly true of oral history, often passed down informally and for instrumental purposes. Since neighborhood histories are often conveyed orally and since oral histories are often conveyed through networks, there are usually different versions and snippets of history that circulate among different networks at any given time.

Setting the context requires sensitivity to the way *different* groups view the history of that place and the way individuals see their place in that history. The task is not simply to study the history of a place and its people but also to understand how people see the history of that place. In so doing, one finds there are many different versions of history, each from a different vantage point. Oftentimes, the social histories that one hears in a community contradict one another, moving one to wonder if the people are talking about the same events. It is no wonder that people come to divergent conclusions about issues in the present. The source of such difference lies not only in the varied experiences of people in a place but also in the wide-ranging sets of collective memories that groups gathered in a place share, as stories are often handed down from generation to generation or from neighbor to neighbor within somewhat separate networks.[2]

In order to provide a historical overview that could serve as a referential orientation, I started with two points in time—past and present—to explore potential "pathways" between certain events in the past and collective recollections of them that were "alive" in the present. I documented recollections of the past during the fieldwork period to identify meaningful moments in history while at the same time mining written historical accounts. In conducting the archival research, I relied primarily on secondary sources, including books and articles on Venice. I also reviewed several primary sources, namely government documents, U.S. census data, and news articles.

I organize this overview according to major periods in the history of Venice that were found in the historical record. The major periods include: Rancho la Ballona; "Venice of America"; World War II and the postwar boom; the civil rights era; immigration, deindustrialization, and income polarization; and gentrification, crime, and the "War on Drugs."

Rancho la Ballona

Venice has enjoyed notoriety for many reasons stretching across the decades. Until the late 1800s, the area of Venice was part of a large *rancho* owned by the Machado and Talamantes families (Adler 1969). They initially settled the land, which had been vested to the king of Spain in 1769; his control ended in 1822. Historical records indicate that the families had stocked the area with long-horned cattle during California's pastoral era around the beginning of the nineteenth century. In 1839, the families petitioned the Mexican governor for a formal grant to the land they called "Rancho la Ballona," named after their ancestral township in Spain (Robinson 1939). Before then, the land had been home to Mission Indians who lived off the fertile lands and estuaries along Santa Monica Bay.

In 1848, the region, along with the entire Southwest Territory—comprised of what would become the five states of California, Nevada, Texas, New Mexico, and Arizona—was annexed from Mexico by the United States after the Mexican-American War and the signing of the Treaty of Guadalupe Hidalgo. A U.S. Land Commission was established to review and adjust the boundaries of what were previously Mexican land grants. In 1854, the commission upheld the Rancho la Ballona grant, and the estates continued to remain in the name of the relatives and friends of the two families (Adler 1969). But the Talamantes and Machado families did not maintain ownership of the land for very long after the U.S. conquest. Tomas Talamantes, one of four owners, allegedly lost his parcel after a failed mortgage on the land. In 1868, the rest of the land was partitioned among the heirs. By the end of the century, speculators and land developers took legal ownership over the parcels closer to the beach (Robinson 1939).

The end of the Civil War and the construction of the transcontinental railroad brought settlers, developers, and land speculators who transformed the entire West. One such speculator named Moses L. Wicks gained control of oceanfront portions of the Rancho la Ballona land. He attracted real estate speculators and sold tracts to prospective developers. Before he completed the sales of his parcels and realized the full potential of land development, the 1880s economic bust ended the short wave of speculation (Adler 1969). This halt, however, was only temporary.

The conquest of Mexican territory by the United States in its westward colonial expansion may not lie in the contemporary consciousness of the majority of southwesterners, but a general colonial history was certainly part of the popular history within Mexican American or Chicano communities and institutions. In fact, during the social movements of the 1960s, activists within the Chicano movement initiated the term *Aztlán* to refer to the land base of the southwestern states that were once part of Mexico as a way to asserting claims of self-determination.[3] In the 1980s and 1990s, the colonial legacy was often retrieved to frame political positions by advocates of minority and civil rights in charged debates over immigration policy, political representation among communities of color, affirmative action, multilingual education and language rights, and other issues of race and politics in California.

"Venice of America"

The turn of the century brought dramatic change to Venice. In 1892, capitalist Abbot Kinney induced the Santa Fe Railroad to extend its rail line to his land tract and led the engineering of "Venice of America," a seaside resort, recreation, and "cultural center." Kinney, a cigarette-manufacturing tycoon, developed a tourist town borrowing Venetian architecture and landscaping, highlighted by canals dredged inland and piers built out over the Santa Monica Bay. Competition among pier developers triggered an imaginative array of roller coasters, games, pools, and funhouses. A series of natural disasters and mysterious fires eventually brought an end to the flurry of recreational construction, but not before tourism had brought more land speculators and developers. By the 1920s, Venice's population was predominately white, Anglo-Saxon, and Protestant, and it featured the lowest illiteracy rate in the state of California (Cunningham 1976).

In the early 1900s, many African American families began to arrive in the Venice area, migrating from the South in search of work.[4] In an era when society remained strictly segregated along racial lines, Abbot Kinney employed African American men and women as manual laborers, service workers, and servants in his entrepreneurial exploits. Many affluent Anglo families hired African Americans as servants in their canal-side homes. Racially exclusive housing covenants prohibited the settlement of the African American population in many sections of town. One of the few places they were allowed to settle was a one–square mile area of Venice that later became known as Oakwood. During this period, some referred to this small neighborhood located north of the canals as the "servant's quarters" of Venice.

This history of Oakwood as a longtime African American community remained meaningful to residents at the time of the gang war. In the Oakwood section of Venice, contemporary discussions of the neighborhood made frequent mention of the historical fact that "Oakwood was the only place that African Americans were allowed to live." This was particularly the case among African American families with ties to the area that spanned many generations. In fact, one of the historic sites in Venice is the home of the Tabor family, one of the early African American families known to settle there. Irvin Tabor worked as a chauffeur and personal assistant to Abbot Kinney. When Kinney passed away in 1920, he left his home to Irvin Tabor. Because of racially prohibitive housing policies, the house was lifted off its foundations and moved to the Oakwood section of Venice. It has been restored and preserved as a historic building in the registry of historic sites in the state of California with the support of relatives and descendants, some of whom remained in Oakwood. The presence of the historic site remains a symbolic reminder of the history of legal segregation that had continued into the 1960s and the de facto segregation that many believed still continued.

Cunningham (1976) argues that Kinney's dominance stunted the development of more democratic institutions in the community and sent Venice on a political trajectory that ended in fragmentation and neighborhood rivalry. Kinney became known as the "founder" of Venice and served as its patriarch. Since Kinney oversaw so much of the affairs of the incorporated city of Venice, it was said that his death in 1920 brought political chaos and financial instability. Five years later, citizens voted to consolidate with the city of Los Angeles. The Great Depression of 1929 and a serious earthquake in 1933 caused further economic devastation to the area. While many had hoped that consolidation into the city of Los Angeles would provide better support, many social and infrastructure needs of Venice were overlooked within the larger city bureaucracy (Cunningham 1976).

Postwar Boom and Continuing Segregation

The period of greatest numerical growth took place directly after World War II, firmly establishing Venice as a relatively stable middle-class and blue-collar community during the postwar era. The war economy and the postwar boom that lasted through the 1950s brought an influx of working-class families of various ethnic and religious backgrounds. Between 1940 and 1960, the population of Venice increased by 65 percent (from 23,263 to 38,365). In the 1930s, Douglas Aircraft Company set up a factory in neighboring Santa Monica and soon aircraft parts manufacturing plants were set up in nearby vicinities, including Venice. Soon, North American and Hughes would open aircraft industry plants in nearby Inglewood, Culver City, and the Del Rey Bluffs, employing thousands who settled along the coast (Adler 1969). Multiplier effects were felt all along the coast, making the Los Angeles leg of California Coast Highway 1, which runs through Venice, a major commercial corridor. Though not all groups enjoyed the benefits of economic growth, many were able to take advantage of the new opportunities. The infusion of federal aid accompanying large military contracts coupled with lower interest rates and reasonable land values led to the creation of stable working-class neighborhoods with high rates of home ownership throughout the region.

The reach of prosperity might have lessened prior racial and class divisions had it not been for rampant discrimination and the persistence of legal segregation. While affordable housing was constructed on the eastern portions of Venice, the southern beachfront stretch, originally tarred by unsightly oil derricks propped up alongside residential bungalows, eventually became the most exclusive parcel of Venice thanks to city-sponsored urban renewal (Cunningham 1976). Segregated military combat units, a racially skewed occupational division of labor, and racially exclusive housing covenants continued to shape race relations and the racial settlement pattern during this period of expansion. While the population became more heterogeneous, most residential subsections remained racially homogeneous.

All nonwhites were adversely affected by racially discriminatory housing practices. Residential segregation was strictly practiced and did not begin to abate until years after the passage of the Civil Rights Act in 1965. The segregation of African Americans in Venice was particularly pronounced. Highway 1 had become a major barrier separating Oakwood from the adjacent Walgrove section. Housing developments on the east side of the highway were built to accommodate the influx of white manufacturing workers during the postwar boom. As of 1960, 3,191 African Americans were recorded in the official census as living in Oakwood. In contrast, only two African Americans lived in the Walgrove section across Highway 1 in an area of similar geographic and population size.[5] In the similarly sized section immediately south of Venice Boulevard, only eleven African Americans were counted and only 64 were counted to the west of Oakwood. The one–square mile neighborhood of Oakwood, though still majority nonblack, became the social and cultural center for African Americans along that stretch of the coast.

Apart from forced segregation, residents formed other cultural enclaves as well. To the west and south of the Oakwood neighborhood, a large Jewish population had settled, including many Russian and Polish immigrants who had relocated to Venice during the Depression (Cunningham 1976). Similar to the African American experience in Venice, institutions that served their religious, social, and cultural needs thrived. Throughout the westside, the Jewish population would continue to grow and became a strong influence in city politics. To the west and along the beachfront, an active artisan and beatnik community had formed during the 1950s and 1960s, though many were later driven out by a series of government abatements. Many Japanese American families had settled in Venice as farmers prior to World War II but were incarcerated as part of the mass removal of Americans of Japanese ancestry from the west coast in 1942. Some did return to Venice at war's end. The

Latino population continued to grow with the help of steady immigration from Mexico. Like other groups, Latino residents established churches and cultural institutions that also thrived over the years.

Within this changing demographic milieu, the 1950s and 1960s saw continued political disorganization. Venice was shifted back and forth between two city council districts and was split between two state assembly districts as well as between two U.S. congressional districts such that there was no clear or single representative at any of the three levels of government (Adler 1969). According to Cunningham, "In the absence of any compelling forces to give them shape or substance, the 40,000 people living in Venice during the 1960s, while seeming to fall apart have, in actuality, fallen back into smaller, more manageable units of identification: neighborhoods became ascendant by default" (Cunningham 1976, 211). Coupled with legally sanctioned racial segregation, a lack of community cohesion, increasing heterogeneity of the population, and an absence of unifying local leadership, Venice was plagued with recurring political and social discord.[6]

The Civil Rights Movement and Racial Solidarity

The civil rights movement in the early 1960s signified an era of increasing racial cooperation among progressives, and this included those living and working in the Venice area. Venice was relatively liberal in its political attitudes. An active Jewish community became influential in liberal Democratic Party politics throughout Los Angeles's Westside. The Oakwood neighborhood of Venice was one of the most influential neighborhoods in Venice politics during the heyday of the civil rights movement. African Americans, Latinos, Asian Americans, and whites joined in significant campaigns to empower a local political base that advocated liberal social reforms. Residents waged intensive voter registration campaigns; sat on local funding boards; established a myriad of social service agencies; conducted voluntary self-help projects; lobbied local, state, and federal legislators; built networks throughout city and county government; and promoted racial cooperation and civic participation.[7]

Various community-based programs were formed in Oakwood during this period. Barrios Unidos, Community Service Organization, Venice Action Committee, Project Action, Venice Teen Post, Venice Drug Coalition, and a variety of social service agencies were founded. Governing bodies such as the Greater Los Angeles Community Action Agency (GLACAA) included local residents and guaranteed some level of grassroots involvement, including the participation of those most disenfranchised and economically marginalized. Neighborhood organizations such as the Latino-based Community Service Organization (CSO) and the African American–based Pearl White Theater worked closely with residents of all racial backgrounds in their pursuit of civil rights. Many of these organizations remained in operation up to the time of the 1990s period of the gang war.

During the 1960s and 1970s, a number of community activists of the civil rights and Black Power movements advocated for and developed affordable housing for low-income residents. Fourteen housing complexes were planned and were sited strategically throughout the neighborhood in anticipation of coastal development. These buildings, initially named the Holiday Venice apartments, were federally subsidized by the Department of Housing and Urban Development (HUD) and represented some guarantee that African American and low-income residents would be able to "hold their ground" in the face of development interests.[8] Reverend Robert Castile was one of the active proponents and galvanizers of this affordable housing effort.

Within the civil rights movement there were deeply felt differences in political ideology regarding issues of racial integration, self-determination, cooperation with government institutions, use of violence, forms of democratic participation, and control over government resources. These differences reflected tensions in the movement nationally between those organizations advocating nonviolence and those abiding by the logic of "by any means necessary."

Nevertheless, the dominant political atmosphere, set under the spirit and slogans of the civil rights period, was inclusionary and forward-looking. As civil rights veteran Pearl White repeatedly states, "We're for *all* poor people in Venice—black, brown, yellow, red, or white." The quality of interaction between neighbors was characterized by a great degree of optimism, openness, and willingness to share. House meetings, community forums, potlucks, sports activities, community classes, and after-school activities reflected more hopeful times. While race was certainly a salient group boundary, the movement for civil rights and equality also enhanced a more encompassing social identity of those who supported its principles and worked together toward its progressive vision.

Deindustrialization, Immigration, and Socioeconomic Polarization

The 1970s and 1980s marked a period of increasing globalization in the world economy. This was accompanied by a change in the demographic composition of neighborhoods and the socioeconomic well-being of families. The growth rate of the U.S. economy began to slow after enjoying several decades of postwar economic boom. The 1980s and 1990s saw major global shifts in production, with southern California undergoing a decline in the manufacturing sector and a rise in the finance and service sectors. One result was the loss of well-paying jobs that did not require higher education. For those who did not complete high school, there were fewer and fewer chances of securing the "American dream," which more and more stressed material goods in a culture of mass consumerism. The polarization between those who earned six-digit incomes and those who struggled to earn a "living wage" was evident in the deterioration of housing conditions alongside new fortress-style housing construction.

Globalization also fueled labor migration, which, coupled with other changes, contributed to rapid demographic change in Oakwood as well as the Southwest region. Southern California was a popular destination for immigrants, especially from Central America. The Immigration Act of 1965 led to, among other things, a sharp increase in legal immigration from Asia, Mexico, and other parts of Central and South America. With growing poverty and dislocation in industrializing countries, the drive for cheap labor in the United States, and mechanisms to facilitate illegal migration to the United States, many undocumented workers also immigrated to the region in search of jobs and opportunities. The passage of the 1965 Civil Rights Act ending de jure segregation coupled with increased immigration led to two types of demographic shifts in Oakwood. The lifting of racial covenants resulted in greater dispersal of African Americans outside of the Oakwood boundaries and into the surrounding neighborhoods. At the same time, Oakwood experienced a steady increase in immigrants from Latin America and Asia.

The ratio of Latinos to African Americans reversed itself in the two decades between 1970 and 1990. In 1970, African Americans comprised 45 percent of Oakwood's population while Latinos comprised 31 percent. By 1990, the proportions had more than reversed—the Latino population increased to 48 percent while African Americans declined to 24 percent. Meanwhile, the white population sharply declined from 1960 to 1970 but began to increase during the 1980s as gentrification began in earnest.

Socioeconomic trends among Oakwood residents between 1970 and 1990 reveal growing economic polarization with a growing gap between the wealthy and everyone else. Longtime low-income residents were aging, while most newcomers were younger and enjoyed greater economic means. The poor were comprised of all racial groups but were disproportionately African American and Latino. Those who were financially better off tended to be disproportionately white and Asian, though not exclusively.

The demographic characteristics of Oakwood as documented in the 1990 U.S. Census of the Population reflected this increase in income polarization and the shift in racial and ethnic composition. While the median household income rose from approximately $18,700 in 1980 to $25,300 in 1990 (in 1990 dollars), the proportion of children under the age of 18 who lived under the poverty line grew to almost 40 percent.[9] A quarter of all Oakwood residents lived below the poverty line, though some racial groups had a higher poverty rate than others (see table 3.1). Poverty rates broken down by race reveal that Latinos (28 percent), African Americans (26 percent), and Native Americans (36 percent) had a relatively higher rate of poverty in comparison to whites (20 percent) and Asian Americans (12 percent). The entire county of Los An-

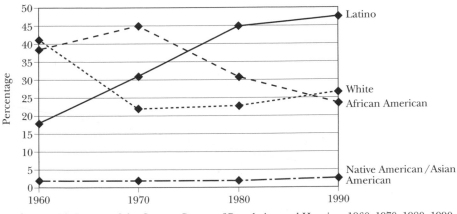

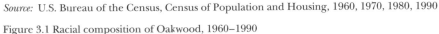

Source: U.S. Bureau of the Census, Census of Population and Housing, 1960, 1970, 1980, 1990

Figure 3.1 Racial composition of Oakwood, 1960–1990

geles experienced a greater widening of the income and wage gaps as compared to the rest of the state and to the nation, as the income of families in
the bottom decile declined 17 percent while those of the top decile increased
22 percent between 1973 and 1990.

The high rate of poverty in Oakwood accompanied a low level of formal
educational attainment. Forty-five percent of residents 25 years of age and
older had not graduated from high school. Among Oakwood's residents, immigrants comprised over a third (37 percent), the majority of whom were
born in Mexico or elsewhere in Central America. In addition, nearly a third
(31 percent) of Latinos did not speak English well or spoke it not at all. Home
ownership in the neighborhood was declining. In 1970, about a third of the
housing units were owner-occupied, but by 1990 that proportion had fallen
to less than a fifth.

In this context of growing economic insecurity and socioeconomic polarization, a political shift took place beginning in the 1980s as liberal views to-

TABLE 3.1
Percentage of Oakwood residents with incomes below the
poverty line, 1989

All persons	25.0%
Children >18	39.1
White	19.5
Black	26.1
American Indian	36.0
Asian/Pacific Islander	12.3
Hispanic	28.1

Source: *U.S. Bureau of the Census, Census of Population and Housing, 1990.*

ward state and civil society relations gave in to conservative positions, some of which meshed more closely with expectations held by many new immigrants. The "personal responsibility" campaign slogan that characterized the presidential administrations of Ronald Reagan and George Bush sent the loud message that one can overcome poverty and become financially and otherwise successful if one only worked hard. Moral appeals for personal responsibility placed blame and shame on those who had become marginalized from mainstream economic and political life.

At the same time, a growing anti-immigrant movement had been building; it eventually led to the passage of the controversial state Proposition 187 in 1994. This ballot initiative was designed to cut off many health and social services, including public education, to undocumented immigrants. Meanwhile, legal and undocumented immigrants were favored by employers for many of the low-paying jobs that often fell below the reservation wage of many U.S.-born workers. The political discourse combined with racial discrimination in the labor and housing markets, particularly against African Americans, was a source of tension that was cited by many of the residents who faced this problem. Social tension such as these in Los Angeles and elsewhere between African Americans and Latino immigrants gained greater attention as a subject of study in the 1980s and 1990s (Oliver and Johnson 1984; Jennings 1992; Jennings and Lusane 1994; Sekou and Seltzer 2002).

Gentrification, Crime, and the "War on Drugs"

During the 1980s, conflicts between groups in Oakwood climaxed over gentrification and crime. On the one hand, the rise in property values spurred gentrification; at the same time, increasing poverty and high rents continued to feed drug addiction, drug-dealing activities, and property and personal crimes. New developers and homeowners began purchasing older buildings, replacing them with higher-density condominiums as well as upgrading single-family homes. Housing immediately surrounding Oakwood commanded increasingly higher rents. Many of the newer structures fit the vision presented in Mike Davis's *City of Quartz*, with multi-level housing shielded behind high fences, elaborate security devices, electronic gates, iron bars, and thorny bougainvillea scaling shielding walls. As the rents and home prices rose, the proportion of affordable housing stock began to shrink (see table 3.2). Sixties beatniks and centers of counterculture were all but driven out of Venice by the skyrocketing rents and the city-sponsored abatement operations to "clean up" the neighborhood. Elderly residents on fixed incomes and families with low incomes struggled to hang on to the dwindling stock of low-rent housing.

Gentrification and increased competition for affordable housing became a source of racial tensions along several social cleavages. One divide was felt between newcomers, including speculators, who were identified by longtime

TABLE 3.2
Median house value in Oakwood,
1969–1989 (in 1990 dollars)

1969	$90,000
1979	$150,000
1989	$280,000

Source: *U.S. Bureau of the Census,
Census of Population and Housing, 1970,
1980, 1990.*
Note: *Adjusted for inflation using
shelter CPI. Estimation based on median
house values for census tracts 2732 and
2733.*

residents as relatively wealthy and predominately white. The new fortress-style architecture of newly constructed homes was interpreted as a message of social distance to neighbors. As one resident described, "They build high walls and hide behind them." Referred to by some as the gentrified people, higher-income white property owners were seen by some longtime residents as "taking over" the neighborhood and driving poor residents out.

Nested within this set of tensions between wealthier, predominately white residents and poorer, mainly nonwhite families was another set of fault lines stemming from competition for affordable housing. As aging housing stock was replaced with new construction, African Americans, Latinos, and whites found themselves in competition over a diminishing stock of affordable units, including HUD-subsidized apartments. Some residents felt that landlords often discriminated against African Americans in favor of Latino tenants, a phenomenon noted in other parts of Los Angeles and the Southern California region (Oliver and Johnson 1984). Coupled with the increasing competition over jobs, health and human services, and educational resources, gentrification intensified inter-minority group tension more than it served as an impetus to unify around a shared need for shelter.

For many residents, anxiety over shelter and fear of dislocation was not new. Many older residents interviewed during the fieldwork made reference to two periods of forced removal suffered by low-income Latino and African American residents on the Westside. One was the result of urban renewal in Santa Monica and the construction of Interstate Highway 10 to the north. Eminent domain powers were used to clear residential neighborhoods for the major highway construction in the 1960s. The rapid commercial development that followed led to the displacement of even more families. The second episode was a series of expansions of Los Angeles International airport to the south with the arrival of the jet age beginning in the 1950s and 1960s.[10] Some residents had been forcibly removed as a result of these developments before settling in Oakwood. Stories of these experiences conditioned their response to the gentrification taking place in Oakwood.

While the presence of HUD-subsidized housing helped to deter new development, the forty-year HUD contracts with building owners set to expire in the 1990s hastened the possibility that the complexes would be converted to market-rate housing. This stirred anxiety among low-income residents, who feared they might lose their homes. Community activists and several tenant associations, including one of HUD subsidy recipients and another of African American and other longtime homeowners and tenants, voiced their concerns over the future of Venice for minorities and the poor. For the many people who advocated for affordable housing, gentrification came to represent a dangerous threat to the maintenance of a historic community and all they had put into it. Since the contest over space became so concentrated in such a small area, social conflict became that much more intense and interpersonal.

At the same time, the introduction of crack cocaine in the mid-1980s had a profound impact on the physical and social health of the neighborhood. Addiction to money at the top and addiction to the drug at the bottom sustained a symbiotic relationship between dealers and users. The addictive power and affordability of crack cocaine led to strong demand for the substance. Low-income neighborhoods became "drive-through" markets for more middle-class and affluent drug users in the surrounding areas. Drug addiction also had traumatic effects on the families and acquaintances of users within the neighborhood. Poverty, particularly among children, ensured a steady supply of workers willing to take the front-line risk for older, high-volume dealers. It is important to note that not all drug dealers were associated with gangs, nor were all gang members involved in illegal drug activity (Klein and Maxson 1994). However, for some gangs in the Los Angeles region including those involved in the gang war, the drug economy had provided a steady income for a fair portion of its members.

The two organized gangs with members in Venice were the V-13 and the Venice Shoreline Crips. The V-13 were predominantly Latino male teens but included some middle-aged and older adults while the Shoreline were predominantly African American male teens and young adults, though there were exceptions to both, including Southeast Asian members of the V-13 and part-Latino members of the Shoreline Crips. Oakwood was a major hub for the Shoreline since many of their social and economic activities were concentrated there. Also, many of those who assumed influential roles in the Shoreline were from the Oakwood neighborhood. The Shoreline also had a presence in the Mar Vista Gardens with a "cousin" organization under the same name. A low-rise public housing complex located a few miles away, their presence there was on the decline, as the number of African American families who resided there had decreased, especially during the 1980s. The V-13 also had a strong presence in Oakwood, but their activities were dispersed throughout the larger Venice area. Both gangs had a fairly large street network numbering at times up to several hundred each with varying levels of involvement. Both had various subgroups or cliques organized by age, location, or friendship ties.[11] The V-13 tended to be more tightly organized than the Shoreline. The age of affiliates ranged from young adolescents to those in their forties and fifties. And both were multigenerational with long histories in the neighborhood.

Like other large cities throughout the country, gang violence in Los Angeles was a growing problem in the 1980s and early 1990s, and the Westside communities of Mar Vista and Venice were no exception. Gang-related violence had become more serious due to several factors, including the easy access to firearms, the use of violence to protect underground economic activities, the effect of mainstream cultural values regarding materialism, the effects of imprisonment on gangs, and the limited opportunities available to many marginalized youths (Hagedorn 1998). Gangs had also grown in size and expanded their influence on "street subculture" and activities, now spanning the social to the cultural and economic. Many gangs grew to have a heavy influence on street life and on the socialization of youths who found themselves on the "margins," often after leaving school (often as a result of expulsion due to zero-tolerance policies), leaving home, or becoming homeless. Especially vulnerable were adolescent young men who had experienced personal or family trauma, marginalization, or victimization and who were in search of social support, protection, camaraderie, and a definition of manhood not available elsewhere (Vigil 1987, 2003).[12]

Oakwood was where the Shoreline were historically based, and their presence along with that of some members of the V-13 had become a focus of law enforcement efforts. One of the outcomes of gentrification was an organized constituency of residents concerned with the impact of crime on public safety and property values. New property owners and real estate interests exerted pressure on law enforcement officials to "clean up" Oakwood by eliminating the robberies, drug dealing, and vandalism occurring at purportedly higher rates than surrounding areas. A vocal group of homeowners took a visible role in speaking out against the drug dealing occurring on public streets and sidewalks. Some of them cooperated with police to videotape criminal activity from their homes at the risk of their personal safety.

Individuals who were seen as cooperating with police were ridiculed by gang members and affiliates as "snitches." Some of these individuals experienced personal retaliation, including personal threats and even firebombing of their home, for this role. One such firebombing took place in the midst of the 1992 civil unrest, when a homeowner who had cooperated with police was victimized. He believed gang members were taking advantage of the chaos of the civil unrest to inflict retaliation against him. Since almost all of those seen as working closely with police were middle-aged white male homeowners and since almost all of those seen as violating the law were either Latino or African American young men, a schism along the prominent dimensions of race, generation, and gender festered over time.

Meanwhile, a group of women, many of whom were active in the civil rights era, had over several decades actively maintained local block clubs (neighborhood watch groups). While they attempted to work with police to reduce criminal activity, many in the block clubs also protested acts of police misconduct against African Americans and other minorities. They and others long argued that job training and recreational and other opportunities for gang members and youths in general could offer a more meaningful alternative to illegal activities. They argued for closer cooperation between families and agencies to resolve the myriad social and economic problems that lead to criminal activity. While many residents, government agents, and community activists agreed with this general concept, cooperation was often difficult to achieve given the complex social history, persistent inequalities, and dwindling amount of resources for social programs.

The problem of criminal activity in earlier days had also left some tension between Latino victims of crime and the young African American men suspected of perpetrating those crimes. During the 1970s and 1980s, new immigrants, mostly from Mexico, fell victim to occasional but persistent street robberies. Many immigrants at that time were known to carry large sums of cash on their person, since many did not use banking services due to fears related to their undocumented legal status in the United States. These robberies were one reason for the initiation of a community credit union by the Community Service Organization that lasted until the late 1990s.

These economic and social conditions set the backdrop for the "War on Drugs" launched in the 1980s. The Los Angeles Police Department developed a high-suppression police plan for Oakwood, titled the "Oakwood Plan." This plan focused primarily on the Venice Shoreline Crips and secondarily on the V-13, the two street organizations that operated in the Venice area. Under this suppression plan, the LAPD, in concert with other local and federal agencies, engaged in gang tracking, surveillance, and undercover and other activities that led to the arrest of scores of youths and young adults who revolved through the county jail and state prison systems. With the adoption of "zero tolerance" policies by the Los Angeles Unified School District, numerous students were expelled from public schools throughout greater Los Angeles. Venice schools were no exception, contributing to the already high dropout rates in the school district. "Zero tolerance" policies combined with intensive police suppression activities and mandatory sentencing laws led to the steady rise in the prison and jail populations statewide. Youths in Venice were also affected by the expanded scope of law enforcement powers, detailed further in the next chapter.

Community Institutions and Organizations

At the time this study was conducted, there were many community-based organizations in Oakwood and the surrounding areas in Venice. Organiza-

TABLE 3.3
Partial list of organizations and institutions in or adjacent to Oakwood, 1994

Churches
New Bethel Baptist Church
St. Clements Church
St. Mark's Cathedral
St. Joseph's Church

Education and youth groups
Venice Shoreline Crips (VSLC)*
Venice 13 (V-13)
Pearl White Theater*
Project Heavy West
Venice Skills Center
Barrios Unidos
Boys and Girls Club of Venice
LIEU CAP (Community Action Program)
Neighborhood Youth Association
Community Youth Gang Services
Westminster Children's Center
Westminster Elementary School
Broadway Elementary School
Venice Arts Mecca
Venice Library

Community, social, and health service organizations
Community Service Organization*
Oakwood United
Jewish Family Service
Venice Family Clinic
Didi Hirsch Community Mental Health Center
Prototypes/Women and AIDS Risk Network
Oakwood Recreation Center
Oakwood Wesley House*
Positive Alternative Choices Today
Santa Monica/Venice Branch, NAACP

Civic and homeowner's groups
Oakwood Homeowners and Tenants Association*
Oakwood Property Owners Association*

Housing and economic development organizations
Venice Community Housing Corporation
Venice Chamber of Commerce

Majority of members residents of Oakwood (not including houses of worship)

tions based outside of Oakwood and even outside of Venice were also present, as outreach workers related to clients and residents in the neighborhood. Oakwood itself was rich in community associations and activities. Table 3.3 lists the major organizations and institutions based in Oakwood along with external organizations that sponsored activities or had outreach workers in Oakwood. Some of these organizations no longer have a presence in Oakwood, and new organizations have since then formed. There are also other organizations that have not been listed that have members who reside in the neighborhood.

Many of these associations and activities involved residents across a spectrum of backgrounds. However, differences in income level, race, education, language, culture, gender, religion, home ownership, and length of residence were noticeable in the composition of organizations and participation in many community activities. Common preferences, interests, and informal social networks shaped the makeup of civic groups and associations. Some gatherings were more homogeneous and others were more diverse. For example, there were five Protestant churches in the Oakwood area that were predominantly African American in membership, while several Catholic churches had predominantly Latino congregations. At the same time, activities held at each of the churches often brought together residents of all racial backgrounds, such as weddings, funerals, and preschool programs. Sports leagues were a mixed bag. For example, the local football league involved mainly African American youths, while young Latino males gravitated toward soccer. But at the same time both racial groups could be found playing together on the basketball court.

Two vocal and often conflicting groups that actively organized during the early 1990s were the Oakwood Homeowners and Tenants Association (OHTA) and the Oakwood Property Owners Association (OPOA). Boundaries of race, class, ideology, and gender intersected in defining the composition of these two groups and their leadership. OHTA was comprised of residents of the HUD-subsidized apartments, longtime homeowners—many of whom were older African American residents—and others who had participated in some of the civil rights activities in the 1960s and 1970s. Members of this resident association came into conflict with the more recently organized OPOA, comprised exclusively of those who owned property in Oakwood. Class differences were the primary cleavage between these two quite outspoken groups. However, the visible leadership and active core of OHTA were older African American women, while that of OPOA were somewhat younger to middle-aged white men.

There were other organizations based in and around the neighborhood that served the needs of many low-income residents and children. Most of these service organizations were racially inclusive of all residents and supported racial cooperation to varying degrees. Two of the oldest grassroots service organizations were the Pearl White Theater and the Community Service Organization. Both had been active during the civil rights movement, conducting voter registration drives, organizing block clubs, organizing activities for youths, and providing various social services. Other organizations such as Venice Teen Post, LIEU-CAP, Oakwood Wesley House, and the Venice Boys and Girls Club also involved residents and provided valuable services throughout the years. In addition, many other institutions serving the Oakwood neighborhood were located there or in close proximity. These included the Oakwood Park and Recreation Center, the Venice Skills Center, the Westminster Elementary School, the Broadway Elementary School, the Venice

Family Clinic, the Venice Arts Mecca, the Venice Community Housing Corporation, and Positive Alternative Choices Today, among others. In 1992, representatives from a portion of these groups formed a coalition called Oakwood United, initially convened as an information- and resource-sharing network; it later embarked on a small economic development venture.

While many of the social service organizations mentioned earlier served what some call "at-risk" youths, there were several agencies that worked specifically with gang-involved youths. Project Heavy West (PHW) was a local nonprofit agency focused on gang prevention activities such as counseling, tutoring, and peer mediation skills. Community Youth Gang Services (CYGS) was a county-funded agency based in East Los Angeles that hired gang intervention workers in other parts of the city, including an outreach worker for the Venice area. In addition to gang prevention and gang intervention workers, various law enforcement personnel worked in the neighborhood. State parole workers and county probation workers had Venice residents as part of their caseloads. Police, city attorneys, and district attorneys were also involved in Venice. The activities of law enforcement agencies are covered in the next chapter.

Even though the Oakwood neighborhood was rich in organizational and institutional resources relative to more isolated urban areas, longstanding conflicts and competition over resources, particularly between community-based organizations and more professionalized human services agencies, often made meaningful cooperation difficult to achieve. Changes in social policy contributed to the alienation between many social service agencies and some of the more vocal and active residents of Oakwood associated with grassroots community groups. Cutbacks in social programs and changes in funding patterns made it more and more difficult for grassroots community organizations to compete for public monies. Funding criteria shifted in emphasis from community-based governance of social programs to the professional management and administration of service agencies. And a change in funding cycles at the city block grant level from one-year to three-year cycles favored larger and more stable organizations. Many of the more grassroots groups, lacking resources, technical expertise, and professional credentials, could no longer compete for shrinking resources. Ironically, the more professional organizations, while often very effective with their clients, tended to have less contact with those most marginalized, including gang-involved youths and their families.

Meaning-making and Multiple Publics

Visions of Venice and the folklore about events of interest go back as far as the social networks and institutions reach. Each neighborhood network circulates its unique recollections. These memories are as divergent as the experiences of different segments of the community. However discordant, they shape the sentiments that people hold about their neighborhood and their visions of its future. Some would like to see the preservation of their community of friends and relations, while others envision change and see themselves as part of its transformation. Demographic shifts, market forces, and government policies and social institutions combine to gather people with different aspirations who play out their fate in the backdrop of multiple and parallel histories. Common touchstones, in turn, reinforce networks of mutual support and obligation. Collective memories form part of the social bond that holds these networks together. They are also grounds for the formation of multiple publics—groups that identify with one another and share interpretive lenses through which they see the world around them and based on which they take collective action in a given situation.

A major stage-setting issue that influenced the formation of multiple publics during the gang conflict was crime and law enforcement policy. It is to this subject we now turn.

Chapter 4

Law Enforcement Policy and the Oakwood Plan

Gang violence in the United States reached historic levels from the 1980s through the mid-1990s. Media touted Los Angeles County as the "gang capital" of the nation, as gang-related violence left over 800 dead in 1992 alone. Meanwhile, social and economic conditions in many urban neighborhoods worsened. The gap between rich and poor across the nation and throughout the region continued to widen. Global economic restructuring, worldwide recession, regressive fiscal policies, cuts in education and human services, retrenchment of welfare policies, wide availability of firearms, and deterioration of social and physical infrastructure in central city areas added further strain to the most distressed of American neighborhoods. Some argued that repressive measures used to quell the activism of the civil rights era in the late 1960s contributed to the fall of the emerging young leadership, particularly in African American communities in cities such as Los Angeles, leaving a vacuum that would be filled over the next several decades by the expansion of youth gangs in areas buffeted by high rates of poverty and instability. With an estimated membership of 130,000 by the early 1990s, gangs in Los Angeles County would become a major target of law enforcement in a policy environment marked by growing public fear.[1]

Gang suppression operations were established in Los Angeles and other big cities across the country.[2] As a whole, these operations employed the following measures: (1) increase the "zone of violation" under which gang members can be arrested and increase penalties for gang-related crimes; (2) increase the powers of law enforcement agencies to investigate and arrest identified gang suspects; (3) create specialized units in various agencies to focus specifically on gang-related crime; (4) set up anti-gang task forces to coordinate the work of various arms of law enforcement; (5) establish information systems to track the movement and activities of gang members; and (6) devise special operations intended to quell gang activities (Klein 1993).[3]

The Oakwood Plan developed by the Los Angeles Police Department (LAPD) in late 1980s was a prime example of a high-suppression plan targeting the gangs in the Oakwood neighborhood of Venice. It provided a general outline for policing strategies up to and during the outbreak of the gang war. The objectives of the plan were to eliminate gang violence, "remove" the criminal element, reduce the level of fear among residents, and establish long-term control over the crime problem in Oakwood. The plan was a twenty-four–page document authored by LAPD's Pacific Division leadership along with key veteran officers in consultation with related agencies.[4] It was originally written in 1988–89 and later updated in December 1993.[5] The updated plan was very similar but placed greater emphasis on community-based policing following the entrance of Willie Williams, successor to Daryl Gates as chief of the LAPD. Both versions of the plan called for a high-suppression approach by a team of officers from the "Oakwood Task Force" in coordination with other agencies, particularly the Office of the City Attorney and the District Attorney's Office.[6] More important, the plan provides the context necessary to understand the LAPD response to the outbreak of the gang war.

But the Oakwood Plan was not devised in a policy vacuum. To the contrary, its core assumptions and approach reflected the larger national policy environment toward gangs and youth violence. The following sections describe the policy environment within which the Oakwood Plan was articulated as well as the Oakwood Plan itself. I also describe the controversies surrounding these high-suppression approaches, especially in light of the problems troubling the local police department. These problems were the focus of an investigation by the Independent Commission on the Los Angeles Police Department (better known as the Christopher Commission) following the incident in which LAPD officers were videotaped beating African American motorist Rodney King. I suggest that the shift toward a decidedly punitive set of criminal justice policies and more suppressive police practices and away from education and social programs changed the quality of the interface between state and civil society, or more specifically government agents and community residents, particularly in distressed neighborhoods such as Oakwood. This had many implications, among them the limited ability of government agencies across the spectrum to develop a fuller and deeper understanding of the problem and the limited leverage of agencies and community organizations to affect situations involving gang violence.

America's "Gang Problem"

Two separate phenomena coincided in the 1980s and 1990s that profoundly shaped law enforcement policies toward gangs. A moral panic over the more general problem of drugs and crime struck the nation from the mid-1980s into the 1990s (Reinarman and Levine 1997). At the same time, the country saw a disturbing rise in the levels of youth violence in major cities such as Los Angeles (Hutson et al. 1995). The timing of the two contributed to a conflation of three distinct problems in the public image—gangs, drugs, and crime. Gangs were blamed as the main purveyors of drugs, who spread the use of violence in defending their turf (Jackson 1993). Gangs became seen as a major "disease" responsible for what many experts assessed as being a great deal more responsible for society's ills than was indeed the case (Moore 1991; Jackson 1993; Hutson et al. 1995; Hagedorn 1998). Though gangs would get more involved in the drug trade nationally over the next decade (Skolnick et al. 1988), gangs were a primary target in the campaign to wage a "War on Drugs" from the start—a campaign that not only led to the apprehension of gang members but also created a set of images that demonized young African American and Latino men in the public eye and cemented a heavily suppressive and punitive policy infrastructure.

Public alarm over the "gang problem" helped to fuel a larger moral panic over crime, lending momentum to the creation of a sophisticated set of law enforcement tools and tactics to address gang proliferation and violence (Jackson 1993). A succession of policy reforms increased the range of violations and the severity of sanctions against law violators. In California, for example, the state legislature created the Gang Violence Suppression (GVS) program in 1981, giving district attorneys greater powers and resources to prosecute perpetrators of gang violence. In 1988, California passed the Street Terrorism Enforcement and Prevention Act (STEP; California Penal Code Section 186.20), which created sentencing enhancements for gang members; many other states passed similar measures. As for federal courts, legislation and court decisions had already increased police powers by expanding federal authority to investigate and interrogate individuals suspected of gang-related offenses.[7] By the 1992 election year, candidates addressed the issue of crime as a major platform issue in the presidential race. In 1994, Congress passed the most sweeping crime bill of this century—the Violent Crime Control and Law Enforcement Act (Public Law 103-322)—more commonly known as the 1994 Crime Bill. The 1994 Crime Bill included the "three strikes and you're out" mandatory life imprisonment without possibility of parole for federal offenders with three or more convictions for serious violent felonies or drug trafficking crimes. It also authorized stiffer penalties for violent and drug trafficking crimes committed by gang members, adult prosecution for those 13 and older charged with certain violent crimes, and expansion of death penalty application to nearly 60 additional offenses.[8]

This period of law enforcement crackdown on gangs and the "War on Drugs" contributed to high rates of incarceration among young male adults in California and elsewhere (Langan 1991). Between 1980 and 1994, the number of sentenced inmates incarcerated under state and federal jurisdiction increased threefold from 139 prisoners per 100,000 population to 389 per 100,000 (U.S. Department of Justice 2004a).[9] By 1994, there were over 5 million persons under corrections supervision, including jail, prison, probation, and parole (U.S. Department of Justice 2004b).[10] By several accounts, the United States had the second highest rate of incarceration in the world (Currie 1998; Walmsley 1999), with only Russia having a higher rate until it was surpassed by the United States shortly into the new millennium (Walmsley 2001). Incarceration rates in U.S. prisons and jails differed greatly by race with African Americans and Hispanics imprisoned in U.S. jails at rates that were seven and three times higher than non-Hispanic whites, respectively.[11]

Subsequently, the 1980s and 1990s witnessed a boom in the growth and political influence of the prison industry. By 1995, California was reported to have carried out the largest prison-building boom in U.S. history. With this came the political influence of the growing ranks of prison guards. That year, the *New York Times* reported that "the California Correctional Peace Officers' Association has transformed itself into the most politically influential union in the state, using its muscle and generous campaign contributions to push not only for better benefits for its members but also for ever more prisons and tougher sentencing laws." In 1992, campaign contributions by the union's political action committee were behind only the California Medical Association (Butterfield 1995). In a relatively short period of time, this industry had created a powerful engine that actively mobilized for its own perpetuation and extension.

As the incarcerated population grew, so did the ranks of large prison-based gangs (Huff and Meyer 1997; Curry and Decker 1998). Curry and Decker (1998) cited growing evidence that prison had the effect of propelling many young men toward gang membership—young men who had never been gang members prior to their incarceration. Links between prison gangs and street gangs were strengthened, as many youths and young adults became affiliated with prison gangs for protection within and outside of prison walls (Hagedorn 1990). Some became involved for economic opportunities, as prison gangs in some cities had become increasingly influential in the underground drug trade (Hagedorn 1998). With the growth in the membership of prison gangs, there has been growing concern over the degree of social control they have come to wield in the prisons, their reinforcement of street gangs, and the increased proclivity among those involved in prison gangs to violence following their imprisonment (Moore 1978; Vigil and Long 1990; Curry and Decker 1998).

Violence among prison gangs, including racial violence, became a serious problem for state officials in many prisons throughout the country (Huff and Meyer 1997; Fleisher and Decker 2001). In California as in many other states, prison gangs were organized largely along racial lines, mirroring the composition of many of the street gangs affiliated with them. During the 1980s, many prison gangs throughout California became entangled in violent interracial conflict. Tensions intensified with the overcrowded conditions, competition within the drug trade, and a changing demographic balance as the proportion of Latino inmates in many facilities began to surpass that of African Americans.[12] Prisons became a major site of racial conflict and animosity that reverberated onto the streets, with violence traveling the full circle. A growing number of California prisons instituted the practice of racially segregating inmates, at least for the first sixty days and often for the duration of the sentence, as a way to avert conflict. While this may have been a prudent tactic to address the immediate problem, sustained segregation continued to reinforce the centrality of racial identities and a racially bound system of social organization.[13]

In Los Angeles, the dominance of high-suppression approaches and the reproduction of racial conflict within the correctional system combined with a number of developments. These included a heightened sense of nationalism among the various gangs, intensified street violence, more desperate social and economic conditions in many urban neighborhoods, continued proliferation of firearms, abysmally high public school dropout rates, and fading government support for social programs. This left a politically and socially polarized environment.

"Moral Panics" and Crime Policy

The concept of "moral panics" describes a state of fear that captures the public in response to a perceived breach in the moral contract of a society.[14] As put by Cohen (1972), "Societies appear to be subject, every now and then, to periods of moral panic. A condition, episode, person or group of persons emerges to become defined as a threat to societal values and interests" (28; also cited in Hall et al. 1978, 16). Hall and his colleagues illustrated how institutions help to define situations, select targets, initiate campaigns, and legitimate their actions in response to a defined problem. He stated, "They do not merely respond to 'moral panics,' but form part of the circle out of which they develop. Thus, they '*amplify* the deviancy they seem so absolutely committed to controlling' and thereby act out a script which they do not write" (52).

One common feature of moral panics is the contradiction between popular perceptions and official evidence. The 1980s panic in the United States was sparked by a perceived increase in the rate of violent crime. The flurry of rhetoric about the rising rate of crime, however, contradicted crime statistics showing that the overall crime rate had not changed significantly since 1973. In fact, crime had decreased since 1980, as shown in figure 4.1 (Chambliss 1995; Torny 1995).[15] Data collected by the Bureau of Justice Statistics and the FBI indicated that the rate of violent crime remained relatively stable between 1976 and 1992. Some categories of crime did increase, but most of the increases reported in the Uniform Crime Reports was due to an increase in the reporting of crime (Bogess and Bound 1993).

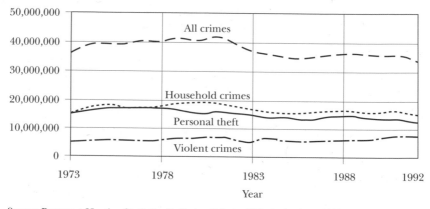

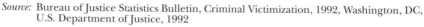

Source: Bureau of Justice Statistics Bulletin, Criminal Victimization, 1992, Washington, DC, U.S. Department of Justice, 1992

Figure 4.1 Victimization trends, 1973–1992, crimes reported by type of crime

The moral panic lent support to cries for increased law enforcement powers despite a history that has shown that increased powers do not necessarily lead to decreased crime (Jacob 1984; Torny 1995). The post–World War II era, for example, was a boon for police, courts, and prisons; police expenditures tripled between 1948 and 1978, yet crime continued to surge. To the contrary, a great deal of research on the sources and correlates of criminality and gang violence suggest that there is not a single "magic bullet"; multiple modes of intervention are necessary. This one-dimensional focus precluded a more integrated strategy that may prove more effective for this complex problem.

Furthermore, the moral panic was imbued with a strong racial tinge. The appropriation of racial imagery animated alarmist stories in politics and the media about the growing criminal threat. One illustrative example was the personification of crime using references to Willie Horton by candidate George H. W. Bush in his 1988 bid for the presidency. Willie Horton was an African American man who raped a white Maryland woman on a work furlough taken while serving a sentence for a murder conviction in a Massachusetts state prison. Willie Horton became a symbol of the "incorrigible criminal" whose life was projected to buttress a tough stance against crime. This and similar caricatures of the problem promoted the cognitive association between crime and race, particularly the association of criminal activity with African American, Latino, and other nonwhite males, perpetuating a long and documented injection of racial meanings into the public discourse (Chambliss 1995; Torny 1995). These helped to reinforce and embellish negative stereotypes, fostering greater public receptivity to punitive rather than rehabilitative measures to address a problem seen as being perpetuated by an "undeserving other."

Los Angeles and the "Gang Problem"

Despite the stable rate of violent crime between 1976 and 1992 nationally, there was a growing rate of gang-related violence in certain cities. The increase in gang-related violence during this period was most pronounced in Los Angeles and Chicago (Block et al. 1996; Maxson 1998). In Los Angeles County, gang-related homicides quadrupled from 1982 to 1992 (see figure 4.2). Near the start of the gang war in 1992, 803 persons were killed in gang-related incidents across the county (Katz 1991, 1993a). This number peaked at 807 in 1995 and later began to decline. An epidemiological study of gang-related violence in Los Angeles showed that the proportion of gang-related deaths increased from 18.1 percent in 1979 to 43 percent of homicides in 1994 (7,288 of 27,302). In 1994, almost 40 percent of gang-related homicide victims were children or adolescents, with African American and Hispanic victims accounting for 93 percent of those victims. Most of the homicides were intra-racial; 82.2 percent of gang-related homicides involved a victim and perpetrator identified with the same racial group.[16] Of the cases studied, 32.7 percent of those killed had no known street gang involvement. And firearms were used in 94.5 percent of the homicides (Hutson et al. 1995).

Los Angeles was a primary source of imagery in the panoply of portraits fueling public alarm. Jackson (1993) and Chambliss (1995) argued that a moral panic over the problem of gang violence struck major metropolitan cities in the United States from the late 1970s through the 1990s. Gangs were proclaimed to be an illness crippling our society. Gang violence came to represent the breakdown of the family, the deterioration of moral values, the decadence of greed, and the product of an overly permissive society. The 1989

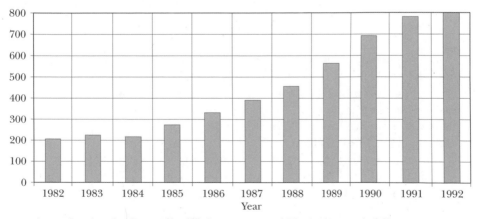

Source: Los Angeles County Sheriff's Department and District Attorney's Office

Figure 4.2 Gang-related homicides in Los Angeles County, 1982–1992

California State Task Force on Gangs and Drugs quoted Sacramento County District Attorney John Dougherty, who stated, "The situation has been called narcoterrorism, a blight, an epidemic, an infection, and perhaps the health analogies are correct, because gangs and drugs attack the community body as other diseases attack the human body" (California Council on Criminal Justice 1989, 12).

By the late 1980s, gang-related violence had gained national attention. High-ranking government officials began referring to the "gang problem" as an issue of national security. Federal agencies were mobilized to address the problem with a national information database to track the movement of suspected gang members. In a statement before the Congressional Subcommittee on Civil and Constitutional Rights of the Committee on the Judiciary in June 1992, Daniel M. Hartnett, then associate director of law enforcement of the Bureau of Alcohol, Tobacco, and Firearms, testified:

> The close working relationships between the Bureau of Alcohol, Tobacco and Firearms and state and local law enforcement agencies enabled ATF to be one of the first in federal law enforcement to identify these violent gangs as not just a threat to one city or one localized area, but as a national threat, one that had to be dealt with at the national level.[17]

Henry J. Hyde, a member of the subcommittee and a representative from Illinois, responded to ethical concerns over the federal government gathering such information into a national database. He supported the idea with an analogy to fighting Nazism:

> I dare say, in time of national stress and security issues approaching even war, who is to say we are not at war today in some of our cities? War has been declared by some people against this society—membership in the Nazi Party, just for example. I would be more comforted knowing that our intelligence services knew who the Nazis were back in, say, 1941, 1940, 1939.[18]

Los Angeles was seen as a center from which the "gang problem" emanated nationally. Then LAPD Chief Daryl Gates warned that "cities of all sizes throughout the United States are now threatened either by an influx of Los Angeles–area gang members or by local gangs attempting to establish dominance" (Gates and Jackson 1990). One of the characteristics of contemporary gangs emphasized by Hartnett in his testimony was that "this new breed of criminals were [sic] highly mobile, with their activities spanning state and regional boundaries."[19] These messages nurtured a fear that if the "gang problem" was not quickly "contained," gangs could proliferate and cause havoc in every city across the nation.

The Gap between Knowledge and Practice

The way in which gangs were problematized in the discourse of moral panic, however, did not reflect our best understanding of the phenomenon at that time and resulted in policies and practices based on dubious assumptions. In the policy discourse on the problem of gangs, for example, it was assumed that drugs and violence were inextricably intertwined. Not only did the three problems come to mean the same thing, the increase in one problem implied an increase in the other two. But research has shown that the relationship among gangs, drugs, and violence was more complex than popularly perceived (Moore 1990; Klein and Maxon 1994; Fagan 1996; Howell and Decker 1999).[20] Though there was a higher rate of violence among gang members and a greater frequency of violent offenders among gangs, not all gang members participated in acts of violence. According to a 1992 report by the Los Angeles District Attorney, it was estimated that half of all gang members in Los Angeles did not participate in violence; the other half participated in violence that for the most part was "minor or isolated in most cases" (Reiner 1992, iii). Furthermore, it was not clear whether or not the increased frequency of gang-related violence reflected the extent to which (a) gangs were becoming more violent; (b) there was a rise in the number of gangs; or (c) there was a general increase in societal violence. It was also recognized that it was often only a few members of any gang instigating acts of violence and that violence was not necessarily the preferred *modus operandi* for the vast majority of gangs or gang members (Jankowski 1991).

There was a similarly complex relationship between gangs and drugs.[21] Not all gangs participated in the sale of narcotics and not all narcotics were distributed by gangs (Klein and Maxson 1994). There were also vast differences among gangs in the extent to which members of various gangs used different types of drugs (Fagan 1989; Huff 1996). Klein (1995) encouraged a distinction between street gangs and drug gangs, due to the fact that most street gangs did not conduct high-level drug distribution beyond their immediate territory. A law enforcement survey of over 200 cities found that drug gangs appeared to comprise less than a tenth of all gangs (Klein and Maxson 1996).[22] At the same time, there were a number of street gangs that were connected with larger prison gangs involved in drug trafficking and other criminal enterprises on a larger geographic scale (Jackson and McBride 1985; Ralph et al. 1996). Though there were gangs involved in the drug trade, researchers observed that most gang homicides did not appear to be related directly to drug trafficking (Curry and Decker 1998; Klein, Maxson, and Cunningham 1991) and the relationship among drugs, drug trafficking, and violent crime remained a topic of much debate (De La Rosa, Lambert, and Gropper 1990). Moreover, most local experts agreed that, at least up to that time, gangs in Los Angeles had not evolved into organized distribution rings (Reiner 1992).

Most researchers agreed that gangs are best understood in the context of a larger societal problem having to do with the marginalization of groups in society and the isolation of youths from the mainstream of opportunities and social life (Spergel and Curry 1993; Curry and Decker 1998).[23] Scholars have emphasized different reasons for gang involvement that include both "push" and "pull" factors (Curry and Decker 1998). Horowitz (1983) suggested that gang subculture was one solution to demands for honor made by the local culture in light of expectations modeled by the "American dream" that seemed for many unreachable. Gangs provided an alternative path for socialization during the critical period of adolescence (Vigil 1988; Thrasher 1927; Thornberry et al. 2003). In some neighborhoods, they not only offered social camaraderie but also economic alternatives that appeared attractive, particularly in the isolation of economically and politically marginalized communities of color (Skolnick 1990; Sanchez-Jankowski 1990; Vigil 1990; Padilla 1992; Fagan 1996). Especially in areas of high gang membership, some joined to seek protection from rival gangs or the other risks of urban life they saw around them. Once initiated, members would be subject to the duties, obligations, and risks of a life from which it was difficult to retreat without serious physical and social consequences. In cities such as Los Angeles, a growing sophistication and organization of gangs accompanied the growth of the urban underclass, ever more distant from those life options deemed "legitimate" in an increasingly polarized society (Moore 1991). And as gangs grew in numbers and "corporatized"[24] their activities, they were able to wield greater influence in the daily movements within a community by marking turf, spatializing ally and enemy relations, and assigning certain areas for exchange and consumption. In so doing, their presence forced others to reconstitute their personal identities in reference to the gang-based social space they inhabited (Venkatesh 1996).

One obstacle to finding appropriate interventions to gang-related crime has been the disconnection between existing theoretical-empirical understandings of the problem and the choice of responses that are most often used (Miller 1990). Scholars have pointed out that there remains a great deal of variation in the structure and dynamics of contemporary gangs and gang crime problems (Hagedorn 1988; Curry and Spergel 1992; Spergel and Curry 1993; Moore 1993; Klein 1995; Curry and Decker 1998). They have also noted variations among cliques within a gang and among individuals within cliques. Different gang structures and dynamics require different tools and approaches for intervention. The task of the practitioner is to find the most appropriate solution given the particularities of the problem in a given neighborhood. The types of options range from community mobilization and the provision of social services and opportunities to law enforcement suppression. Each type includes a vast suite of tools and can be combined into any number of approaches.

But seldom are interventions well integrated or based on an informed assessment of the particular case. Even more seldom are strategies adjusted over time as conditions change, based on built-in mechanisms for social learning. Thus far, few evaluations have been conducted on attempted interventions, and those that have been conducted have not been conclusive. More careful evaluation of social interventions and further experimentation with innovative approaches has been stunted by the rush toward punitive policies and programs. As Curry and Decker (1998) noted, "One problem is that those who have the ultimate responsibility for developing and implementing programs are policy makers and practitioners who do not have extensive training in theory, while researchers, who have extensive training in theory, do not often have a significant role in the practical aspects of responding to gang problems" (162).

The lasting legacy of the moral panic was a policy trajectory based on a one-dimensional understanding of the problem—completely devoid of the intricacies, complexities, and subtleties that may have prompted a more holistic approach to dealing with it. The racially veiled demonization of gangs eroded public empathy for the plight of those youths. This was aggravated by a retreat from the concerns of the urban underclass more generally (Cummings and Monti 1993). In the midst of policy debates that vehemently objectified youth gangs, little attention was paid to the multidimensionality of youth violence. Few policymakers understood the impetus for gang involvement, the varied nature of gang activity, the social dynamics of youth gangs, the relationships between gang members and the larger community, and the variables that contributed to certain types of gang activity. Variations among the targeted population were flattened and swept into a less discerning system of social control dominated by law enforcement institutions with relatively skimpy resources allocated to other modes of intervention. The result was a set of extremely blunt policy instruments to address a highly complex problem.

The Oakwood Plan

The Oakwood Plan reflected the prevailing law enforcement perception of the problem in Oakwood and how police believed they could best address it.[25] For the purposes of this book, it provides the context to understand the response of the LAPD to the gang war and gives some sense of their relations with African American and Latino residents. Though the written plan was an internal LAPD document, some residents in Oakwood had knowledge about the plan and its contents. Their understanding of the plan also figured into their interpretation of events during the war. The following describes the original plan launched in the late 1980s, representing the policy approach at the outset of the gang war. An eventual shift in emphasis toward a somewhat more community-oriented approach yielded more positive community relations in the later stages of the conflict.

Targeting the "Predators"

The LAPD and other law enforcement agencies identified the Shoreline Crips as one of the most "notorious" gangs in Los Angeles. They were also one of more than twenty gangs in Los Angeles County targeted by the FBI for investigation of federal violations following the civil unrest in 1992.[26] Locally, the LAPD identified the Shoreline along with the V-13 as a source of a large proportion of criminal activity in the Venice area. Oakwood had been designated a Gang Related Active Trafficker Suppression (GRATS) hot spot.[27] The LAPD's GRATS program was launched in 1988 "to focus on the narcotic aspect of the Black street gang problem."[28] For the LAPD's Pacific Division, located in the westernmost division in the LAPD's jurisdiction, Oakwood was a major focus of police operations. Its proximity to the world-famous Venice boardwalk also contributed to the high level of political attention to the area.

The Oakwood Plan used the term "predator" to describe perpetrators of criminal acts in Oakwood. One of the patrol units was named the "Pacific Area Predator Arrest Team" (PAT), assigned to identify, apprehend, and prosecute those listed using "every available Department resource." The Oakwood Plan stated:

> Currently, PAT personnel have identified over thirty predators who either live in or apply their evil trade in Oakwood. Most of these individuals are also members of either the Venice Shoreline Crips or the Venice 13 gangs. Past police experience in Oakwood has determined that much of the criminal activity is being perpetrated by members of various criminal gangs. (13)

Webster's dictionary defines a "predator" as "one that preys, destroys, or devours" or "an animal that depends on predation for its food." This projection painted a portrait of a group of primal creatures that pose an ominous threat to society at large.

The plan named an intersection in Oakwood as the second most active narcotics street sales location citywide and described the Shorelines as "a confederation of cocaine selling groups bound together by loyalty to the neighborhood" (8). The plan noted the proliferation of automatic weapons made available by the sale of cocaine. The active participation of members in the drug trade was seen as responsible for the increased frequency of attacks on police officers. "The street sales of narcotics, guns, and stolen property cannot take place with the presence of police officers. The gang member, who uses intimidation, fear and death to control rival gangs, victims of their crimes, and the neighborhood where they live, are attempting to use the same tactics on the officers who patrol the streets" (9). The plan noted the increased frequency of attacks on police officers and LAPD officers were regularly reminded of the dangers gangs presented to their safety.

A plan that targeted gangs in the geographic area of Oakwood would by default focus on the activities of the Venice Shoreline Crips (VSLC), despite the presence of V-13 members, due to the mere fact that the activities of the Shoreline were concentrated in Oakwood whereas the V-13 was more dispersed throughout Venice. While the plan also mentioned numerous Latino and "mixed race" gangs whose territory lay in the boundaries of the Pacific Division, it stated that "the primary problem gang in Oakwood is the Venice Shoreline Crips." (7).[29]

One of the sensitive features of the plan was the subtle implication of the larger African American community as logically suspected of local criminal activity. The plan described the social ties between gang members and a network of longtime families. But in doing so, it raised suspicion about the larger African American population, many of whom may have been related to gang members but who themselves may have led crime-free lives. The plan distinguished the Shoreline Crips from other gangs by their integration in the social fabric of the local African American community, stating:

> The Shoreline Crip community is different than any other black gang because of its homogeneous roots. Essentially, the gang is a web of criminal associations within a larger network of historical criminal association between about a dozen repeat offender families. The more the families of Oakwood are studied, the more it becomes apparent and the more you understand that almost everyone is related through either marriage or out of wedlock births. (7)

Various families were mentioned by name as "prominent criminal families where repeat offenders have spanned generations" (7). Family relations were also described to illustrate the degree of intermarriage within the community.

The plan also named political organizations tied to African Americans in Oakwood, such as the Santa Monica chapter of the NAACP and the Rainbow Coalition, as problematic to the extent that they exerted political influence restricting the activities of the LAPD. These local organizations assisted residents' efforts to curb police misconduct by filing charges on behalf of residents. The implied "incestuous" behavior of gangs, residents, and political organizations created tensions between law enforcement agencies and constituencies that would otherwise be considered "legitimate."

One of the dangers of the plan's depiction of the community was in its simplification of the much more complex nature of attitudes that residents held toward police and of the nature of group affiliations. Many African American residents interviewed, for example, were willing to cooperate more closely with law enforcement officers to curb criminal activities if (1) there were positive alternatives that youths could be steered toward, (2) officers would show a greater attitude of respect toward members of the African American community, and (3) antidiscriminatory reforms would be made in the establishment and enforcement of criminal laws. Some asked, for example, why drug buyers, the majority of whom were white males, rather than sellers were not targeted in any sustained manner to balance the supply-side equation of the problem. Many voiced sadness about the deteriorating social effects of drugs on friends and relations but did not feel able or empowered to bring about a turnaround. Many objected to the violence and tried to use whatever leverage they did possess to try to halt the fighting, while others scrambled to find alternatives for youths, whom they saw as being unnecessarily swept into the fray. The dominant portrayal as reflected in the plan, however, was one that raised general suspicion of those who may have been more open to cooperating with law enforcement efforts under a more community-based policing model that made finer distinctions between various sectors of the population. The "broken windows" approach of heavily enforcing minor infractions such as broken taillights was often seen as making life harder and more burdensome for those who were struggling the hardest merely to survive, let alone for those trying to address more serious problems within the neighborhood.[30]

Some officers interviewed perceived the underlying problem in Oakwood as one of moral corruption. An LAPD detective who specialized in gang-related homicides in Oakwood discussed what he saw as the adoption of alternative moral codes by many residents that led them to condone the use of violence. He explained:

> You have to understand that in some of these groups, they truly don't morally believe the same things that you do. . . . Their value system is completely different. Oakwood is a prime example. They're very educated people. This is a conversation I had with a very educated man—a white guy who lives in Oakwood, in his forties, went to Berkeley, all these good schools, and everything like that. And this is what he says. He says, "You have to understand that Oakwood requires a certain amount of violence . . . is absolutely necessary because it makes the neighborhood less desirable for development." And, therefore, it is totally acceptable that there's an occasional killing, periodic shootings and drug dealings. It's completely acceptable, because it's a source of economic [relief]. So, there's a value structure that does not believe in the same values that are involved in the penal code.

The officer's interpretation was that, for many residents who made this observation, "that's justification for a real value structure that doesn't believe that killing is wrong."[31]

The implication, however, that African American and other residents in Oakwood operate on a value system that belittles the value of human life is a hazardous one. While it is true that crime lowers rents and housing prices, the conclusion that most condone murder for the sake of affordable housing entails a certain leap in logic. Many residents were very aware of the risks involved in gang life, including the premature death of many of the youths. And many accepted the possible loss of life as a risk and reality of gang involvement. There were certainly different realities and norms among gangs that varied widely across groups. The perception, however, that whole communities or neighborhoods subscribed to a moral code that "doesn't believe that killing is wrong" projected a more sweeping view of an "amoral other" than was appropriate under the existing conditions. The danger of such a projection is its psychological power to justify, in turn, amoral action against whole groups. Sweeping generalities about the community concealed the great amount of diversity in norms, beliefs, and attitudes that did exist. Such a negative perception of the neighborhood did little to engender cooperation from those segments of the population who had been effectively branded as supporters of gang activity; the truth was that many strongly opposed the violence that ensued.

A High-Suppression Strategy

The mission and objectives of the Oakwood Plan included eliminating gang violence through policing heavily, removing "criminal predators," and reducing the level of fear in the community and among the officers. The major phase of the plan exemplified the prevailing high-suppression approach. Central components included (a) the formation of an interagency Oakwood Enforcement Task Force, including representatives of the city attorney, the LAPD, the district attorney, and the parole and probation departments; (b) additional policing by the LAPD's Operations-West Bureau's Community Resources Against Street Hoodlums (CRASH) unit; (c) application of the 1988 Street Terrorism Enforcement and Prevention (STEP) Act to extend state prison sentences; (d) short-range measures such as the expedition of booking and processing of arrestees; and (e) various long-range control measures such as the abatement of "nuisance" locations and the intensification of investigative efforts on known "criminal predators."

The plan reflected an awareness of the need for broad-based community consent of their actions. The LAPD brass recognized that community perceptions of their operations were important. The plan stated:

> Although this operation is designed to provide a high level of enforcement, it must not be viewed as an "occupying force" by the general, law-abiding population. Officers who have demonstrated a strong service attitude would convey a positive attitude to the community and would reduce the negative perceptions which might arise from a continual presence.

Selection criteria for the Oakwood Task Force included knowledge of local gangs, narcotics expertise, a history of "pro-active" enforcement, a service-oriented attitude, and a desire to join the task force. Ethnicity and personnel complaint histories would also be considered in the selection of officers.

Thus, the Oakwood Plan was a high-suppression policing plan designed specifically for the Oakwood section of Venice that included state-of-the-art policy tools and operations developed during the "War on Drugs" in the 1980s, such as the use of surveillance powers and abatement procedures. Many of the practices used in this case were being used in selected communities across the nation. The following sections provide the background and context for the strategies employed in Oakwood.

The Gang Suppression Controversy

There was ongoing controversy among law enforcement agents, policymakers, and the general public over the effectiveness and appropriate use of high-suppression approaches to quell gang violence. While many agreed that focused and coordinated assaults by law enforcement agencies on high-crime neighborhoods was effective in certain situations, the general approach as well as the selection of appropriate situations and the frequency of their use remained hotly debated. Four major problems associated with gang suppression approaches arose: (1) "over-labeling" youths as being gang members, (2) unintended results and "boomerang" effects of suppression tactics, (3) misuse of discretionary powers, and (4) questionable long-term effectiveness of such approaches.

Over-labeling was the problem of identifying individuals as gang members even though they may not be. Across the spectrum of law enforcement agencies, specialized gang control units were created (Needle and Stapleton 1983). These special units served as a double-edged sword in that their establishment and expansion may have contributed to over-labeling (Huff and McBride 1993). Hagedorn (1988) and Huff (1989, 1990) noted that some gang members attributed their first real identification with a gang to over-labeling by law enforcement. Anderson (1990) discussed the problem of labeling in terms of color-coding, expressed in the anonymous black male who was often considered guilty until proven innocent. Labeling by others can shape or reinforce an image of the self or nurture an "oppositional" identity based on a rejection of the norms of the dominant group (Ogbu 1990).

A second issue was what Klein (1993) referred to as "boomerang" effects. He asserted that messages relayed in deterrence and suppression approaches were blocked or reinterpreted by group processes. Gang suppression programs may backfire because the receiving gang members could alter their implicit message and deterrent properties. He cited longitudinal research indicating that peer pressure was the most important proximal contributor to drug and delinquency involvement. He also cited research by Moore and Vigil (1989) suggesting that gangs maintain an oppositional subculture. Klein feared that suppression approaches "may deter a few members but also increase the internal cohesiveness of the group," resulting in a "boomerang" effect (107). Klein and Maxson (1994) observed that drug suppression tactics

such as the massive street sweeps conducted by the LAPD, when simultaneously declared as part of the "war" on gangs, might only heighten gang identity and status. Additionally, they warned that the national gang identification
roster system might have the side effect of increasing gang cohesiveness. Many
questioned the benefits and ethics of a national gang database, particularly
in light of evidence that there may be individuals included in the database
who were not active gang members (Reiner 1992). Elijah Anderson (1990)
noted that "because the young black man is aware of many cases when an 'innocent' black person was wrongly accused and detained, he develops an 'attitude' toward the police" (196).

A third concern lay in the increase in discretionary powers given to law enforcement officials and the potential for unchecked abuse of powers. Numerous writings document the problem of unchecked police corruption that
periodically mired various law enforcement agencies throughout the nation
(Duchaine 1979; Donner 1990). Increasing the powers of police agencies that
were suffering from problems of police misconduct could conceivably lead to
greater abuse of power. The nature of institutional decision-making processes
within law enforcement makes policing agencies more vulnerable to harmful
abuses of power than other types of agencies. In particular, juvenile justice
policies are heavily dependent on "street level bureaucrats" (Lipsky 1980).
Law enforcement agents possess relatively greater discretionary powers due
to the private and physical nature of contact between officers and civilians.[32]

Finally, some argued that law enforcement agencies relying solely on suppression approaches were unlikely to be effective in the longer term because
(a) new gang members may simply replace those arrested owing to similar un-
met needs and the continuing availability of criminal opportunities and (b)
where incarceration follows conviction, the gang problem often is partially
displaced into the correctional system as gang members become active inside
the institutions, only to return to the community and resume their activities
with the gang (Huff and McBride 1993).

Jankowski (1991) argued that a major problem of gang suppression policy
was its inability to address the individual and collective aspects of the phenomenon simultaneously. Law enforcement agents did not always understand
the organizational dynamics and world views driving gang behavior. Nor did
they fully understand that the root causes of violence were such factors as individual fear, ambition, challenges by peers, and frustration, rather than the
specific situation. Jankowski argued that it was important to understand the
internal dynamics and thinking of gangs in order to reduce gang violence.

In addition, traditional approaches to crime control would prove counterproductive in the long run if they undermined community values (Akerlof
and Yellen 1994). Community cooperation with local police was essential to
law enforcement. Fear of reprisals, the perceived consequences of weakening
the local gang (i.e., outside gangs entering the neighborhood in the absence

of a local gang), the fairness of penalties (either too high or too low), and attitudes toward police had direct bearing on the willingness of community members to cooperate with law enforcement. Akerlof and Yellen (1994) noted that gangs have an incentive to commit crime right up to the point where people will cooperate with the police. The community's willingness to cooperate is heavily dependent on the level of trust and cooperation that law enforcement entities maintained with affected communities. High-suppression law enforcement activities often alienated those whose trust and cooperation were necessary for effective crime control.

Controversy over these and other issues persisted, due in part to the lack of more conclusive research and empirical evidence regarding the outcomes of existing policies.[33] Huff and McBride (1993) suggested that "a continuing display of professionalism, personal concern, and fairness—both on the streets and during incarceration—can help curb gang involvement and encourage cooperation with law enforcement's gang control efforts" (409). But others did not completely agree. Jankowski (1991) argued that gangs and the community in which they operate establish a working relationship, each providing the other with certain services. Often, gangs fulfill the role of a neighborhood militia, protecting residents from outside gangs or intruders. However, since gangs need community support more than the residents need gangs, they are usually subject to the will of the community. He found gangs to establish a similar exchange relationship with government officials and institutions, though in less intimate forms.

Controversy in the realm of public policy discourse was also mirrored in local communities subject to high-suppression activities. Differences over these approaches often enflamed social divisions in communities, especially when policy decisions had a very direct impact. Those who believed in their efficacy were at odds with those who protested their use. It was not necessarily the case that either side condoned criminal behavior or racial bias. But those who opposed certain practices were often accused of condoning crime. The choice between "tough love" and "criminal sympathizer" left no room for those who favored a policy response that would squarely confront criminal behavior while also ensuring fairness in its application and offering viable alternatives in light of historic inequalities and injustices.

Racial Imagery within the LAPD

The Los Angeles Police Department (LAPD) was the line of first response to the local problem of gang violence. During the gang war, the LAPD was the lead agency in the implementation of gang suppression operations. But increased powers and an expanded law enforcement infrastructure for gang suppression were not limited to the LAPD. Special gang units were established in almost every law enforcement agency in the region. Additionally, federal agencies including the Federal Bureau of Investigation (FBI) and the Bureau of Alcohol, Tobacco, and Firearms (ATF) shifted resources to gang intelligence and enforcement. By 1992, the ATF was committing over a third of its special agents to investigate "violent gang groups."[34]

Top-ranked LAPD administrators promoted a quite animated racial imagery of gangs that permeated the agency. The assessments of different gangs and their threat to police and society varied, with race being the main distinguishing characteristic. In 1990, LAPD chief Daryl Gates articulated the meaning of racial distinctions among Los Angeles gangs in an article he wrote with Robert Jackson that appeared in *The Police Chief*. Titled "Gang Violence in L.A.," he described the growing danger of gang violence and the distinctions between black and Latino gangs:

> Differences between the black and Hispanic gangs became apparent early on. The violent crimes committed by the traditional turf- or neighborhood-oriented Hispanic gangs were typically centered around longstanding rivalries. Indeed, some of the feuds have gone on for generations.
>
> Although black gangs also engaged in inter[-]ring battles, it was obvious that they shared a common goal that set their criminal activity apart from the traditional gang-against-gang battles. The thrust of the black gang actions both then and now is the premise that money buys power, which is then enforced through violence. Those who have something the gang member wants—even if they have very little—are the quarry for the predatory black street gang members. Black gang member activity started with robberies within their own neighborhoods and then expanded to include more affluent areas where victims and money are more plentiful. *It has been said that a Hispanic gang member will die for his dirt, while a black gang member dies for his gold. Gang homicide reports attest to the accuracy of this statement.* (20; emphasis added)

The top brass among the LAPD had long held the belief that African American gangs possess a predisposition to violence and a penchant for political resistance, as demonstrated in the social movements of the 1960s. In contrast to other gangs, African American gangs are portrayed as lacking moral judgment and of having little respect for human life. Gates continued:

> Violence is a given for all gangs. What is it, then, that sets the black street gangs apart? Although the fixation on crime for profit is one difference, *by far the more significant difference lies in what seems to be a total disregard for human life—including their own.*[35] (emphasis added)

According to Gates, black gangs had no moral code of conduct to inhibit their quest for money and power. Coupled with the concern over increasing attacks on police officers, this image of African American gang members shaped police behavior toward black male suspects and affected their interaction with African American residents more generally.

This distinction between black and Latino gangs was reiterated in the LAPD Gang Awareness School training manual. In describing Hispanic gang members, the manual stated, "Hispanic gangs invariably name their gang after a geographical area or 'turf,' something they feel is worth fighting for and defending. Foremost in each gang member's mind is the belief that '*the gang is more important than the individual member.*'"[36] In contrast, African American gangs were described as more prone to violence and more concerned about material gain. The training manual states, "They are not considered turf gangs and are more involved in crimes for profit."[37]

In these documents, African American gangs are portrayed as dangerously preoccupied with the pursuit of material gain to the point that they pose a much more menacing threat to society. In contrast to "traditional gang-against-gang" battles, black gangs are presented as preying on the non-gang community, roving outside of central city boundaries to "more affluent" areas. They are seen to victimize poor and rich alike with no regard for others. "Hispanic" gangs, on the other hand, are portrayed as often operating as a "family affair." Implicit in this description is the perception that Latino gangs are more humane, since "family values" and the familial structure are maintained, albeit within the culture of the gang. Police officers specializing in gang-related crime saw this characteristic as a stabilizing force, as family members could help mediate rivalries that may get out of hand.

One LAPD officer in a specialized gang unit operating in Oakwood at the time of the study echoed this distinction between the familial structures of black and Latino gangs:

> Now the Hispanics are a very close, family-connected, organization. Hispanic gangs, not all of them, the ones in Oakwood are very visible. Very, very strong family ties. . . .
>   Now the black side, the family structure isn't there. When we talk about families, they have the same name, but boy, it's not, I mean, there's no father present. There's no grandmothers present like there used to be in the traditional black family. Literally, it's just people coming in and out, so you don't see the family structure in the black groups.[38]

One notable public omission in the widely projected racial imagery was the acknowledgment by law enforcement agencies that white gangs were among the most violent in California, yet these gangs had not garnered the attention that minority street gangs in urban areas had in the media. The Los Angeles Police Department estimated that there were approximately 370 "outlaw motorcycle gangs" in California, more than a hundred of which were criminally active. In the California prison system, white supremacist prison gangs were considered the most vicious. According to the Los Angeles Police Department's Gang Awareness School training manual, "the Aryan Brotherhood (AB) is the most violent of the prison gangs."[39] Violence was also a problem observed among Southeast Asian gangs. The problem of gangs in the popular media, however, seemed to dwell on the two most vulnerable and economically impoverished groups in the region.

The danger of stereotypical depictions is that they serve as a cognitive map for officers who may not have a deeper understanding of the life experiences, histories, cultures, and sensibilities among the diverse groups in U.S. society. Many officers recruited from states with less diversity often had little experience working closely with the multicultural population of Los Angeles. For federal agents recently returning from their tour of duty in Europe and Asia with the breakup of the Soviet Union and redeployed to domestic duties, these depictions did little to anchor a more grounded understanding of the local conditions into which they now found themselves.

Stereotypes are often based on "points of fact" that can be supported by measured evidence. There are some researchers specializing in the study of gangs, for example, that have made the observation that Latino gangs are more strongly oriented toward family and group than their African American counterparts (Curry and Decker 1998). But if lifted out of the context of a fuller, multidimensional description of gang formation and community life, "points of fact" can paint gross caricatures that flatten one's perception of a much more complex reality. In the act of homogenization and simplification, important variations and explanations are overlooked. Groups become objectified with the effect of dehumanizing categorical groups.

This creates a major problem in policing. While there may be a wide range of individuals who are affiliated with a gang, it is seldom the case that all of the younger followers fit the profile of a serious "criminal predator" as defined in the Oakwood Plan. But the younger "soldiers" who do the bidding of an entrenched gang leadership are often treated by law enforcement as being in the same category as more seasoned veterans. Oftentimes, law enforcement officers confront those who are not themselves gang members but are related by friendship or family relations to gang members. The tendency in a high-suppression mode of operation is to classify all who fit a certain profile into the most serious threat category and to treat them accordingly.

This approach had profound implications under the guidance of Chief Gates in Los Angeles. The use of racial imagery in what has been termed "racial profiling" led to an "over-identification" of certain groups, namely African American young men, as suspected criminals. This was especially the case in gang intelligence, where the Los Angeles County District Attorney's Office expressed concern over the high proportion of African American males in Los Angeles who were identified as gang members. In a 1992 report, they noted that nearly half (47 percent) of all African American males between the ages of 21 and 24 had been entered in the national Gang Resistance Education and Training (GREAT) database. The authorities even admitted that "that number is so far out of line with other ethnic groups that a careful, professional examination is needed to determine whether police procedures may be systematically over-identifying Black youths as gang members" (Reiner 1992, v). In contrast, 0.5 percent of Anglo youths, 6 to 7 percent of Asian youths, and 9 to 10 percent of Latino youths were documented as participating in gangs. The over-identification of youths has been observed to have serious negative consequences, hardening oppositional identity among targeted youths and pushing them into the spotlight of law enforcement operations as well as rival gang activities (Huff 1996).

These one-dimensional portrayals of youths associated with gang life also fostered a sense that the loss of a gang member's life was somehow less of a loss than that of an "innocent" victim. Since so many African American youths were identified by law enforcement agents as being members of a street gang, there was the danger that their deaths would be portrayed as somehow less tragic than the deaths of others. The flavor of the discourse left little appetite for policies that explored more creative alternatives for the problem of gang-related violence, heavily favoring incarceration rather than diversionary alternatives in the face of larger social crises.

The LAPD in the Limelight of Controversy

Reactions to LAPD's practices within Venice were nested within larger controversies concerning the police as a whole. The LAPD had a controversial past, and scandals continued to plague the department beyond the period under investigation here. Its most critical observers portrayed the police force as "protectors of privilege," a militaristic organization that has served as one of the major agents of social control over the activities and movements of racial minorities in Los Angeles, particularly African Americans and Latinos (Donner 1990; Rothmiller and Goldman 1992). Its advocates portrayed the beleaguered department as the city's David confronting Goliath in the unruly city of Hollywood-inspired death and decadence. In the official realm, major external investigations of the LAPD had been highly critical. The LAPD's practices were the focus of several major governmental investigations initiated after incidents of police brutality, including the Kerner Commission Report in 1968, the Christopher Commission Report in 1991, and a subsequent report evaluating the implementation of the Christopher Commission recommendations five years later in 1996.[40] During the period of the Venice gang war, the LAPD was embroiled in heated debates surrounding the videotaped beating of African American motorist Rodney King and the subsequent acquittal of the police officers involved, which sparked the largest civil unrest in U.S. history since the draft riots of the mid-1800s.[41]

The 1991 Christopher Commission Report conducted after the police beating of Rodney King called attention to the LAPD's use of excessive force, the ineffectiveness of internal investigations into police misconduct, and evidence of racism and racial bias among police officers. A 1991 feature in the *Los Angeles Times* reported that the number of complaints filed against LAPD officers increased over 70 percent, from 1,065 to 1,826 between 1979 and 1990 (see figure 4.3). The number surged to 2,425 in 1991 (Murphy 1991). The commission reported that of the 2,152 citizen complaints of excessive force filed between 1986 and 1990 examined by the Commission, only 42 (2 percent) were ruled in favor of the filing party.[42] Nearly a third (30 percent) of the 650 senior LAPD managers randomly surveyed by the Christopher Commission agreed that "the use of excessive force is a serious problem facing the Department."[43] A quarter (24.5 percent) agreed that "racial bias" on the part of officers toward minority citizens currently existed and contributed to negative interactions between police and the residents. And more than a fourth (27.6 percent) agreed that "an officer's prejudice towards the suspect's race may lead to the use of excessive force."[44] Popular concern over the problem of excessive force grew with the increase in officer-involved shootings. The number of people killed or injured by LAPD officers reached a decade-high figure of 77 in 1992.[45]

According to the Christopher Commission report, the LAPD's institutional culture helped to perpetuate the practice of excessive use of force. The LAPD historically used an aggressive use-of-force policy. This was instilled in the training of officers within the academy as well as in the ongoing training activities required of officers. One LAPD patrol officer assigned to Oakwood described the stance they were trained to take toward suspects:

> It don't matter whether you're black or white, it's a mentality that these guys have that you gotta be the aggressor, that you gotta be strong, that you gotta destroy the enemy. Because they teach you in the academy to stop their action. But then the anger gets all riled up. All that stuff that we talked about at roll call, all the stuff you've seen on TV, all the stuff you've read in the papers, every nasty ugly call you've gone to, builds up. And this one person, and I tell you, when somebody tries to attack me, we are trained to destroy them. You let them know that they don't do that anymore.[46]

Educational sessions were conducted at roll call to keep officers abreast on shooting policies. These sessions were designed to keep officers updated on beat activity and changing policies as well as to maintain their morale. But the impact of the implicit and explicit messages, along with the daily duties of patrol, tended to "harden" many of the officers:

> Every month they gotta do a [refresher on] shooting policy. They'll show a film of some officer getting shot, or somebody else getting shot. And so every time you see that, to me, it leaves an impact—a scar. . . . They'll show a film of an officer getting shot or a white boy's life, trying to inspire you to keep fight-

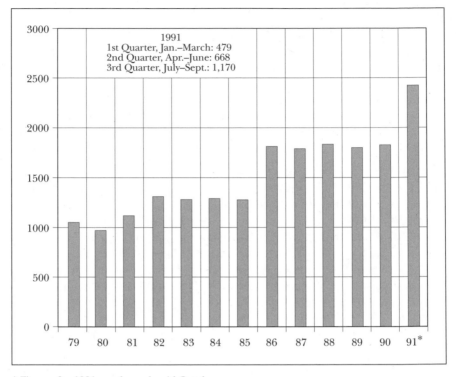

1991
1st Quarter, Jan.–March: 479
2nd Quarter, Apr.–June: 668
3rd Quarter, July–Sept.: 1,170

* Figures for 1991 are through mid-October

Note: Figures listed for 1979–1989 are numbers of complaints processed and deemed "closed" by the department. Because of continuing investigations of some complaints, however, the figures exclude a small percentage of the total complaints received. The LAPD reports a surge in personnel complaints in 1991, making it a record year. Through mid-October, 2,425 complaints were filed against police by citizens and department personnel. About half of the complaints came after the release in early July of a highly critical report on the LAPD by the Christopher Commission. By contrast; fewer than 360 of the complaints were filed prior to the police beating of motorist Rodney G. King in March.

Source: LAPD, reported by the *Los Angeles Times,* October 17, 1991

Figure 4.3 Complaints filed against LAPD personnel, 1979–1991

ing. But it reinforces the reality of "you can get shot." Or "you might have to pull your gun out today and kill somebody." Neither side is easy.

I was in a shooting back in [the 1980s] and to see another person's life gone like that. People think, "Yeah, just take 'em out and shoot 'em," but is a lot more to it than just pullin' that. . . . I mean, yeah, you can pull a gun out, and a lot of guys shoot people and they become numb to it. These same individuals are dangerous individuals because they have lost compassion, for people. They really went into a Vietnam mode, I call it. Their sensors are singed to compassion. This is a human being. This isn't a deer. You didn't catch a wild boar. A human being. A lot of them have forgotten that.[47]

Seventy-seven people were killed or injured in Los Angeles Police Department shootings in 1992—the highest total in a decade.

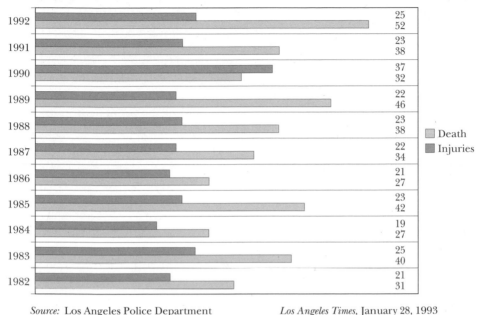

1992	25 / 52
1991	23 / 38
1990	37 / 32
1989	22 / 46
1988	23 / 38
1987	22 / 34
1986	21 / 27
1985	23 / 42
1984	19 / 27
1983	25 / 40
1982	21 / 31

■ Death
■ Injuries

Source: Los Angeles Police Department   *Los Angeles Times,* January 28, 1993

Figure 4.4 LAPD officer-involved shootings, 1982–1992

Since officers are recruited nationally, there were many who were not familiar with Los Angeles neighborhoods or the cultural diversity that existed in the city. Potential recruits were not screened for their understanding of different groups, defined racially or otherwise. As a result, many officers adopted prevailing racial stereotypes and those holding racist attitudes remained in the ranks. The same officer who once patrolled Oakwood confirmed:

> And so you got a lot of racist guys on the job. That's just there. That's another reason there's so much trouble in our department, too. In the streets, you got some guy that comes from Iowa, they come from different places where they have no contact with blacks or Hispanics, and therefore they believe the hype. They believe that all Orientals know karate. They think that all blacks are violent. . . . that all of them are criminals.[48]

He witnessed actions on the part of other police officers that he believed used unnecessary force in the apprehension of individuals in Oakwood:

> Now in Oakwood, I've been down there, and they've used a lot of unnecessary force. There's been guys down there that took dirty underwear off the ground

and stuck it the guy's mouth. One guy had a gun stuck in his mouth—the barrel in his mouth. These were complaints being made. I've seen guys kicked in the groin. . . . I've seen tons of guys dragged across the street, handcuffed. This is why they don't forget. I didn't forget it. They go, "Oh, here we go again, more abuse by the police department." So, people go, "Why are people so mad?" Well, if your son got beaten up unjustly, and even if he was guilty, the policy says "use the amount of force necessary to activate an arrest."[49]

There were some officers that were recognized by residents within the neighborhood as clearly and consistently abusing their powers. These officers occasionally fell victim to threats from within the neighborhood. An LAPD officer recalled one such instance concerning an officer who worked in Oakwood:

There have been officers that were taken out of the division because of the death threats on their lives. Like I said, none of it's warranted. But this one guy was down there—it was put in the paper so I could mention his name is Womack. A year or two ago, they had this [article] in the L.A. Times.[50] They had the top forty officers in the city that were "excessive force" guys. Well, he was one of them. And this guy would kick in doors at apartment buildings, totally violating rights. No regard for [search] warrants. Just come in there, kick in the doors, drag you out of there, take them to jail, I mean, just totally defying the law—making up their own law. . . . So that's why we got the guys on the street that are totally resistant to anything the police do or try to do, any programs they try to do, because they don't trust them.[51]

The rogue cops that were allowed to continue without reprimand did a great deal to undermine public trust in the police department. This created extremely difficult conditions for those officers who made diligent efforts to gain community trust and cooperation. Though the police was concerned about attacks against officers, and legitimately so, some residents believed that those officers shot were often those who repeatedly "crossed the line." Though no one interviewed condoned violence against police, there were those who explicitly sympathized with those victims of police misconduct.

The subsequent resistance to police enforcement among negatively affected segments of the community continued to wear on the already low morale of patrol officers. The LAPD was hampered by internal discord and lack of cohesion during this period. Like any community, LAPD officers are not a homogeneous group. Ideological, religious, political, racial, ethical, and moral identities, beliefs, and attitudes differed widely among the ranks.

On the heels of the civil unrest of 1992, internal differences within the LAPD grew even sharper with the replacement of LAPD Chief Daryl Gates by Willie Williams, the first African American appointed to the post of chief commanding officer. In the context of the tensions that accompanied the change in leadership, public criticism on the heels of the Rodney King beating, the aftermath of the civil unrest, extended union contract debates over salary and workplace issues, and the flight of many of its most seasoned career officers, the LAPD was in the midst of its own crisis. This added to an already desperate situation in a neighborhood overwhelmed with a stew of problems.

Gangs, the War on Drugs, and the Prison Boom

Gang suppression and the war on drugs had a particularly severe impact on black and Latino communities during the 1980s and 1990s (Tonry 1995). A disproportionately high percentage of minority youths were involved in the cycle of crime and caught in the web of law enforcement. In the early 1990s, the incarceration rates for African Americans were nearly seven times higher than those for whites nationally. This has been attributed to various factors, including the contrasting patterns of criminality among racial groups, intensified policing in minority communities, and biased patterns in arrests and sentencing.[52] Between 1979 and 1992, the proportion of African Americans among those admitted to state and federal prisons increased from 39 to 54 percent (Tonry 1995). By the early 1990s, the extent to which black and Latino communities interfaced with law enforcement personnel was astoundingly high. In 1991, nearly half (395,245 out of 824,133) of those incarcerated in state and federal correctional authorities were African American, while African Americans represented less than 13 percent of the total U.S. population (U.S. Department of Justice 1992a). The 1995 report of the Sentencing Project estimated that in 1994, almost one of every three (30.2 percent) black males in their twenties was in prison or jail or on probation or parole on any given day. This proportion had increased from almost one in four (23 percent) in 1990. They estimated that the proportion of Hispanic inmates in state and federal prisons since 1980 had doubled by 1994 (Mauer and Huling 1995).[53] These figures were similar in California, where approximately 33 percent of all African American men between ages of 20 and 29 were either in jail, in prison, or on parole or probation during the late 1980s (Center on Juvenile and Criminal Justice 1990).

Incarceration rates among youths in California were exceptionally high. Austin (1995) reported the youth incarceration rate in 1989 as 463 per 100,000 juveniles in the state, a ratio more than double the national average of 207 per 100,000 juveniles.[54] Not only were rates much higher, the proportion of minority youths drastically increased in the 1980s and 1990s.[55] Among minority youths, African American males were the most overrepresented in relation to their proportion of the population (34.4 percent of the prison population compared to 4.5 percent of the state population). The proportion of Latino males in custody was also higher than their proportion of the state population, while Anglo and Asian American young men were in custody in proportions lower than their percentage of the state population.

Much of the increase in the prison population nationally was a result of the war on drugs. Tonry (1995) stated that "by trying to reduce the supply of drugs rather than the demand for them, by adopting a prohibitionist crime control approach, rather than a harm-reduction approach, policy makers chose strategies that had little prospect of succeeding but a high likelihood of worsening racial disproportion in the criminal justice system" (116). The number of incarcerated drug offenders rose 510 percent from 1983 to 1993 (Mauer and Huling 1995). The proportion of African Americans arrested for drug offenses increased from 24 percent in 1980 to 39 percent in 1993. This rate was much higher than their reported rate of drug use, which was comparable and lower for some substances when compared to other racial groups.[56] A 1990 national household survey by the National Institute on Drug Abuse (NIDA) indicated that African Americans comprised 13 percent of monthly drug users, but comprised 34.7 percent of arrests for drug possession (National Institute on Drug Abuse 1991). African Americans and Hispanics comprised 80 percent of offenders sentenced to state prison for drug offenses.

Advocacy organizations had begun to raise objections to the rising rate of minority confinement while also pointing out the discriminatory sentencing policies that affected large numbers of young African American and Latino men. One oft-cited example of discriminatory sentencing was the differential in sentences for those convicted of selling *crack* cocaine as compared to those convicted of selling the substance in *powder* form. African American dealers sell crack in higher proportion than cocaine, which is more often sold by white dealers. Under federal sentencing guidelines, judges are directed to multiply quantities of crack by 100 to determine the length of prison sentences, giving much harsher sentences to crack offenders than to cocaine offenders. This policy exists despite the fact that crack is pharmacologically indistinguishable from powder cocaine (Tonry 1995, Hatsukami and Fischman 1996).[57] Tonry (1995, 41) refers to one federal court of appeals as reporting that 95 percent of federal crack defendants are African American.

The incarceration of a rising number of young men in California intensified another problem. Racial division became especially acute in the L.A. County jails and the California prison system, both sites of some of the most physically violent and organizationally tied inter-minority group conflict within any publicly run institution. During the 1980s, the racial balance of the county jail and state prison population shifted, with an increase in the proportion of Latinos, which partially reflected the increase in the state population. By 1991, Latino jail inmates narrowly outnumbered African American inmates, 40 percent to 37 percent (Meyer 1994). As the ranks of the inmate population swelled, so did the ranks of prison gangs that, in California at least, were racially organized. The Mexican Mafia, Black Guerrilla Family, the Aryan Brotherhood, and the Consolidated Crips were the major prison gangs organized within the southern California penal system. Fights in the prison system became endemic in the late 1980s and 1990s. Race riots ended in the deaths of inmates, while gangs held significant control over the territorial use of space within the prisons. Major race riots between African American and Latino inmates reached crisis proportions in November 1994 when an estimated 1,000 inmates, at the alleged instigation of the Mexican Mafia, became entangled in a racial brawl at Pitchess Honor Rancho correctional facility that left eighty inmates injured (Meyer 1994). As prison authorities began a broader practice of segregating inmates by racial group to avoid fights, inclusive boundaries were reinforced and cross-racial interaction was stunted more than ever (Tamaki 1996). If one did not sense racial antagonisms before going to prison, it was impossible to leave without an acute awareness of the racial divide.

The Changing Interface between the State and Civil Society

With a more punitive set of social policies, more suppressive law enforcement practices, and a shift in resources away from education and community-based social programs, in many distressed neighborhoods such as Oakwood the quality of the interface between state and civil society subtly but profoundly became transformed. In a less punitive era, residents had a much wider spectrum of dialogue with a broad array of public servants, including teachers and school administrators, social work professionals, counselors, community outreach workers, public health professionals, park directors, and other neighborhood-based service providers. But with a shift in resources away from educational and human service institutions and the implementation of unforgiving zero-tolerance policies in schools and other institutions, many of the past connections to families facing the greatest challenges and hardships slowly faded.

The retreat of the state from social programs is most glaring in the failing record of urban public schools. A California Department of Education report showed that in the Los Angeles Unified School District (LAUSD) in the period covered by this book, nearly half (44 percent) of high school students dropped out before graduating—a disturbingly high statistic. This was more than twice the dropout rate of the state as a whole, which stood at an already troubling rate of 20 percent.[58] Many youths were left to roam the streets, including those who were expelled from schools under zero-tolerance policies and not allowed to return to any other school in the LAUSD. With fewer recreational activities to involve youths and fewer social services, a growing number of youths were losing hope of succeeding in a discriminating job market. For those who became entangled in gang activity and found themselves tangled in the web of the criminal justice system, there were few opportunities in sight to change life's direction. In acutely affected neighborhoods, many residents experienced their interface with government through police precincts, courts, and prisons more than they did through schools, social service agencies, and town hall meetings. From 1984 to 1998, the state of California opened only one college—and twenty-one new prisons. This shift in resources and attention had many implications, among them the limited leverage of government agencies across the spectrum of roles to intervene effectively in problems in need of pro-social solutions.

This was not the first time such a shift had taken place. Juvenile justice policies have swung like a pendulum between lenient and harsh punishments,[59] cycling back and forth at least three times over the past 200 years (Thomas 1992).[60] Juvenile justice policy in the 1990s was largely determined by the ideas of the "get tough" movement advocating swift, certain, and severe punishment for youthful offenders (Thomas 1992). In contrast to periods in the cycle that emphasized "rehabilitation and reform," suppression-era policies emphasize punishment and incarceration. A principal assumption underlying high-suppression approaches toward gangs was the idea that gangs and gang members should not be tolerated or even helped (Spergel et al. 1989). Between the two polarized positions remained a sorely neglected third position: one that supported the use of selected suppression tactics but within a more comprehensive strategy based on a much more fine-tuned understanding of the complex social dynamics at play (Spergel and Curry 1990; Spergel 1995). In cases of gang conflict such as in Venice, a more sophisticated strategy might have tapped into community sentiment and disparate community efforts to secure peace—efforts that could not be mobilized without a more balanced vision of prevention and rehabilitative measures along with mechanisms to ensure fair application of policies across racial groups and class strata.

Though this was not the first swing of the pendulum toward harsher punishment, what made this turn so weighty was the fact that it also coincided with drastic cuts in public funding for education and a myriad of social services during the Reagan-Bush era. Between 1980 and 1990, the federal government reduced its contribution to education by half. For the first time in U.S. history, beginning in the 1980s more public expenditures were spent for criminal justice than for education by state, county, and municipal governments combined (Chambliss 1995). In Los Angeles County, the shift in interface toward law enforcement was further prompted by a growing reliance on state funds that allocated increasing dollars for "public safety" (Niblack and Stan 1992). Education, mental health, child care, tutoring, counseling, substance abuse, youth development, youth recreation, elderly assistance, and other programs faced major cutbacks. Furthermore, as shrinking allocations increased competition among nonprofit service providers, social service organizations also became more professional. Many of the programs that survived the various waves of budget cuts were those that had highly trained professional staff and did not necessarily have strong bonds with the segments of the population facing the greatest threats and challenges.

Not only was there a shift in the state's interface, there was also a shift in the balance of power within the residential population of distressed neighborhoods. With cuts in community-based programs, community leaders lost much of their ability to influence the inner workings within the neighborhood. In earlier times, community leaders had many of the tools that came with social programs to provide assistance, guidance, incentives, and opportunities to families. This allowed them to help shape the activities and behavior of youths to a significant degree, in many cases steering them away from risky behavior and toward wiser decisions for their safety and well-being. But as funding disappeared and as the economic influence of gang members increased, there was a shift in the loci of influence as the influence of gang members over the social dynamics within their neighborhoods grew. Venkatesh (1997) documented such a phenomenon in a midwestern housing project. He observed a case in which a more corporatized gang worked to become a more legitimate social actor in the community through monetary donations and the provision of services that residents wanted or needed but that were not provided by anyone else, such as recreational programming. They were able to garner a resident support base and undermine the established leadership structure, at least temporarily.

Thus, two phenomena came together to create a "perfect storm," toppling any power lines that may have once connected to those close to the center of the tragedy and disabling potential intervention efforts. First, the shift away from "rehabilitative" social programs toward "punitive" law enforcement solutions changed the balance in the mix of government and private nonprofit agencies with ties to distressed communities. This shift severely limited the range of avenues through which government could respond to gang violence, with law enforcement left to lead the charge with the "stick" and little in the way of even ancillary "carrots." Police-community relations forged in a high-suppression policy environment were strained, particularly with segments of the population in a more opportune position to influence the situation. Second, even those who had historically been able to exert some influence from the base of residents no longer had the same backing of resources to readily influence decisions of individual youths involved in the quagmire. The influence of key community leaders had declined as gang influence over the territorial control over space and the social dynamics within it rose. Tensions not only festered between law enforcement personnel and residents but also among the residents themselves over the role of law enforcement officers in the community. Both types of friction made it that much more difficult to intervene effectively in the problem, since collaboration is often necessary to develop sustainable solutions. Furthermore, the mantra of "zero tolerance" created a policy environment that paid little heed to the existence of multiple publics and the differences in interpretive lenses through which diverse groups experience a phenomena or view a problem. Law enforcement agents were equipped with a wide array of high-suppression tools and technologies. But as the following chapters illustrate, the heavy reliance on suppression tactics alone would prove too blunt an instrument for this complex problem that had no clear end in sight.

Chapter 5

The Racialization of a Gang War

It is the peculiarity of social controversy that it sets in motion its own dynamics; these tend to carry it forward in a path which bears little relation to its beginnings.
—JAMES COLEMAN,
Community Conflict

Throughout the 1990s, interracial gang violence broke out in many sections of Los Angeles County, one of the largest and most diverse counties in the nation, with an estimated 12 million residents spread across eighty-eight cities covering 4,084 square miles. Historically speaking, most gang violence was *intra*-racial, that is, among members of the same racial identity group (Hutson et al. 1995; Curry and Decker 1998). Persistent patterns of *inter*-racial gang violence, that is, across racial boundaries, was a fairly new phenomenon that gained public attention in the 1980s, particularly as race riots in the California prison system hit the mainstream media. By the 1990s, interracial gang violence had become a grave concern in some Los Angeles County neighborhoods, including sections of Long Beach, Azusa, Hawaiian Gardens, Inglewood, along with the Harbor Gateway, South Central, Mar Vista, and Venice neighborhoods of Los Angeles city (Umemoto and Mikami 1999). Los Angeles gangs, which were for the most part racially or ethnically homogeneous, that were involved in interracial gang conflicts spanned the spectrum of ethnic groups, including Cambodian, Laotian, Mexican American, Salvadoran, African American, and Armenian, among others.[1] One striking pattern was the active role of Latino gangs. This followed a rapid increase in the Latino population throughout the region, with Latino youth making up over half of the public school population. There was a surge in nationalism among Latino gangs seen in the "ethnic cleansing" of numerous gangs that corresponded to their rising numbers within many California prisons and a rise in dominance of prison gangs, such as the Mexican Mafia, also referred to as "La Eme." In some neighborhoods such as Mar Vista, interracial gang violence followed a racial "tipping" in the population, in this case from majority African American to majority Latino, shifting the balance of power from one racially defined gang to another.

The episode of gang violence in Venice was one of the more intense of these racialized gang conflicts. Gang conflict between the largely African American and Latino gangs originated in two different but nearby locations—the Mar Vista Gardens public housing complex in Culver City and the Oakwood neighborhood of Venice (henceforth simply Mar Vista Gardens and Oakwood). The specific origins of the conflict in each of these places differed in their details, but both were embroiled in a battle over territorial turf and reputation.

This chronicle of the evolution of the conflict focuses on Oakwood, where conflict began as an interpersonal tiff and, over time, grew to generate widespread public fear and racial distancing throughout a much broader population, well beyond those directly involved in physical confrontations. From late summer 1993 to early summer 1994, the scope of conflict in Oakwood expanded, starting with individual confrontations and soon drawing in family members and eventually members of several gangs. Conflict between members of the warring gangs became increasingly racialized, pulling larger segments of the community into a tide of social polarization along racial lines. In a ten-month period, over fifty victims were reported, including seventeen deaths, with most of the incidents occurring within a one-mile radius of Oakwood.

The scope of conflict and the shifting line of cleavage can be traced, starting from individuals and families to gang loyalty and moving toward racial group identification. This trajectory of escalation can be charted along the following group boundaries, as illustrated here:

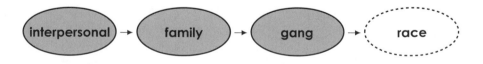

Each successive stage of the conflict as illustrated above represents a shift in the definition of the problem as well as in the salient boundaries around which groups coalesced.

Throughout the gradual escalation of social conflict and racial distancing among residents in the affected communities, this book examines, among other things, the evocation of "race" in the physical and discursive struggle for turf, power, and peace among multiple publics. I apply the metaphorical concept of morphing to describe how race became an increasingly prominent identifier in the pattern of victimization in the gang war (at times superceding the interrelated but also distinct boundary of gang membership). I also explain how events took on racially charged meanings and how racial distancing began to spread through the surrounding population. The morphology of the conflict detailed in the following chapters reveals the tensions between the pull toward polarization and the efforts at reconciliation. While the gang war created deep antagonisms and racial divisions among major segments of the community, some people tried desperately to quell racial discord and reframe the conflict, that is, "deracialize" it and define it more strictly as a gang battle or a class issue. The reframing of the conflict eventually helped to open opportunities for truce negotiations, but only after the entire community suffered a great deal of trauma.

While most studies of racial conflict in the United States have treated racial division apart from other social cleavages or as a social division assumed to be stable over time, I attempt to show how racial lines of division can ebb and flow relative to other social boundaries over the evolution of a conflict. I argue that contemporary urban conflicts often "morph," undergoing transformations in definition, axis of division, and level of intensity over time. Groups in conflict do not remain static; they change in size and constitution. Nor are their goals always stable. Sets of issues over which conflicts arise may change in focus or priority. Conflicts may begin between individuals primarily over competition for scarce resources such as housing or employment and later evolve into a contest over group rights, however those groups and rights may be defined. As the substantive issues of conflict transform, so too do the constituencies that mobilize around them.

In the Venice gang war, over the course of various interactions and attempted interventions, tensions increased in scope and intensity, enveloping larger segments of the community in conflict along racial divides. The character of these conflicts also shifted from mere disagreement to outright antagonism. Left unchecked, the conflict intensified, especially with the outbreak of violence. As in other cases of intergroup conflict, participating groups tended to close ranks, drawing greater numbers into a chain of reciprocal actions (Parsons 1951; Coleman 1957; Light and Spiegel 1977).

Gang violence is not altogether different from other forms of intergroup violence where retaliatory actions prompt the escalation and scope of tensions. Decker (1996) applied the idea of "contagion" to describe gang violence, stating that the growth in gangs and gang violence occurs when there is a spatial concentration to the violence, a reciprocal nature to the assaults, and an escalation in assaultive violence. Most scholars and practitioners agree that violence often comes with membership in gangs but is more serious among groups that actively secure territories for illegal profit-making activity (Goldstein 1985; Fagan and Chin 1989; Chin 1990; Taylor 1990; Sanchez-Jankowski 1991; Decker 1996). As the crack cocaine market grew starting in the mid-1980s, many observers noted an increase in violence and a greater proliferation of firearms as established gangs mobilized to protect their turf (Curry and Decker 1998). This is one account of what took place in one Los Angeles neighborhood.

Precipitating Events and the Outbreak of Conflict

The conflict originated somewhat differently in the Mar Vista Gardens public housing complex as compared to the Oakwood neighborhood. In Mar Vista Gardens, the conflict erupted over economic turf between the established gangs—the Culver City Boys and the Shoreline Crips—whose members resided in the low-rise public housing complex and the surrounding area. In the Oakwood neighborhood of Venice, however, the conflict began with a set of interpersonal altercations involving associates of the Venice 13 (V-13) and a related set of the Shoreline Crips headquartered in Oakwood. While some events in Mar Vista are relevant, the main focus of this chapter is the escalation of gang conflict and the generation of racial tensions in the Oakwood neighborhood. In the description and analysis of the conflict, I begin with the origins of the "war," as everyone called it, and later chronicle the process of racialization that led to wider social polarization. I also describe some of the efforts made to reverse the tide of polarization and reach across racial divides.

A Backdrop of Shifting Gang Alliances

Several events precipitated the tragic and deadly gang war. But the backdrop against which these precipitating events took place was paradoxically positive. In the early 1990s, gang truces had been negotiated across the city between the predominately African American Blood and Crip gangs that had been warring for decades and among several Latino gangs, including those on the westside of Los Angeles. There was also an edict declared by the Mexican Mafia, one of the largest prison-based gangs in California with ties to many Latino gangs throughout the southern California region. The edict prohibited the drive-by shootings that had for many years led to the deaths of many Latinos and innocent bystanders who happened to be in the line of fire. The results of the truces and edict were a reduction in gang-related homicides and greater peace within neighborhoods across the region.

Unity and greater consolidation in the Latino and African American gangs had a secondary effect that would manifest in Oakwood and elsewhere. One former member of the Shoreline believed that the newfound strength of unity within African American and Latino gangs emboldened each group in confrontations with each other:

In actuality, it probably started . . . it started positively. There had been various truces being made on the westside. You had Latino gangs were no longer fighting one another. On the entire westside, you had black gangs who had come together to set aside their differences. This was positive. Where the negative part came in was when these particular entities wanted to, I guess you might say, flex their muscles. They felt good about what was going on and they felt like they could handle things, you know. . . . Prior to the truce being made between the Latino gangs and the black gangs, they might have overlooked one another—somebody saying something that was derogatory towards the other or whatever. They probably would have overlooked it. But, because of the show of force that both parties had, they felt, "Hey, we can do this." And basically, I think that's what it was.[2]

As gang truces commenced, competition between gangs over the drug market began to shift from an intra-racial character to an interracial one, particularly after Latino gangs became more heavily involved in the crack cocaine trade alongside the more established African American gangs. Economic competition led to the reinforcement of gang boundaries, within which race had become highly salient among many networks of southern California gangs.

Many of the more established street gangs in southern California had ties to one of several large prison gangs, such as the Mexican Mafia, the Black Guerilla Family, or the Aryan Brotherhood. Membership in prison gangs was racially defined. Prison gangs such as the Mexican Mafia were a growing force in the underground drug trade as well as in the prison system. This translated into increased competition among racially aligned street gangs involved in narcotics sales. The director of a local gang prevention program summed the situation up in a 1994 public radio interview: "It's pretty common knowledge on the street that [La]Eme has said they want to take over the drug trade in any community where they have people, and to move the Black gangs out."[3] The concurrent rise in nationalism, particularly among Latino prison gangs, was especially influential in shaping racial attitudes. In several East Los Angeles neighborhoods, gangs had instituted a form of "ethnic cleansing" that resulted in the purging of non-Latino members or an organizational split along racial lines.

Within this backdrop, there were two separate series of incidents—one in Mar Vista and another in Oakwood—that eventually converged in Oakwood, where the gang war played itself out. In its initial stage, each set of conflicts involved a separate set of players. In Mar Vista Gardens, the main players were members of the Shoreline Crips, some of whom resided in that housing project, and the Culver City Boys, whose geographic base was concentrated in Mar Vista Gardens. In Oakwood, the initial set of participants were associated with the Shoreline Crips residing in Oakwood and the V-13s, who were dispersed throughout Venice, including the Oakwood neighborhood.

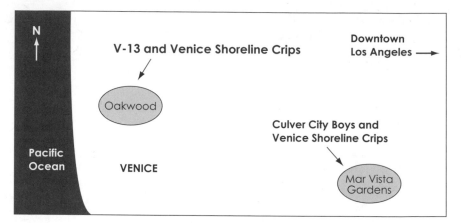

Map 5.1 Geographical origins of the gang conflict

Both conflicts involved clashes between gangs whose active membership was comprised primarily of African American and Latino teen and young adult males, respectively, save for a few exceptions. Two different Latino gangs were involved, one in Oakwood and one in Mar Vista, while related sets of the Shoreline Crips were involved in each of the two locations (see map 5.1). Relations between the Culver City Boys and the V-13 were not in the least amicable. In fact, the Culver City Boys was one of the few westside gangs that did not participate in a westside area truce involving over twenty Latino gangs, of which the V-13 was one.

Turf Competition in Mar Vista Gardens

One set of the Shoreline Crips lived in the Mar Vista Gardens public housing complex, while a larger group of Shoreline Crips was concentrated in the Oakwood neighborhood of Venice. The Mar Vista–based Shorelines and the Oakwood-based Shorelines were closely associated and predominately African American in membership, although there were a few Latino members. The V-13s and the Culver City Boys were both predominately Latino in racial composition with some Southeast Asian members. These two Latino gangs were in the middle of an ongoing feud, even though family relations occasionally crossed gang boundaries. An important difference in gang relations between the two sites was that in Mar Vista Gardens the Shoreline and Culver City Boys had developed increasingly antagonistic relations, while in Oakwood, members of the Shoreline and V-13 had experienced a fairly long history of amicable relations.

The spatial location of these communities served as an ideal setting for the establishment of lucrative street sales of narcotics among all four gangs. Both neighborhoods sat in the middle of more affluent residential tracts, with the upscale Marina del Rey area only a few miles away from both Venice and Mar Vista. In contrast to the surrounding affluence, Oakwood and the Mar Vista Gardens housing project were home to the highest concentrations of low-income residents on the westside (see map 5.2). Affluent buyers in close proximity to populations with a narrower range of opportunities for employment in the formal economy made for a symbiotic relationship. Both sites became known as "drive-thru" areas where one could purchase various drugs without leaving one's car. Not all who dealt drugs in these sites were members of gangs, nor were all gang affiliates involved directly in narcotics sales. For those who did participate, however, the drug market provided a fairly steady and sometimes sizable income for themselves and their families.

Demographic changes in the Mar Vista Gardens shifted the balance of competition between the Culver City Boys and the members of the Shoreline who based their sales in Mar Vista Gardens. The relative decline in the African American population and the increase in Latino and Asian populations throughout Los Angeles County between the 1970s and the 1990s led to an increase in competition over limited resources in many niches where defined interests overlapped; the drug market was no exception. The Shorelines had long dominated the drug trade in the Mar Vista Gardens, creating some resentment among the Culver City Boys, who felt they were not receiving their proportionate share. As the population of Latino residents in the housing complex increased, it became much more difficult for the Shorelines to defend their traditional turf.

But demographic change was not the only factor intensifying competition over the drug market in the Mar Vista Gardens. The Los Angeles Housing Department made a change in the physical terrain that inadvertently intensified competitive relations in Mar Vista Gardens. In the years prior to the war, one main road curved through the complex, and buyers were known to drive through this corridor, which began on the west side of the square-mile project and curved around to its north side. The Shorelines were known to sell at one entrance and Culver City Boys at the other, and the physical distance helped to alleviate visible competition over buyers. In the early 1990s, however, the north entrance gate was closed permanently in an effort to seal off traffic related to the drug trade; the goal was to curb sales and thereby make the streets in the project safer. One unanticipated consequence was the intensification of competitive relations, as the Culver City Boys moved to the west entrance, where the Shoreline operated. As antagonisms grew, residents believed to be members of the Culver City Boys firebombed the homes of African American residents; the Shoreline retaliated in kind. The popular understanding among African American residents was that the Culver City Boys wanted to run the Shorelines out of the projects so that they could control the street economy there. The Culver City Boys, on the other hand, felt the Shoreline had been getting far too large a share of the drug sales. This perception was magnified by the much more assertive style of business practiced

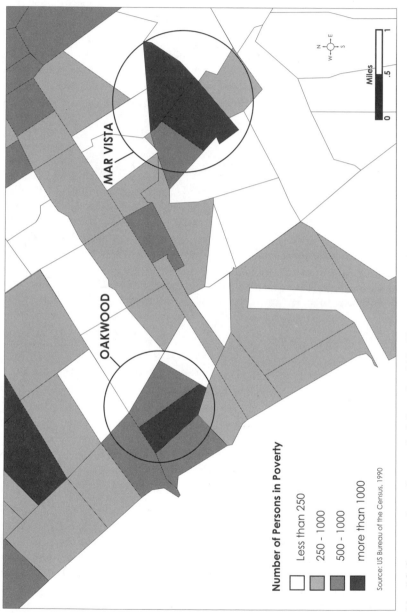

Source: US Bureau of the Census, 1990

Number of Persons in Poverty

- [ ] Less than 250
- 250 - 1000
- 500 - 1000
- more than 1000

MAR VISTA

OAKWOOD

Miles

N
W—◇—E
S

0   .5   1

Map 5.2 Concentrations of poverty in Oakwood and Mar Vista

by the Shoreline as compared to the more discreet style of the Culver City Boys.

The increase in prison gang rivalries in the state prison system also had direct bearing on events at Mar Vista Gardens. A confidential intelligence report by the Housing Authority Police Department stated that members of the Mexican Mafia were paroled to Mar Vista Gardens at around the time that members of the Black Guerrilla Family, a rival prison gang, were also paroled there. The *Los Angeles Times* reported that the releases occurred "just about the time the street gangs turned on each other." The article quotes the intelligence report as stating that "the problem is much larger and vastly more complex. The fight is not racial or territorial, but financial. The local gangs are proxies in a larger war" (Katz 1993b).

In February and March of 1993, a series of firebombings rocked the projects. Many African American families moved out of the area, and physical skirmishes increased between the remaining Shorelines and the increasingly bold Culver City Boys. Several violent confrontations ensued, including a shoot-out. The war between the Culver City Boys and the Mar Vista clique of the Shoreline was decidedly on. Eventually, the Shoreline left the projects and moved to various parts of the city. Some sought refuge in Oakwood with their fellow Shorelines about a mile away.

Personal Conflicts and Family Matters in Oakwood

Meanwhile, in Oakwood, tensions arose between the Oakwood-based Shoreline and the V-13 under very different circumstances. First of all, members of the two gangs living in the neighborhood had longstanding ties of friendship spanning several generations. As described in chapter 2, Oakwood was a place where, as longtime resident and community activist Pearl White put it, "Blacks and browns have always gotten along."[4] Though there was one previous conflict between the V-13 and the Shoreline back in 1978, the two neighbors had a relatively peaceful coexistence. Furthermore, the population turnover during the 1980s and early 1990s in the community of Oakwood was not as drastic as that in the Mar Vista Gardens public housing complex. The major reason for this was the relatively higher rate of home ownership in Oakwood.

The study of racial polarization in Oakwood is important precisely because of the history of close cross-racial bonds largely characterized by respect and cooperation. As mentioned in chapter 2, many black, Latino, Asian, and white progressives had worked closely together during the civil rights movement during the 1960s. Better economic times saw community-wide activities that promoted cross-racial interaction. Many community organizations in Oakwood, such as the Community Service Organization with roots in the Chicano movement of the 1960s, had long worked with groups such as the Pearl White Theater, based primarily among African American youth and their families. There was a stable base of native-born Chicanos. This was in contrast to the

Mar Vista Gardens, where the majority of adults were new immigrants from Mexico, Central America, and Southeast Asia who were not able to communicate as easily with their English-speaking neighbors. The established relationships in Oakwood offered various means to moderate the level of social tensions despite any conflicts that might arise.

The rich history of social organization, cross-cultural cooperation, and longstanding friendships in Oakwood made the tragic turn of events that took place around the same time as the firebombings in Mar Vista Gardens all the more ironic. In Oakwood, a series of interpersonal conflicts escalated into gang conflict. The series of incidents in Oakwood began with an argument between two friends—an African American woman and a Latino man, both Venice residents—who were allegedly sharing some weed on the steps of a church in January 1993. Newspaper and oral accounts agree that Mark Herrera and Diane Calhoun had an altercation. Diane Calhoun stabbed Herrera with a knife, and Herrera died. Herrera was allegedly connected to the V-13. It was said that relatives of Herrera gave Diane Calhoun time to leave town, warning that her life would be at risk if she stayed. She apparently refused to leave the area and was shot to death in early April, a little more than two months after the death of Herrera. It was said that the Shoreline allowed time for the shooter to leave, which the individual apparently did.[5]

There may have been connections on the part of Calhoun and Herrara to the Shoreline and the V-13, respectively, but individuals affiliated with each of the groups took deliberate steps to define the two killings as an individual and family matter and not a conflict involving the two gangs. The process to reach a shared definition of the problem and to agree upon terms of understanding was mediated by individuals who had standing with both groups. According to popular accounts, the two parties reached terms that were seen as being fair, including alternatives for Calhoun to leave or stay, along with consequences for violating those terms. Since there were lines of communication between members and affiliates of both gangs, it was still possible to avert greater conflict. In the eyes of the parties involved, there was a level of order in the way that this incident was handled. Restraint was maintained between the two gangs in the handling of the dispute. For the next five months, there was relative peace.

From a Family Matter to a Gang War

The ability of the Shoreline and the V-13 to limit the parameters of the interpersonal conflict along "family" boundaries demonstrated a substantial level of communication and trust between the members of each group. The enforcement of their agreement also demonstrated a level of control that the gang as a form of social organization maintained among those who operated under or abided by their rules. The deliberate attempt by family members and members of each gang to define the parameters of the problem limited the further involvement of gang members in the dispute. It also represented a willingness on the part of members of both gangs to resolve their issues cooperatively.

A series of incidents over the summer months, however, led to a transformation of relations between the two gangs. This series of incidents began to blend together in a larger narrative that defined the conflict no longer as a set of interpersonal disputes but as a battle between the gangs themselves. Throughout the series of events and interactions, the conflict expanded in scope, encompassing not only members of the two gangs operating in Venice but those from Mar Vista Gardens as well. Divisions widened between gang members in Oakwood, overshadowing many of the interpersonal friendships and cooperative dealings that had long existed across gang boundaries.

An examination of a series of events reveals the process through which a breakdown of trust and dialogue evolved between the two Venice gangs—the V-13 and the Shoreline Crips—leaving room for multiple and divergent interpretations of the other's acts. Narratives explaining the cause and motives behind each action led to depictions of the "other" that helped to justify retaliatory acts in response. Events and participants' interpretations of them resulted in an eventual declaration of war between the two gangs. The redefining of the conflict signaled a shift in the major line of cleavage from family to gang boundaries in Oakwood.

Spillover from Mar Vista to Oakwood

The migration of the Mar Vista–based members of the Shoreline to Oakwood created tensions between the V-13 and the Shoreline, who had long coexisted there. Economic competition in Oakwood increased as the small but active Shoreline group from Mar Vista moved their drug dealing activities to the Oakwood area of Venice following their ouster. However, their presence in Oakwood lured in members of the Culver City Boys in search of their rivals. In addition, in the eyes of some V-13 members, incoming members of the Shoreline did not demonstrate the expected signs of "respect" toward the V-13 into whose territory, shared by the Venice Shorelines, they had sought refuge. As described earlier, the Shoreline members from Mar Vista had very antagonistic relations with their Latino rivals, the Culver City Boys. Upon entering Oakwood, those entering Shorelines did not always make a clear separation between their relationship with their nemesis Culver City Boys and their reactions to the Oakwood-based V-13.

Members of the Shoreline who lived in Oakwood came to feel that their Shoreline cousins from Mar Vista were jeopardizing their somewhat fragile peace with their longtime V-13 neighbors. V-13 associates even questioned their Shoreline neighbors as to why they would allow their cousins from Mar Vista to take refuge in Venice. As one source explained:

> We [the V-13] did talk to [the Shorelines]. You have these guys [Shorelines from Mar Vista who fled to Oakwood] running around [Venice] when they got kicked out of someone's neighborhood. That's cowardly. Go handle your business. Why don't you shoot over there instead of running to Venice. The Shorelines say, "They're family." But Culver City wants these guys. They're going to drive through. Shorelines say, "How do we know they're not V-13s?" We tell them, "You should get rid of them then." But they say, "They're family. We can't kick them out."[6]

Despite the added potential for complication, Shoreline members in Venice remained in unison with their cousins from Mar Vista. In fact, they pulled together more tightly in the face of rumors that Latino gangs bigger than either the Culver City Boys or the V-13s had their eye on the African American gangs' share of the street trade.

Narrative Spins and the Breakdown of Trust

A series of incidents that rolled into one another in a narrative stream created social momentum for an eventual war between the V-13 and the Shoreline. Three incidents in the early fall of 1993 took place under separate circumstances between separate groups of people. Though these incidents were not clearly connected in any retaliatory sequence, they fused together like frames in a film, welded by causal explanations that created a larger interpretive picture of changing relations. It was in this sequence that the object of contestation and lines of division began to shift.

One of the earliest incidents began under circumstances similar to the altercation described earlier between two acquaintances. According to accounts by members of the Shoreline, what began as a one-on-one fight between a Shoreline member and a V-13 member ended in a drive-by shooting that many believed was committed by associates of the V-13 member who Shoreline associates thought may have felt humiliated by the fight. Drive-by shooters sprayed the house of a Shoreline member with bullets while family members were inside. The Shoreline took the actions by the V-13 to be an affront, as they had regarded the initial dispute as having been fairly resolved. They took offense to the attack, since it endangered friends and relatives in a family residence. Because of that incident, Shoreline members became suspicious of the intentions of certain members of the V-13.

Nearly three weeks later, on 27 September 1993, a murder occurred in an alley in Oakwood. According to official reports, Benjamin Ochoa, a familiar and well-liked man referred to in press accounts as a "transient" of Oakwood, was standing with a woman alleged to be a local prostitute. Ochoa was shot in the head and died at the scene. The suspect arrested was someone the V-13 believed was a member of the Shoreline. Though the incident may not have been intended as retaliation for the drive-by shooting earlier in the month, it nonetheless caught the attention of V-13 members, who had known Ochoa. One affiliate of the V-13 described the sympathy among his peers: "The first guy killed [Ochoa] was fifty years old. Used to be from V-13, grew up in Venice, maybe in the '70s. But 'cause he happened to walk down the street, he was killed. People felt for him 'cause he was a bum."[7] Though the man arrested was identified by the V-13 as a member of the Shoreline, it was not confirmed at that time that the man arrested was indeed the shooter. Nevertheless, over the following week distrust grew on the part of the V-13 toward the Shoreline, as about a half-dozen assaults and attempted murders against Latinos were reported in the Oakwood area.

Two weeks following the murder of Ochoa, on 4 October 1993, a well-known and popular member of the Shoreline by the name of Anthony Bibbs was hit by multiple gunshots in the presence of two women who had been accompanying him to a residence in Oakwood. Both women were injured; Bibbs died at the scene. Bibbs had come from a lineage of well-known Shorelines. He was not only popular among gang members, but he was liked by his peers in the broader community. Residents close to the incident shared stories that promoted him to a larger-than-life figure. Accounts praised his bravery, as he was described as flinging himself in the line of fire to protect the two women standing next to him.

The day before the murder of Anthony Bibbs, the V-13 and Shoreline had come to an alleged cease-fire agreement. The shooting of Bibbs came as a shock to members of the Shoreline, many of whom came to believe that they had been betrayed by the V-13. Before the identity or affiliation of the shooter could be determined, the Shoreline lost all trust toward the V-13, believing that they were responsible for the murder. One individual with ties to the Shoreline described their surprise, disbelief, and eventual loss of trust:

> Nobody thought about, even, not even me, thought it was them that shot Bibbs. Even though these guys had sat down together and had said, "We're not in it. We're not going to do anything about it." All of a sudden, Bibbs gets shot, you know. Then everybody thought, "Why they do that?," you know. They just wanted us to put our defenses down so that they could get us, you know. We ain't going to do that no more. . . . Oh, there was no more talking after Bibbs got shot, until June. That was the first time anybody sat down and talked was in June after all those people had died.[8]

Immediately following his murder, various rumors spread among the Shoreline and their social networks as to the reason for the killing. As one rumor had it, he was hit because he was a known narcotics dealer. This narrative reinforced earlier suspicions on the part of the Shoreline that Latino gangs intended to "eliminate them and then take over the whole west side," including the lucrative drug market. As one resident and youth worker explained, "See, they had West L.A. They had Santa Monica. They had Culver

City. And they didn't have Venice. And Venice had the most money. So that's why they wanted to knock Venice [Shoreline] out of it."[9] Some believed that prison influences were behind the actions of the Latino gangs, since an earlier rumor had circulated that the major Latino prison gang in southern California, the Mexican Mafia, had issued a directive to its affiliated street gangs to take stronger control over the street economy. This reading raised questions among the Shorelines as to the forces behind the Bibbs killing. In particular, it raised the possibility that there might be coordinated efforts among those Latino gangs that had negotiated a westside truce earlier in the year, which included the V-13.

A second rumor added to the salience of race among the Shoreline members and friends in relation to the murder. It was hypothesized that Bibbs was targeted because he was known to date Mexican women. For those who believed this rumor might be true, Bibbs's murder was interpreted as a message from Latino gangs that there was to be no "taking" of Mexican women by black men. This reading sent an ominous message not only to members of the Shoreline but also to the large segment of the community with close relations with Mexican Americans.

Longstanding friendships and personal ties between individuals in the Shoreline and the V-13 became strained under the weight of events, which loomed larger than any of the individual incidents. As far as the Shorelines were concerned, Bibbs's death was interpreted as an official declaration of war from the Latino gangs. The alleged agreements between the V-13 and Shoreline evaporated. The legitimacy of those individuals who attempted to mediate between the gangs became tainted, at least within the Shoreline, which had not been prepared for such an attack. Within several hours of Anthony Bibbs's death, three Latinos, allegedly from another westside area gang, were shot at while stopped in their car. One teenager, John Kelley, was killed in the incident. Kelley, however, was not affiliated with either the V-13 or the Culver City Boys.

Certainly, there were many facts about all of these incidents that were unknown to those outside of the circle of direct participants. Many questions lingered. Who actually committed the crimes? Were they acting on behalf of a group or as individuals? What were the intended messages and objectives of the attacks? Were the attacks meant to serve as warnings or declarations of war, or were they committed by groups or individuals completely unrelated to the two parties? Did these attacks emanate from orders made by prison gangs?

It is due to precisely such blurriness that discursive contests over the meaning of events take on such power. As people try to make sense of such dramatic events, the desire to understand what is taking place creates a vacuum that is filled by narratives spun with both facts and speculation. Morphing involves filling in partial images so that the larger picture may be clearer and so that there is some reasoned understanding of the sequence of events. Narratives not only connect a series of snapshots through a storyline that tries to achieve some level of comprehension, they also prime viewers to pay attention to certain features of future events, setting the stage somewhat for the next round of interpretation. For instance, suspicion that an opposing gang is on the attack may sensitize members of that group to see any and all acts of violence in the area as attributable to the opposing gang and then assume that those acts were directed at their entire group. Whether attacks were directed at the respective gangs by the suspected gang was not always verifiably clear. For example, it was possible, based on evidence at that time, that the murder of Bibbs might have been planned by individuals not affiliated with the V-13.

The adoption of one narrative over another often hinges on the believability of one explanation over another and on the "legitimacy" of the source in the minds of the listeners. Stories can tie together events into a causal narrative, but stories cannot stray too far from pieces of "known" evidence. Some facts are difficult to dispute publicly. However, stories can assemble evidence in many different ways and can tie together pieces of evidence with a variety of causal linkages. Discursive contests serve to facilitate the sorting and sequencing of facts by wedging various explanations and predictions between them. Discursive contests, particularly among organizations or publics that do not communicate with one another, can result in varied and conflicting interpretations of the same event.

These early incidents and the explanatory narratives that fused them drew both gangs into direct conflict. As trust and communication between members of the gangs gave way to rumor and suspicion, both sides drew conclusions as to the other's motives and strategies based on interpretations of events as they perceived them. Bare spaces in the canvas of events were filled in with threatening images in an atmosphere of growing fear and anxiety. Each gang attributed responsibility to the other group for the attacks they perceived to have been perpetrated against it. Shoreline members read the murder of Bibbs as a betrayal on the part of the V-13 and their compliance with larger prison-based gangs. The V-13 read the murder of Ochoa and subsequent incidents against their peers as cowardly and senseless acts of aggression by the Shoreline. The personification of both Bibbs and Ochoa by the Shoreline and the V-13, respectively, heightened a sense of injustice on one's own side and projected a charge of moral breach on the part of the other side. The articulation of a moral breach served as a justificatory foundation for acts of retaliation. As each side closed ranks, the interpersonal relations that reached across the Shoreline and the V-13 were momentarily suspended.

As mentioned in chapter 1, the escalation of conflict can be measured along two dimensions: (1) the degree of uniformity displayed by members of the in-group in their behavior and attitudes toward an out-group and (2) the decrease in variability in the characteristics and behavior of the members of the out-group as they are perceived by members of the in-group (Tajfel 1981, 1982). In regard to the first dimension, it was Sumner (1906) who wrote that the "exigencies of war with outsiders are what makes peace inside" (12). As the Shoreline and the V-13 each closed ranks, each acted with greater uniformity toward its rival. This may have been, as some psychologists would explain, the result of a shared perception among members of each gang that their individual fates were intertwined with and dependent upon one another (Lewin 1948; Rabbie 1971). Alternatively, for some gang members the closing of ranks may have accompanied a heightened sense of ethnocentrism (Tajfel 1981).

In regard to the second dimension, each gang tended to perceive attacks by individuals whom they associated with the rival gang as deliberately planned actions on the part of the rival gang as a whole, despite instances where the individuals may have acted on their own initiative. This can become a more frequent problem when there is greater social distance between the conflicting parties. Both the degree of internal group cohesion and the degree to which groups view each other as internally homogeneous affected the intensity of intergroup conflict. So far, the most salient cleavage fell along gang boundaries. This would slowly change, as race would become increasingly salient in relative terms.

The Rising Prominence of Race

As the gang conflict ensued, racial markers became a more pronounced feature of conflict in two ways—as an identifying marker of victimization relative to gang membership and as a focal issue in the discursive contests over the meaning of events. Residents and public officials, among others, expressed growing concern about what appeared to them to be "random racial targeting" of victims by the gangs involved. They expressed fears that many of the victims who were not members of gangs may have been targeted because of their perceived racial group membership. There was public debate over whether the "gang war" was turning into a "race war."

Whether or not the war actually had become a race war was less important than the *perception* held by many that it was becoming one or might become one. If one treated the conflict as though it were a race war, one tended to respond accordingly. Paradoxically, treating the situation *as if it were* a race war would inevitably turn it into one.

This underscores the dialectical and iterative relationship connecting experience, interpretation, and action. An event takes place, an interpretation is made, and a response occurs. In the successive back-and-forth interplay between the gangs, each act of violence was answered with a retaliatory act. If gang members believed that the opponent was targeting victims based on the victim's perceived racial identity rather than on gang identity, they could decide to retaliate against the rival gang similarly through racial targeting regardless of the actual basis of victim selection on the part of the other gang. The interpretation that violence was directed randomly at a member of their racial group, as opposed to their gang, seemed to spur retaliation against a victim whose racial identification matched that of the rival gang, regardless of gang membership. Instead of recording the "score" according to victimized gang members, the scoreboard soon became tallied according to the racial identity of the victim.

Both the V-13 and the Shoreline believed the other guilty of racial targeting, whether intentionally or by using race along with other physical markers as a default to select victims when uncertain of gang affiliation. Rumors and suspicions that the gang war was possibly turning into a race war, circulating internally within the gangs and externally by the local media, may have contributed to a self-fulfilling prophecy. Also, as rumors of racial targeting circulated among the broader population, there were more and more instances of social distancing along racial lines among residents in the neighborhood who had no direct gang affiliations.

Four major processes contributed to the racialization of the gang war: (a) the increasing reliance on phenotypic markers of "race" by those involved in the conflict; (b) the transmission of racial tensions across other existing racial fault lines; (c) the racialized construction of the issue, especially by the media, in the public discourse; and (d) real or perceived institutional biases that were most pronounced according to racial categories. We now turn to the first three processes while the next two chapters include the role of real or perceived institutional bias.

Reliance on Phenotypic Markers of Race

Race is a phenotypic categorical construction; it is a socially constructed category of identification based, in its crudest form, on the physical features of an individual—features such as skin tone, hair texture, and facial characteristics. Race and ethnicity are central components of gang identity in most cities, reflecting the social and familial histories of gangs, the characteristics of neighborhood change, and the centrality of race and ethnicity in the nation as a whole. When race is evoked as a prominent feature of gang membership, the phenotypic character of the racial category becomes abused as a partial proxy for organizational identification, particularly in conflicts involving violence where perpetrators rely heavily on visual clues in the selection of targets. In the absence of clearly marked organizational uniforms as used by official armies in battle, phenotypic features such as those defined by constructed racial categories combine with other physical markers—gender, age, skin tattoos, and attire—to identify members or affiliates of opposing groups. Especially under the duress of violence, combatants often rely on phenotypic identifiers rather than a more complete knowledge of a potential adversary.

Many became victims because of mistaken identification as a gang member. In many cases, the only attributes those victims may have had in common with the targeted gang was race, gender, and sometimes age and attire. By fall 1993, at least three different gangs were involved, and the members of each gang did not all know one another and could not always recognize members of the other gangs involved. The size of the gangs, estimated at several hundred each, made it nearly impossible for gang members to recognize who was or was not a member of an opposing gang. Since members of the V-13 lived in a much more dispersed area than members of the Shoreline who were concentrated in Oakwood, it was especially difficult for Shoreline members to accurately identify their opponent in battle. The number of gangs and the size of membership magnified race and gender among the default characteristics in the identification of victims and perpetrators.

The Shoreline members who had fled from Mar Vista to Oakwood did not know the individual members of the V-13 in Oakwood. Unlike the Shoreline members who had grown up in Oakwood, the Shoreline members from Mar Vista did not have the same social history in the neighborhood and did not know the individual players from the V-13 as their cousin Shorelines did. Similarly, the Culver City Boys in search of Shorelines from Mar Vista did not know the individuals in the Shoreline who had long been based in Oakwood. Race was becoming a prominent fallback proxy in identifying adversaries. A former Shoreline affiliate explained:

> In my opinion, there was more than one gang at war here. You had other gangs that were outside of this particular community that were comin' in. They don't know [Shoreline] gang members per se as V-13 might know 'em. So people come in to do shootings. They see black. They don't know who, what, where. They see black. And it's an innocent person. Now that automatically puts the black person that is at this warfare on the same level. [They say,] "I don't care, shoot 'em. It doesn't matter. . . . And what I'm looking for, is just Latinos." So in my opinion, it's kind of how that got thrown in there. It intended and it started with gang members only, but who's to define a gang member when you're comin' down the street where you don't know [the people]. You see a black person standin' out there, you shoot 'em.[10]

Both sides seemed to feel that the other gang was guilty of wrongly victimizing non–gang members. On the part of the V-13, one associate expressed frustration with the Shoreline's choice of targets, contrasting it with the V-13's actions: "They [Shoreline] were killing people who were not even V-13. On the black side, all [victims were] connected to the Shorelines. But like the two guys in front of Venice High, no one in V-13 knew 'em."[11]

From the standpoint of members of the V-13, they were practicing restraint and were not targeting the non-gang population, as they believed the Shoreline were. But from the Shoreline members' point of view, it was the V-13 who was victimizing the innocent based on racial identification. Shawn Patterson, Cleo Young, and Harold MacDaniel were among those individuals they felt should not have been targeted. Patterson worked as an orderly at the UCLA Medical Center. He was walking home from the bus stop when two young Latino males rode up to him on a bicycle and fired shots at him. He died on the scene. Harold MacDaniel was sitting in his parked car outside of a liquor store on Lincoln Boulevard on the border of Oakwood when he was shot and killed. Neither was known to be active members of the Shoreline. One resident and youth worker explained their interpretation: "It didn't matter because if you were black or affiliated [with the Shoreline], you were a target. The Mexicans got off just hitting everyone black, like the woman Cleo. They started getting anyone but a gang member."[12]

According to one individual with ties to the V-13, however, the V-13 did not view the murders by V-13 members as breaching any code of the street, since they viewed the victims as having some former affiliation or relationship with the Shorelines. They could not speak for other gangs, but they did not feel they were targeting on the basis of race. MacDaniel and Patterson, in their eyes, represented a strike against the Shoreline specifically and not against African Americans generally. For example, in reference to Shawn Patterson's death, one associate explained: "I'm sure people who went to school with him know [he's not active Shoreline], but he still lives in Venice. He may not have been from Shorelines but he's tied into them. On the flip side, the Shorelines would back him."[13] But for the friends of these two men who respected their independence from the Shoreline, Patterson's murder was read as added evidence that blacks were being targeted based on their race, regardless of gang membership.

Meanwhile, the high number of retaliatory attacks on Latinos was raising the ire of the V-13 and the Culver City Boys who saw the Shoreline as the main perpetrators of racially motivated attacks. The murder of several Latino men with no remote gang associations or physical appearance of gang involvement raised the anger of Latino gang members and fear among residents. The most highly publicized was the shooting of Anselmo Cruz in the presence of his two young children and a neighbor's child. Cruz was preparing to drive the three children to school one morning when, according to witnesses, a masked man in dark clothing approached his car and fired shots at him. He died soon thereafter. Cruz was a cook in an L.A. restaurant. His murder sent shock waves through the broader Latino community across the city. The number of assaults on Latino young men with no known gang associations increased, culminating in the murder of two Latino male high school students in front of Venice High School in June 1994.

Thus, over a ten-month period, seventeen people had been killed. Of those, less than a quarter of the victims were claimed by either gang as bona fide members. Over fifty others were injured or filed reports as victims of attempted assault. As the conflict evolved, many who fell victim to violence had no connection to the adversaries at war other than phenotypic features associated with notions of gender and race.

Was the gang war turning into a race war? Were attacks based on random racial violence against anyone identified as black or Latino? For their part, the V-13 deny that it was the case. Shoreline members did not deny racial targeting but viewed it as an act on the part of all parties involved, including LAPD officers, who they believed were targeting African Americans over Latinos for arrest and investigation, as the following chapter further details.

Discrepancies in perception were exacerbated by differences in organizational norms and structures between the two gangs. It is difficult to determine whether or not the attacks that took place during the ten-month period were coordinated acts or to what degree decisions shaping the pattern of violence were centralized. It is important to note, however, that the organizational structure of the Shoreline seemed to allow for greater individual freedom, including phasing out of active membership, than for members of the V-13 or the Culver City Boys. This makes it difficult to know whether the murder of Cruz and other Latinos with no gang affiliation were the act of the Shoreline as an organization or of specific members acting individually or under a general nod of consent by other Shoreline members. Deep resentments against Latinos were commonly expressed during this time, but whether this translated into deliberately random racial attacks on Latino men by the Shoreline as an organizational policy is difficult to confirm.

In addition, differences in organizational norms may have caused V-13 members not to distinguish between active and former Shoreline members in their identification of targets. If the perspective held by V-13 members was that former membership or close family ties with the Shoreline constituted a near-equivalent to formal membership, they may not have seen their actions as hurting "innocent" people, even though the Shoreline may have viewed it quite differently. In any case, there were a greater number of injuries reported by Latinos than by African Americans over the course of the war. According to LAPD incident reports, of the close to sixty recorded victims (killed, injured, and uninjured), the ratio of reported victims of those with Spanish surnames to those without Spanish surnames was approximately 9:5.

Transmission across Tangential Fault Lines

A second process that contributed to the racialization of the conflict was the transmission of social tensions across tangential "racial fault lines." Like earthquake faults that etch a pattern of lines across the landscape, there were racial tensions present in other arenas of conflict throughout the region. And like earthquake fault lines, a tremor along one fault line often reverberated along another, distributing energy between them. One of the arenas of conflict most directly connected to the events in Venice and Mar Vista was the racialized gang conflict within the county jail and state prison systems. As mentioned earlier, these facilities had been the site of an ongoing feud between prison gangs within many California correctional facilities. Several years before the gang war, race riots had begun to erupt more frequently in the state prison system. Many of these riots were related to longstanding feuds among various prison gangs, including the Mexican Mafia, the Black Guerilla Family, and the Aryan Brotherhood (Meyer 1994; Tamaki 1996). These feuds simmered over a wide range of issues, from control over space, equipment, and privileges within the prisons to their influence in the drug trade beyond the prison walls. Prison riots normally broke out along racial lines, following the racial composition of the prison gangs. Memories of prison fights were carried back onto the streets after inmates were released.

One member of the Shoreline described how conflicts in prison "transferred" to the streets:

> You probably see the Mexicans that you was in prison with that live in the area. He probably tried to stab you [in prison], so you gonna go after him because he already tried to kill you once. So you already thinking in your mind, "Well, I'm gonna see him again, [and] next time he might have a gun or something." So it just escalates. You know what I'm sayin'? I really can't say how it is, but that's the way I feel, you know, that it transfers in there to the streets.[14]

It was in this way that antagonisms that formed or escalated between inmates in prisons and jails carried over into communities upon their release.

And just as conflicts in prison bore upon conflicts on the street, the gang war in Venice also added to racial antagonisms in prison. A former Shoreline who was in prison during the outbreak of several race riots explained how the Venice gang war helped fuel several race wars behind prison walls. He described the social dynamic during the time of his incarceration:

> Well, you find that, like if you was from Shoreline, Latinos looked at you differently. There was a definite war goin' on out there [on the streets] that, throughout the Latino community in the jail system, they knew about. So Shoreline had to watch out not just from V-13s, but from all within [prison]. And as a result of that, it didn't reflect as a Shoreline-Latino thing, it was reflected as a black-Latino thing. And if you do somethin' to this black, it's automatically a race war. And it happened on several occasions. Like it happened once or twice when I was in there . . . a race war. In fact, it started behind a Shoreline thing, but on the back of the other blacks backing the individuals that happened to be from Venice in there, it escalated into a racial thing, instead of just an individual thing. So, it happens real easily.[15]

Since the social organization within the prison is highly structured by racially organized prison gangs, conflicts in prison between street gangs quickly transfer to prison gang membership and, from there, to race. The salience of race is even higher in the prison system with the practice of racially segregating inmates within the prisons in California. This practice was employed starting in the 1980s in an attempt to decrease prison violence and had expanded through this period.

Thus, the pattern of social relations in the prison system tended to replicate itself outside of the prison walls, as many of those involved in gangs would circulate in and out of revolving prison doors. The era of zero-tolerance and suppression-oriented policing led to high incarceration rates among many gang members and non-gang members alike. As participants in prison riots returned to their homes, they often brought with them the racial animosities, vendettas, and distrust that stewed in jails and prison complexes.

There was also spillover from other arenas of conflict, somewhat less directly but still adding to the salience of race in the conflict. One arena was competition within the affordable housing market, particularly in the Section 8 subsidized market where low-income families stood on long waiting lists for the limited number of HUD-subsidized units in Oakwood. Community activists involved in the civil rights movements of the 1960s had fought for the development of subsidized housing in Oakwood. Rev. Robert Castile, a long-time advocate for African American concerns, was one of many who spearheaded this effort. Fourteen buildings housed Section 8 tenants and were scattered throughout the Oakwood neighborhood. Though the buildings were historically racially mixed, the demographic balance was slowly shifting, with an increase in the proportion of Latino and Southeast Asian residents and a decline in the number of African American residents. Meanwhile, African Americans continued to face harsh discrimination in the private housing market. This situation, resulting from competition in the public housing market and racial discrimination, added an additional veneer highlighting racial cleavages in the social fabric. This type of tension resulting from competitive relations was also felt in the labor market as people competed for scarce jobs, as well as in the human service arena as more and more people sought social and health services that were shrinking because of conservative retrenchment.

These arenas of conflict, though distinct, linked together like earthquake fault lines, with a tremor along one fault line reverberating down another. Energy along one fault line had the power to fuel another, feeding energy back and forth along subterranean plates. As the ground began to shake at the epicenter in Oakwood, the movement tended to suck energy from within tangential arenas of conflict while feeding into them at the same time. This convergence of racial tensions magnified the resonance of racial constructions in the exchanges that took place in relation to the gang war, connecting it to the larger map of social discord.

Media Discourses and "Race-making"

A third process in the racialization of the war was the elevation of race in the mass media discourse that shaped public perceptions among the local residential population. The local print media closely covered the events throughout this period. Mass media, specifically news media, have the capability of reproducing select discourses and constructing their own narratives, thereby helping to frame the problem in the public's eye (Hall et al. 1978; Gamson and Modigliani 1989). The *Los Angeles Times* was the main regional newspaper and did feature periodic news stories of events related to the gang conflict. But the news medium that was most influential in shaping public perceptions of the conflict locally was *The Outlook* newspaper, the major subscription daily paper marketed to the coastal communities in Los Angeles. *The Outlook* also had a free weekly issue called the *Venice-Marina News* that was delivered to all residences in the affected and surrounding areas.[16] *The Outlook* was one of the main sources of public information about the violence that was occurring at that time, since this daily consistently followed the unfolding events. Subscriptions to the paper rose sharply during the period of intense gang conflict.[17]

News reporting can have a profound effect on race relations, depending on the situation, the substance of the reporting, and how readers receive the information. News reports of the gang war in *The Outlook* and the *Venice-Marina News* had two cumulative effects that affected race relations: it raised the level of fear and racial distancing within the broader population, and it intensified competition among named gangs whose reputations were now perniciously linked to media coverage of the conflict.

By early November 1993, there were growing concerns that racial targeting of victims may be taking place. There was a rising awareness among residents in the immediate neighborhood that some of the victims had no gang affiliation. Several African American victims who were known not to be gang members were suspected to have been killed by Latino gang members, and several older Latino men who were not gang-affiliated were suspected to have been killed by African American gang affiliates. While a growing number of residents feared racial targeting, there were disputes as to the degree of targeting and the specific motives behind these particular attacks.

But these disputes were muted when a mid-November 1993 issue of *The Outlook* ran the following headline: "Deadly Gang War Turns to Race War" (See figure 5.1). This article, with an almost identical bold, front-page headline, was also reprinted in the *Venice-Marina News.*[18] This article reported on the rising number of incidents that month. In characterizing the violence, the article read, "In the beginning, it appeared gang members were targeted, but in recent weeks targets were apparently chosen because of their race."[19] If there were questions among participants and direct witnesses as to whether or not the gang war had turned into a race war, there was little question about it among the broader media audience. And whether or not it was actually seen as a race war between the gangs involved, reports that it "really" was a race war only exerted greater force in that direction.

Through their regular coverage of the events surrounding the violence,

◁| VENICE - MARINA |▷

· A COPLEY
LOS ANGELES
NEWSPAPER

News

Thursday, Nov. 25, 1993
Zone 14A
Vol. 32 / No. 47

Deadly Venice gang war turns to race war

By Marilyn Martinez
REPRINTED FROM THE OUTLOOK

Police see violence in Venice widening

One man was killed, two people were wounded, and the homes of two families were firebombed over the weekend in incidents police linked to the broadening war between two Venice gangs.

Police on Nov. 21 also arrested two Venice teen-agers, one of them 14 years old, believed responsible for one of the killings.

"It's obvious it's part of the continuing war," said Los Angeles police Detective Bernard Rogers of the latest two homicides.

In recent weeks, a nearly three-month-old gang rivalry between the Venice Shoreline Crips, a black gang, and the V-13, a Latino gang, has taken

on the appearance of a racial war. In the beginning, it appeared gang members were targeted, but in recent weeks targets were apparently chosen because of their race.

In almost all the cases, the victims and assailants were of opposite race.

On Nov. 21, Lenard Keston, 21, of Venice, was gunned down at the southwest corner of Indiana and Seventh avenues in a drive-by shooting at 8:10 p.m., Rogers said. Keston, who police described as a gang member, died at the scene.

A second victim, LaTonya Harrell, 25, of Venice, was wounded at Seventh Avenue and Indiana Court, about a

half-block away. She was shot several times but is expected to live.

Minutes before the shooting, another man was shot at Sixth Avenue and Broadway. But residents told police that family members had taken the victim to a hospital. No police report was filed.

Following the shootings, police saw a brown Jeep Cherokee described by witnesses as the gunmen's car in both incidents. Officers chased the Jeep from the Oakwood area to Tivoli and Ida avenues in Mar Vista, where two passengers jumped out. The driver of the car escaped.

Police arrested Felipe Sandoval, 18,

of Venice, and a 14-year-old Venice boy. Both were arrested on suspicion of murder.

Police said several handguns were used in the shootings. Residents near the scene said they heard at least a dozen shots fired.

The weekend killings bring the number of homicides in the area to 11 since October, police said. That number includes two people who had no ties to gangs and were apparently shot because of their race. One girl, who had no affiliation to gangs, was fatally shot when gunmen opened fire on a gang member who was riding in her car.

"That's a lot of killing in a very

short seven-week period, and that's only the killings," said Rogers.

On Nov. 19, 20 and 21 residents reported that gunshots could be heard nightly in the Oakwood neighborhood of Venice and the area near the Mar Vista Gardens housing projects.

Home firebombed

In Mar Vista, a Molotov cocktail was thrown through the bottom-floor window of Lonnie Loudermilk's apartment in the 11900 block of Allin Street about 11:30 p.m. Saturday, police said.

Although two bombs were thrown at the house, only one ignited. It started a fire in the kitchen. The flames were quickly extinguished.

GANG WAR/A7

Figure 5.1 Front-page headline of *Venice-Marina News*, 25 November 1993

The Outlook and its free weekly were able to intensify the prominence of race as a cleavage in the war through its method of reporting, which relied heavily on law enforcement protocols for providing information, and in the simplification of complex stories in which emphasis was placed on the racial dimension of the conflict to the larger public audience.

It is common practice for news reporters to rely on local law enforcement for any "official" information regarding crime and arrests. One writer, Marilyn Martinez, wrote the majority of articles covering the gang war in *The Outlook*. Her main source of information was the LAPD, which has formal guidelines for the release of information to the public and the media, just as there is a standard protocol for the filing of police crime and arrest reports. The common method of describing crime incidents was to give the victim or arrestee's name, race, gender, and age (unless under 18 years old). Law enforcement agents disclosed a gang affiliation if one was known. Normally, the police release little information on the circumstances, causes, precipitating events, motives, found evidence, and prior victim-suspect relationships related to the reported crime until investigations were completed. Thus, the media-receiving public is left with a compressed and incomplete understanding of incidents, relying primarily on abridged police accounts.

The limited and selective description of incidents emphasizing racial identification and phenotypic descriptors tended to reinforce their significance. Reporting the racial identification of victims and suspects had the effect of creating a public scoreboard for all to see, with body counts tallied along racially split columns. As race became an increasingly prominent descriptor in media reports, as prominent as gang affiliation or even more so, racial categories were reinforced as a substantive object of contest. Many articles reported the racial identity of victims and perpetrators without mention of any gang affiliations since they were not always known or did not exist. The public scoreboard created by the media by reporting in racial terms had the effect of exaggerating the importance of race among the gangs themselves whose reputations were at stake. The wider the media announcement of victim counts by race, the greater the internal pressure placed on gangs to maintain a lead in the body count, marked in the public venue by race. In other words, the more the media emphasized the racial characteristics of victims and suspects, the more salient race became in the counting of bodies for purposes of public scorekeeping.

Not all media made this same proclamation of a "race war," nor did all emphasize the racial descriptors so strongly. The *Los Angeles Times*, for example, aired competing views as to whether the conflict was primarily one between gangs or a racial conflict. For example, in a 19 December 1993 article, *Times* staff writer Ken Ellingwood quoted LAPD officer Brad Merritt that "some of the victims are being killed because of their race, not because they're gang members." But the article juxtaposed this perspective with that of a resident, Carmen Gonzales, who rebutted, "It is not a racial war. It is a *gang* war."[20] Many residents registered protest against *The Outlook*'s representation of the conflict, arguing that the depiction of the gang war as a race war was premature at that point in time and was only adding to the escalating problem.

One irony of the media's role is that those closest to the war tended to resist labeling the conflict as a race war, whereas those furthest from the immediate situation defined it as such early on. This was because the coverage in the print media tended to frame it in racial terms more squarely than did residents who had access to more details surrounding the various incidents. Residents' narratives were much more complex and more complete than those reported in newsprint, especially within networks connected to those close to the events. Those in closer range of the violence knew that race was only one of many descriptors in the identification of victims. For those close to the scene, there were other possible explanations aside from racial targeting in some of the cases that might explain the pattern of victimization.

While race was central among salient identities, it was also clear that the attacks were based on other considerations in addition to race. Women, the young, and the elderly were not targeted, though several women were shot or killed in the company of men. The vast majority of the victims were young males in clothing that could be read as gang attire. However, gang-inspired dress had become part of popular culture, and it was difficult to make assumptions about gang membership based on style of dress. Skin tone, dress, age, and other visual cues indicated the pattern of victimization of Latinos and African Americans.

In fact, physical markers that distinguished one as *not* being a gang member were important "safety devices" for protection from the conflict. One African American mother of several children and resident of Oakwood in her early twenties shared a story that illustrates the significance of visible gender identifiers, of which she and other women became very conscious in their choice of attire. She recalled an event that began in the morning as she prepared to take her kids to school:

> And I just combed my hair back. I forgot to put my earrings on. So I didn't have no earrings on and I had a black, you know, the big puffy jackets? . . . So then my friend was in the car and we was facing one way and my other girlfriend was facing another way. And we were sitting there in the middle of the street talking and, all of a sudden, my girlfriend who was in the car with me looked up and said, "Ahh! Go [name]! Go bitch, go!" And I see my friend hit the corner. She hit the alley real quick and took off, so I just took off and the car was coming. And I said, "Oh, I hope it's no cars coming." So I speeded through and he speeded behind me. And I turned the car and it was, like, turning on two wheels. And the car was behind me and I was speeding real fast. And he was just chasing me. So I thought to take him back to, you know, where the guys were hanging out at, but not knowing they had already been through there and did a shooting and was coming around the corner. [He] thought I was a guy in a car, and chased me down. Because my hair was short and I had on one of those big puffy jackets. I mean, you know, it was scary. She was in the car with me. My baby was in the car with me. She was little. She didn't know what was going on. She just bouncing around the car, laughing. . . . But I guess as they got closer and closer, they seen I was a girl, and they just went on.[21]

With a chuckle, she said that from that day on, "every time I get dressed, I get up and put my earrings on!"

While gender identifiers served to give some residents some sense of protection, flying bullets did not always discriminate. Many of the shootings involved multiple rounds, sending stray bullets in random directions. Many knew that some individuals were at risk of being targeted more than others, but the fact that bullets did not always hit their intended targets instilled fear and trepidation, changing the lifestyles of many families.

Constructing Race as an Explanatory Variable

The morphology of racialization involved a chain of events including interpretive and performative acts engulfing broader segments of the population in a tide of polarization. The readings on both sides that the opposing group was targeting individuals based on racial considerations apart from gang membership led to a redefinition of the substance and tenor of the war. The feeling on the part of both gangs that people were committing acts of racial targeting confounded the stakes of the war. Not only did they see themselves defending their "turf" and their respective group reputations, the stakes of the conflict were increasingly tied to their respective racial identities as Latinos and African Americans. There were two implications to this substantive shift in stakes. First, reputations linked to racial identities began to overshadow the economic issues that may have been the initial impetus for the war. In defending the reputation of their gang, they were also under pressure to defend their race. Second, the self-perception as defending their race opened a floodgate of appeals to the broader community for support in their greater defense *as a race*. These combined effects set the stage for a broader redefinition of alliances and divisions that would polarize larger segments of the neighborhood along racial divides. The conflict, in effect, morphed in substance, character, and salient lines of cleavage.

From the period between November 1993 and June 1994, what began as a set of individual conflicts escalated into a gang war loaded with racial overtones. For over seven months, the war continued unabated, stalled only by the Christmas holiday season and the January Northridge earthquake, which brought an uncomfortable hush to the neighborhood. Unfortunately, this quiet did not last long, and the war soon resumed. From January to June, the number of violent incidents reported to the LAPD resumed an upward trend.

Racial Distancing in a Polarized Field

The course of tragic events and the growing popular perception that the gang war may be turning into a race war spurred deep divisions that reverberated throughout the community. Old friendships between black and Latino families were sometimes strained. Black and Latino children began to fight on the playground of the local elementary schools. Visits between friends and neighbors were postponed. A general feeling of sadness, distance, and occasional distrust fell upon many treasured relations. Throughout the ordeal, boundaries and lines of division and alliance were constantly negotiated and renegotiated in both public and private realms far beyond the circle of the gangs.

The fact that lives were being lost carried emotions to heights that led some individuals to feel and think in ways uncharacteristic under normal circumstances. The violence and pain brought sadness and rage to the surface, expressed in actions and reactions common to wartime. One former member of the Shoreline explained: "I mean, people who wouldn't normally be involved emotionally in these things were involved emotionally. The entire community was upset. And you had people possibly saying, I mean older people, people that are settled in life who wouldn't have condoned what was going on, but after a point, seven or eight deaths, it was like 'Do them or you get done,' you know. . . . So it escalated like that on both sides."[22] The level of fear and anxiety created an atmosphere filled with distrust. He continued to describe the situations in which some found themselves: "It got real serious. People were carrying guns. I mean, not to hurt nobody, but just to defend themselves. At any given point, you move the wrong way, you drive the wrong way. . . . it was at the point that you pull up to a stoplight and have to look to see who's in the car behind you or sittin' in the car next to you. And I think in one instance, they actually had a shoot-out from being just stopped at a stoplight."[23] Under highly combustible conditions, the violence escalated the conflict with great speed and intensity.

The racial polarization that took place between the Shoreline and V-13, at least for the duration of the war, was uncharacteristic of their past relations, except during a previous conflict in 1978. Many residents who had known members in both gangs reminisced of instances of mutual support. Distancing and polarization led to a breakdown in communication between many individuals. This made it more difficult for gang members, old-time *veteranos* and OGs, and their friends and relations to communicate across color lines.[24] While some attempted to maintain communication and found windows of opportunity to mediate the conflict, the tide toward polarization was difficult to turn. Severed communications also caused further complications. It was not uncommon for one group to construct an explanatory narrative that differed from another. Particularly in a situation where intentions and meanings are not verified or verifiable, which is often the case in violent conflict settings, interaction between groups was fraught with misunderstanding, which added to the strained relations.

Conflict and polarization was not confined to the gang population but spread to many segments of the residential community. As more residents came to suspect that the violence represented a race war, there grew greater resentment, fear, and anger. The racial distancing seemed to be more common among younger residents than older adults. There were many older residents for whom the gang war had little impact on personal relations across color lines. But for children and teens in their formative years, the gang war played a large role in defining race relations and personal identity. One parent worried out loud about how the kids perceived the events around them and the impact it had on their understanding of the world. She reflected on her observations: "Some kids was wondering if that's what life is really about. If that's what they have to do to be grown, you know. And that was kind of scary when some kids was like, 'Dang! That's what you have to do to be a man.' You know? And some kids believed that doing this would make 'em a grown-up. A lot of kids got that [idea]."[25]

Longtime friendships among adults were also tested under the strain of the situation. Many proved resilient, but neighbors felt a great deal of pressure from peers and were nevertheless deeply affected by the tragedy of events around them. One young woman in her thirties who was born and raised in Oakwood, worked in the neighborhood, and identified as Latina had close bonds with an older African American neighbor; she told of an encounter after the murder of her friend's son. After hearing of her friend's son's death, she visited her friend's house.

When I was met at the gate and the family is all black, and here I am Latina going into their home. . . . I really felt bad, you know, to know that one of my people had killed him. It was hard for me to even go over there. But I wanted to go pay my respects because I've known that family for a long time . . . she and her daughter's kids that she had raised. So I felt close to that family. And that's why I went. But I still, being met at the gate by a lot of blacks, I felt like out of place and kind of, not so much afraid, but just, I don't know, hurt, sad. But then when we went in and [she] received us with open arms, I felt more comfortable, sitting down and, you know, talking to her. And then . . . I don't know, you know. What do you say? What do you do? You know. It's hard. I mean, you give your condolences, you know, and you offer to help in whatever you can. But, I mean, I don't think she looked at us any different, you know. But . . . (laughs) once I was outside that gate, you know, I don't know. It was like I could feel, you know, the tension.[26]

This recollection reveals the tensions between privately expressed affections of love, caring, and concern across color lines juxtaposed against a publicly framed problem that imposed racial divisions upon established relations. The two friends embraced and shared condolences in the privacy of the home but did not feel the same ease to express their feelings publicly given the highly divided social atmosphere that had developed.

Some of the young adults who had friends across color lines felt that the war took a heavy toll on their relationships. Because so many lives were lost and so many people had been injured, it was difficult to know where the pain and anger might lie and how it might be triggered. It was also unclear who was directly involved in the war. While direct contact between individual Latino and black friends might be more manageable, mixed company at larger gatherings came with a great deal of uncertainty and risk. One resident explained:

I had a lot of Latino friends that was some good friends and we couldn't communicate. We would see each other, you know. You didn't know if you should speak or not speak because you didn't know what the outcome of it was going to be. This girl I had worked with for years—I couldn't even go to her baby shower. And it was hurting. She was like, "I want you to be there, but I don't want nothing to happen to you."

You never know who would be there. You never know who would trip, see. You never know who was with it and who wasn't with it until it happened. You know. And you never . . . you don't know who's initiated . . . or what's going on.[27]

The complicated and often unseen web of group affiliations accentuated racial distinctions in everyday social interactions. Because of unknown connections that may be discovered, as expressed above, friendships across racial boundaries suffered.

Both African American and Latino residents often acknowledged the fact that both racial groups faced similar problems of inequality, discrimination, and economic marginalization. One resident pointed to what she considered the senselessness of the war: "We both from minorities. We both at the bottom of the totem pole. I mean, they're no better than us. We're no better than them. You know. And I can't understand why people like to fight over turf because nobody . . . *you don't own this land.*"[28] Despite fairly widespread acknowledgment that neither racial group enjoyed socioeconomic status equal to other groups in society, the felt realities of conflict had generated a momentum of its own.

While class boundaries had been the more salient division prior to the war, as described in chapter 2, race superseded class in defining publics under the new circumstances. Tensions between renters and those some referred to as the "gentrified people" receded in relative salience. As one member of the Oakwood Property Owners Association, a middle-aged Caucasian male resident and homeowner, explained the impact on himself and his family, "How did the gang war affect us? Well it took a lot of pressure off us."[29] Low-income residents led by longtime African American advocates turned their attention to the immediate problem of gang violence. This is not to say that class cleavages were entirely forgotten. In fact, the "gentrification conspiracy" remained the overarching narrative among many African Americans and low-income residents, as described in following chapters. The situational salience of race did, however, become primary during the gang war, despite the enduring centrality of class.

Hands across the Racial Divide

It would be a mistake to overlook efforts to build and maintain interracial cooperation against the tide of division in such polarized environments. Those seen as socializing with the "other" can be chastised or viewed with suspicion among stalwarts. But despite the division, covert and sometimes overt acts of racial solidarity were expressed, especially between friends and relations in Oakwood. There was real reason to fear for one's life if one were African American or Latino, given the number of assaults and murders of non-gang members who were identified by racial categorization, gender, family ties, or physical attire. Despite this environment, many individuals made great efforts to maintain personal relationships, while many actively sought to bridge the racial divide.

For many of the older adults, expressions of cross-racial solidarity were more boldly and openly shown, due to long-established relations as well as less risk of victimization due to age. These "acts of solidarity," whether it be in the name of friendship or peacemaking or whether overtly or covertly expressed, attest to the persistence of human bonds that held across racial cleavages—

bonds that prevented the violence from creating even greater racial antagonisms than it already had.

One family, for example, had a close acquaintance—a middle-aged African American female resident—who was deeply affected by one of the shootings. The acquaintance expressed resentment against Latinos for the harm they had done to her brother. Members of this family grew concerned and set up a lunch appointment between their acquaintance and one of their longtime Latino friends. This exchange helped to put the conflict into perspective and temper the emotional animosity that had been channeled against another racial group. One of the family members explained, "The one that got killed, his sister was hating all Mexicans. I said, 'How can you hate *all* Mexicans 'cause *all* Mexicans didn't do the shooting?'" They explained to the sister of the slain victim that "you can retaliate, go shooting the Mexicans, but that's not going to bring your brother back."[30] The lunch get-together with her Latino friends and former classmate "eased her" and helped to place events and their meaning into broader temporal and situational context.

There was also cross-racial cooperation between Latino and African American residents in assisting those affected by the war. This included everything from collecting victim's insurance to finding attorneys for cases. Activist Pearl White had long worked with residents of all racial backgrounds in the Oakwood community and was among the many African American civil rights workers of the 1960s. She and Melvyn Hayward of the Pearl White Theater both reached out to one of the Latino youths who shot and injured their friend Jimmy Powell, a youth outreach worker for Project Heavy West and an Oakwood resident, also African American. Powell had been walking along the sidewalk in Oakwood when a Latino youth of his acquaintance fired shots from across the street. Powell shared his thoughts about the incident and how they were able to work through the events that transpired and continue their relationship: "The guy who shot me apologized to me. Melvyn talked to him and Pearl went to court with him. He [later] called Pearl. He wanted to go back to school. Venice High School called me and he had to come talk to me."[31] They smoothed out their relationship, and Powell continued to work with Latino and African American youths on campus as well as in the community. His exemplary actions in helping groups to mediate conflicts across color lines at Venice High School even after the shooting sent a message that people can overcome great obstacles to work for peace. He reflected, "Maybe it was good I got shot. Maybe I could be an example. I could have gone and just stayed home [after that]."[32]

Another story told by a member of the Shoreline who was incarcerated during the war shared an incident in which he made a personal agreement with a friend and fellow inmate who was a member of the V-13. The agreement was that if there was a race riot, they would be obliged to join the fight, but they would not hurt each other. He recollected the discussion with a fellow V-13 inmate:

1. Flora Chavez and Pearl White, longtime civil rights activists, were among the many individuals who worked across color lines to assist victims and advocate for peace.

But I can tell you this right here, it was two Mexicans up in there from Venice that I knew from the street that I kicked it with. We just kicked it before the war jumped off in prison. And they got at me. They told me, "Check this out, homie. If something ever jump up between the races, man, just go your way. I'm going my way. You know what I'm saying? You just get at another Mexican. I get at some more blacks, but we ain't touching each other like that. . . . You know what I'm sayin' . . . 'cause we grew up together." I respected that and when it happened, they did that. You know what I'm saying? And all the people that's black from Venice did the same thing. You know what I'm saying? That's the respect that we had.[33]

In these instances, bonds of friendship transcended racial divides even in the most combative situations. These acts, however, were mainly covert and hidden from those who might have judged such gestures as signs of disloyalty. They follow a long legacy of acts such as those during wartime where human ties transcend nationalisms and other constructed group divisions.

As the war went on and more victims fell, these ties were put under the test of increased pressure. As greater numbers of "innocent" people were hurt, however, anger toward the actions of gang members rose within the neighborhood at large. Individuals and groups began to take more direct steps to try to halt the violence. Peace marches were held. Ministers preached peace to their congregations. Meetings were organized. Messages were relayed to the gangs. And alternatives such as jobs were offered by several community organizations and businesses to involve youth in "positive" activities.

Race and the Escalation of Conflict

To summarize, as racial descriptors became more prominent relative to gang identification in discursive and physical acts, the conflict began to "morph," transforming in appearance and narrative substance from a gang-bounded conflict to one based on broader racial symbols. As in the case of morphing in visual arts, where there is no one particular frame that marks a transformation in an image, there was no single event that signified the transformation in the meaning or reading of the conflict. Narratives strung events together and gave the entire sequence of events greater racial meaning over time, with some events and narratives punctuating the transformation more loudly than others.

Like the vulnerability of one who yearns, these narratives satisfied many different needs, whether explanatory, justificatory, or anticipatory. As an explanatory variable (i.e., "it was because of his race"), race can become a powerful construct in the evolution of social relations. Justificatory narratives ("because it was race") can be invoked to rally troops in combat or inflame group protest. Anticipatory narratives ("it will be because of your race") can instill widespread fear and strengthen racial group solidarity. In this case, race served as a descriptor in the characterization of events but also as an explanation as to why someone may have fallen victim to violence. As an explanatory "reason" for an event, race was also invoked to justify a retaliatory act, elevating race as both an object to defend and a moral stake in an expanding territorial battle. As an anticipatory narrative, racialized discourse led to social distancing and polarization, even among those who were not direct party to the conflict.

The process through which racial meanings were embedded in the conflict was a gradual one. In the ongoing interplay of conflict, each action or event was interpreted by the affected individuals and publics. Discussion and debate over the meaning of events ensued. This interpretive discourse included the portraits of the "self" and "other," causal explanations of events, motives of groups and individuals, and moral judgments regarding actions. Interpretations were made individually as well as through public deliberations. The interpretations of events were also influenced by the media, which reached a broader audience than those directly witnessing the events themselves. Based on conclusions drawn by individuals about these events, the picture of the problem was often reshaped and the relative salience of their multiple identities was reinforced, reconstituted, or reshuffled in relation to one another. Publics emerged based not only on events but through discursive contests over their meaning. Because multiple publics did not see the world in the same way based on differences in vantage points and interpretive frames, the meaning of symbols and actions were not the same for all groups. There was great room for ambiguity in meaning as publics encoded and decoded symbols and actions. Sometimes, groups imputed meanings to the actions of others in ways in which those "others" never intended, especially where there was more limited interaction and lack of overlap in interpretive frames across publics. Over iterative rounds of events, the scope and substance of the conflict expanded. Race became the substantive focus of the problem as well as a primary cleavage in the escalating interplay between an array of groups.

While the salience of racial identities became a primary boundary of group division for many, acts of cross-racial cooperation showed that it was not necessarily central for all. In the midst of the widening racial divide, many bonds of friendship and trust remained strong. Cross-racial publics were present throughout, though their presence was not always visible. Acts of solidarity surfaced from an important resource that could be leveraged on the road to peaceful resolution. How these resources and community-based efforts were seen and whether they would clash with or complement those of law enforcement agencies was yet to be known, for two distinct approaches had emerged within the law enforcement community—one a "firefighter" approach and the other a "mediator" approach. The two chapters that follow describe each of these and their effects on the situation at hand.

Chapter 6

Firefighters

Suppression from Without

Police and other law enforcement institutions were the most visible and direct agents of government intervention in response to the gang war, with the Los Angeles Police Department (LAPD) dispatched as the first line of intervention. Meanwhile, a broad range of civic, religious, educational, and community service organizations in the Venice area mobilized their resources. Individuals with some standing within the circles of the active combatants also wielded their influence at critical moments. Each of the institutions and organizations that attended to the crisis had different sets of objectives, motives, and tools of influence. At times, disparate efforts among various groups and individuals worked at cross-purposes. At other times, efforts seemed to complement one another. At no point in time, however, was there any consensus across law enforcement and community groups as to the approach that would be most effective in ending the violence.

Two distinct approaches to the problem did emerge. The most immediate and dominant was a high-suppression, "firefighter" approach that focused on apprehending as many gang members as possible to "stamp out the flames of violence." I borrow the term from an interviewee who likened the approach used by law enforcement agencies to firefighters who "clear the brush" around a fire and simultaneously "smother the flames." This strategy emphasized intensive suppression methods to remove identified gang members from the area and to restrain the movements and activities among the remaining gang members. Tactics included the use of search and seizure operations, increased patrols, surveillance, and the tracking of arrested suspects to ensure maximum sentencing. The second approach that surfaced shortly into the conflict was a "mediation" approach that tried to get the gangs to negotiate an end to the war internally.[1] It was based on an assessment of competing interests and viewpoints among the various players and on a strategy of coupling government and community initiatives to engage participants in weighing incentives with the mounting disincentives of continued warfare.

These two strategies were based on two vastly different problematics, that is, definitions and analyses of the problem. They also engendered different responses and led to different outcomes. In this chapter, I describe the "fire-fighter" approach, followed by Chapter 7, where I focus on the "mediator" approach. It was this latter "mediator" approach that eventually led to a truce in June 1994 after ten long months of fighting. I analyze the interpretive narratives by which various publics made sense of the events that ensued as well as the responses by them to various interventions.

Multilayered Law Enforcement Agency Networks

The multilayered systems of law enforcement and criminal justice involved many different institutions tied together by unevenly coded interagency agreements.[2] The local jurisdictional agencies responding to the gang war included the departments of police, parole, probation, city attorney, district attorney, fire, and housing. Federal law enforcement agencies were also operating in the neighborhood, namely the Federal Bureau of Investigation (FBI) and the Bureau of Alcohol, Tobacco, and Firearms (ATF). Each agency had its own mission, powers, tasks, incentive structures, decision-making processes, leadership and institutional culture, range of discretion, and specific policy instruments. Each agency had internal protocols as well as interagency protocols.

Individuals acted upon their agency mandates but also upon their own moral convictions and personal biases, much in the way that Lipsky (1980) described the workings of "street level bureaucracy." Agents of those institutions enjoyed broad discretionary powers so that individual beliefs and attitudes were also reflected to some degree in official responses. Networks of law enforcement agents across institutions coordinated their work based on agreements over strategies and assessments of the problem. A shared identification as law enforcement personnel coupled with a shared approach to the problem tied together individuals in working networks.

There was no one single coordinating body among government agencies in response to the gang war, even though several interagency bodies existed to coordinate law enforcement and community activities. The Interagency Gang Task Force under the District Attorney's Office was a standing committee of social service organizations and law enforcement agencies, but it did not serve as a coordinating body to oversee this specific conflict in a consistent way. A neighborhood coalition called Oakwood United was also a standing consortium of community organizations and representatives from government agencies, including the LAPD, concerned with problems in Oakwood. This consortium facilitated the sharing of information and initiated an economic development project for youths, but it had no official capacity for co-ordinating government and community responses to the gang war. The LAPD also initiated a committee consisting of law enforcement and other governmental agencies, community organizations, and social service agencies serving the Oakwood neighborhood. Participation in the LAPD-initiated network was on an invitation-only basis and served information-sharing purposes only. In addition to this, there were two more covert law enforcement task forces, including a task force within the FBI and an interagency task force that included representatives from the city attorney, police, parole, and probation offices that focused specifically on Oakwood.

None of these served as a main umbrella body to coordinate the various strategies to deal with the gang war, due mainly to the absence of a unified view as well as a lack of trust and cooperation among many of the groups and individuals involved. Instead, ad hoc interagency bodies and informal networks were formed, out of which specific strategies and actions coalesced. The result was a set of parallel network-based interagency attempts to intervene in the war, some of which worked in seamless tandem and others that, at times, stumbled clumsily over one another.

Solving a Predefined Problem

When the gang conflict broke out into violence, the majority of law enforcement agents took the approach of rounding up as many gang affiliates as possible. The logic was that the more gang members who were off the street, the less energy there would be to fuel the war. The expectation was that the war would eventually die down through attrition. According to the firefighter approach, it was important that law enforcement agencies pursue all avenues to arrest suspected gang members on any applicable charges and detain them for as long as possible. As Councilwoman Ruth Galanter explained: "We flooded the area with law enforcement because people in danger of being murdered need to be protected. So that was the first thing. Let's just cool it out. Try to stop the killing. Try to get hold of as many killers as we can. Get their weapons off the streets and get them off the streets."[3]

The prescription for intervention entailed numerous operations coordinated among a variety of agencies. The FBI would intensify surveillance and apprehension of the Shoreline Crips as part of their county-wide gang surveillance project. This was part of their fight against organized crime and drugs. They worked with the ATF, which focused on the confiscation of firearms. The LAPD would increase patrols in the area and carry out a variety of suppression operations. The LAPD worked closely with city and district attorneys, who would prepare abatement proceedings or subpoenas for a variety of charges related to the gang war and any previous infractions of the law, from civil codes to criminal codes. Probation and parole offices would rearrest probationers and parolees on the slightest of violations. Special units of the LAPD such as Community Resources Against Street Hoodlums (CRASH), the narcotics division, and the vice squad would allocate additional resources to operations in Venice. Arrestees would be more carefully tracked and receive the maximum sentence if convicted. All of these efforts were designed to "remove the firewood" and "smother any remaining flames."[4]

The foundation for this approach can be more closely examined in the LAPD plan of operations in Oakwood, titled "The Oakwood Plan." As reviewed in chapter 4, the "criminal element" in Oakwood was referred to in the text as "predators." The Pacific Area Predator Arrest Team (PAT) of the LAPD's Pacific Division was "responsible for developing, maintaining and updating a list of those persons who by virtue of their demonstrated aggressive repetitive criminal behavior, can be classified as criminal predators."[5] Pacific Division officers had worked closely with other agencies and had developed an infrastructure with networks and protocols that could be used to respond to the rising violence. The additional local and federal resources funneled to Venice during this period buttressed this existing foundation and boosted the strength of high-suppression operations.

Dispatching the Firefighters

Thus, the strategy of the Oakwood Plan relied on an arsenal of high-suppression interventions whose use was intensified in the face of growing violence in the neighborhood. A high-suppression approach to gang violence was led by a network of personnel in two city agencies, including the LAPD and the Office of the City Attorney, with cooperation from other agencies including the Los Angeles County District Attorney's Office, the County of Los Angeles Probation Department, and various city agencies. The Office of the City Attorney and the LAPD had been working together on a number of high-profile gang abatement operations for several years before the Venice gang war, including a controversial but officially praised "clean up" operation on Blythe Street in the city's San Fernando Valley. The approach of "high suppression" was what the law enforcement and criminal justice systems had come to know. It was a normative practice, codified in rules and embedded in habitual routines of daily operations.

There were individuals in the two agencies with a long history of work on cases involving Oakwood residents. From their experience, they believed that a substantial proportion of crime on the westside involved members of local gangs. For them, the V-13, the Culver City Boys, and the Shoreline Crips were some of the "most wanted." They had a strong commitment to ridding the neighborhood of crime and its perpetrators. The two city agencies were also central to the formulation and implementation of the Oakwood Plan. Though the atmosphere of teamwork had diminished with the turnover in the LAPD administrative leadership and with the appointment of a new captain in the LAPD's Pacific Division, there remained interpersonal ties between the key personnel of the two agencies. Moreover, similarities remained in their approach, as already described.

The LAPD's main strategy was to flood the area with patrol cars, which it did after it was clear that the violence was escalating.[6] Lieutenant John Weaver of the LAPD's Operations-West Bureau (OWB) stated that there were times when there were over a hundred officers assigned to Oakwood during a 24–hour period. That translated to ten to twelve patrol cars with several officers per car at all hours of a given day. A fellow officer added, "That is almost a car in every third block because it's such a small area."[7] Indeed, this was an unprecedented number of officers assigned for any amount of time to an area of approximately 1.2 square miles. In order to staff the area at this level, officers were brought in from other units in addition to the Pacific Division, including the CRASH unit and the metropolitan division, which specialized in gang-related and drug activities respectively. In addition to increasing the number of officers assigned to Oakwood, the LAPD worked with the city attorney's office and other agencies on larger coordinated operations.

One of the first major joint operations was a night "raid" in the early stages of the war on 27 October 1993. Numerous law enforcement agencies under the lead agency of the Department of Fire and Safety gathered over 200 documents in a subpoena against a number of men identified as members of the Shoreline Crips who were suspected of participating in acts of arson earlier in the year. A search warrant was issued by the Los Angeles County Superior Court on 21 October 1993.

The search and seizure operation had been under preparation prior to the gang war in response to arson activities starting in early 1993 that were not related to the gang conflict that later ensued. The police suspected that members of the Shoreline were responsible for a set of firebombing incidents aimed at Oakwood residents who had spoken out against gang activities in the neighborhood. The judge issued the warrant "as a result of an ongoing investigation of a series of fire bombings that occurred in the Oakwood area of Venice, California during a six-month period, from February to August."[8] The timing of the search and seizure operation occurred at the beginning of the war in Venice, following the murder earlier that month of Anthony Bibbs, whose death, along with the murder of Benjamin Ochoa, contributed to the initial escalation of conflict. Whether or not the precise timing of the warrant was altered in light of the war's outbreak is unknown. It was certainly the hope of these law enforcement officers, however, that the arrest of the Shoreline affiliates listed in the warrant would help to quell the current violence.

This highly organized LAPD search and seizure operation involved predawn raids of eighteen residences in search of thirteen named suspects. West Bureau CRASH, the Pacific Division, West Bureau Narcotics, the Oakwood Task Force, and Metro divisions of the LAPD coordinated their tasks and assignments. The majority of homes, thirteen of the eighteen, were located in Oakwood. Police accounts indicate that approximately 200 officers were involved on the morning of the operation. One hundred and fifty officers met at the West Los Angeles station at 2 a.m. to begin the search. LAPD officers issued warrants and served subpoenas at the homes at approximately 3 a.m. Among the items listed to be seized were matches, lighters, lighter fluid, empty bottles, utility bills, dyes, evidence of gang affiliation with the Shoreline Crips, Nike tennis shoes with black or blue laces, Los Angeles Raiders jackets, photos of gang members, phone and address books, evidence of the sale or use of crack, financial records, and firearms. Summary reports state that at the end of the operation that morning, five men were arrested for charges named in the warrant, four were arrested on unrelated charges, and forty firearms were seized along with $40,000 in cash.[9]

This search and seizure operation was the largest gang-suppression operation in Venice in terms of the utilization of resources for a single activity during the period under study. On a more ongoing basis, other features of the firefighter approach took the form of increased coordination among law enforcement agencies, the securing of maximum sentences for gang-related offenses, strict enforcement of civil and criminal laws, and closer tracking of criminal cases related to the gang war.

Effects of Early High-Suppression Operations

Perceptions of Institutional Favoritism

In light of the fact that the raids were directed exclusively at the homes of African Americans in search of members of the Venice Shoreline Crips, some began to argue that the Shoreline was being "targeted" over their Latino counterparts, raising suspicions of law enforcement favoritism. Interviews revealed that many African American residents spanning a cross section of ages and political persuasions suspected bias against their racial group over Latinos in the balance of the conflict.

The police retorted that the racial composition of the suspects listed on the warrant was simply a result of the fact that the raid was in response to *earlier* arson investigations of the Shoreline and *not* the ongoing gang war. However, such details proved to have little resonance. The timing of the operation in the midst of the racialized gang war fueled the public perceptions that the police were targeting the Shoreline over the Latino gangs. The search and seizure operation was not the only incident that drove this perception of police motives and actions, but it dovetailed with other incidents that were strung together in a seemingly cohesive narrative among certain publics to present a picture of collective victimization.

That raids were conducted exclusively at the homes of African American residents lent greater credence among a wide spectrum of African American residents to the idea that police responses to the violence were part of a larger plan to remove African Americans from Oakwood. The preexisting meta-narrative of "gentrification" discussed in chapter 3 had not completely faded in the noise of gunfire but was rearticulated to fuse a series of events into a more cohesive plot that spelled out a conspiracy between real estate developers and police. Suspected collaboration between police officers and real estate speculators led many who feared being driven away by gentrification to believe that many police officers had no true interest in stopping the violence. Indeed, the more violence that was unleashed, the lower real estate prices dropped, making property attractive to speculators who had the patience to wait out the violence. There was also a sustained trickle of African American and Latino residents moving out of the area to escape physical danger.

A female resident employed at the Venice Skills Center located in Oakwood echoed the anxiety many African Americans felt and described her view of police in furthering a black exodus: "They covered a lot for the Latinos. They picked up black people, not a lot of Latino guys. They picked up the black people because they wanted them dead. So that was a lot of tension because it was a one-sided deal. They only wanted the blacks out of here. They said they wanted Oakwood and this was a way for the white superiors to get Oakwood back, is to kill up the black people in here."[10] While some scoffed at the idea of a conspiracy, there remained a fairly widespread belief that at least some police officers were not truly committed to stopping the violence due to their personal connections with real estate speculators, held especially by young African American adults residing in Oakwood. Several added that even though police were targeting African Americans, they believed that it would be only a matter of time that low-income people of all racial groups would be driven out of the neighborhood.

The fact that the captain of the Pacific Division was of Latino descent raised questions among some residents about the motives behind police actions, as the same resident speculated: "If they raided the Mexicans' houses, and if they took some of them in and took some into jail, then maybe we wouldn't feel that way. . . . When they made those raids, that's when people thought it was a racial thing. We had a Mexican captain at that time. I'm not sure if that had something to do with it. I don't know."[11] Others did not assign any significance to racial differences within the ranks of the LAPD. Another resident with associations with the Shoreline did not see the racial identity of the Pacific Division Captain as the cause for bias: "The police is the police. Whatever color they come in has nothing to do with nothing. You know. It's their whole attitude—the makeup of the police and what they're all about."[12]

Police officials vehemently denied charges of intentional "targeting" of African Americans over Latinos. They did not view the search and seizure operation as discriminatory or as a means to handicap the Shoreline in the war.

In their view, it was an operation related to arson investigations that had begun even before the gang war started. In regard to routine arrests on the streets, several CRASH officers had their interpretation of perceptions that African Americans were targeted. They acknowledged a difference in the enforcement of African American and Latino gangs, but they attributed it to the ease with which they could apprehend the Shorelines rather than a choice designed to favor one group over another. An LAPD lieutenant and his detective explained the difficulty of apprehending members of the V-13 or the Culver City Boys with equal success due to their style of illegal operations:

> LIEUTENANT: They deal drugs different from black gangs. Hispanic gangs don't stand on corners and sell rock. They sell it in their homes or in apartments or places like that, so you don't see them standing out in the street like you do the black gang members. Which is very frustrating when you're trying to work the drug problem.
> DETECTIVE: The other thing in the Hispanic is this family and community thing, so to get into it, you have to be part of it. You just don't get an undercover police officer to go in. There's more of a family, community. . . . I mean, there's part of that within the black gang, but it's not nearly as strong. Not even a small percentage as strong. But in the Spanish gangs, it's very strong.[13]

These explanations appeared consistent across law enforcement agencies. Michael Genelin, head of the Hardcore Gang Unit in the Los Angeles County District Attorney's Office, noted that the perception of racial bias was of concern to their office and offered an explanation for the FBI's decision to target the Shoreline as one of the gangs under federal investigation in Los Angeles:

> But the reason the [FBI] task force targeted Shoreline was for several reasons. One, Shoreline is more amenable to targeting because they do a tremendous amount of street dealing. . . . You could use all kinds of investigating tools to get them. Whereas the V-13 did a lot of dealing behind closed doors where it's hard to get to. And there were a number of informants that were available with relationship to Shoreline that were not available to V-13.[14]

Genelin was concerned about community perceptions that there may be racial targeting of African Americans, but he stated that it was hard to avoid given the different modes of operation between the Shoreline and V-13. He explained, "We tried to make that clear [that we were not interested] in favoring anybody. We just wanted the shooting war to stop, and so we tried to figure out ways to also penetrate or to attack primarily V-13. And it was very difficult, again, because of the way one gang operated vis-à-vis the other gang."[15]

Increased Rage and Desperation

While law enforcement agents had their logic and rationale for what was perceived by the Shoreline and many African American residents as racial targeting, one of the impacts of the raids was to increase the level of rage and
desperation among Shoreline members, who read police actions as "disarming" their forces and aiding their Latino adversaries. From the point of view
of Shoreline members, the raids and other law enforcement actions were an
effort by the police to undercut them in their battle against the Latino gangs.
One resident who had family members associated with the Shoreline explained the impact of the raids on the perceptions among members of the
Shoreline whom he knew: "They [the Shoreline] were already feeling mis-
treated. The blacks felt like it was a race thing. When they raided the houses,
how many Hispanic homes was raided? They were disarming us. Taking our
weapons. And they was taking people's guns from people and didn't give
them slips. They just took the guns and let [the people] go. They probably
took them and gave it to the Mexicans."[16] The confiscation of the cache of
arms was compared by some to the embargo of arms against Bosnia in their
war against Serbs in Bosnia-Herzegovina.

Shoreline members came to define the war not as a "Black vs. Brown," but
as a "Black vs. Brown-and-Blue" war. Many Shoreline and their relations believed, as was often said, "It wasn't just a Black and Brown thing, it was a Black,
Brown, and Blue thing. So the Blacks had to worry about the Brown *and* the
Blue." Shoreline members felt that police targeted African Americans for arrests throughout the war, so they viewed their adversaries in this particular war
as both the V-13 and the police. One member who, during the war, had been
in state prison shared his personal observations from his time there:

> It seems that the police, they knew what they was doing because they was, you
> know, arresting majority of black people. Cause if you just go to jail, from the
> whole war, all of them is black. They got, like, . . . out of the whole war, they
> got, like, six Mexicans that's in jail. [They got] 'round about at least thirteen,
> fourteen, fifteen [blacks] and all of them for murder. But they only got, like,
> six Mexicans. And they knew what they was doing.[17]

The V-13 were aware of the law enforcement crackdown on the Shoreline,
but they also believed they were under high law enforcement scrutiny. As it
was later revealed, the FBI was covertly conducting a separate investigation of
the Mexican Mafia, one of the prison-based gangs, which brought some of
their associates on the street under surveillance. These investigations led
to arrests several years later (Ramos 1996). They also felt that the Shoreline
had a geographical advantage to defend themselves better since they were
concentrated in a small residential area. The V-13 tended to be residentially

dispersed over a wider area without the protection that geographic concentration provided. One V-13 associate explained: "Blacks have an edge 'cause they families live there. If V-13s wanted to get someone, they had to go in. A Mexican can't hide themselves. They're stopped by police or hit by blacks."[18] These V-13 members did not believe the police targeted them any more than the Shoreline. Some referred to the police as a "third gang," but they did not see the police siding with them against the Shoreline, as the latter believed.

A rumor circulated that the Shoreline would "hit three Mexicans for every black" hit by gunfire. Whether this rumor was true or whether the rumor was spread by Shoreline members as a tactic to stave off further attacks upon them is not clear. From incident reports, however, it is certain that there were a greater number of Latinos who filed police reports as victims of assault or attempted murder compared to African Americans, at a ratio of 9 to 5. So there were almost twice as many reported Latino victims compared to African Americans, indicating that there may have been some truth to the rumor, assuming that the perpetrators of attacks against Latino victims were members of the Shoreline. It is possible that the perception among the Shoreline that they were the prey of "two gangs"—the "brown" and the "blue"—moved them, morally justified in their own minds, to take more drastic actions.

Altering the Balance of Power

A third, and possibly the most profound, effect of the search and seizure operation was to alter the balance of power within the Shoreline toward those holding more extreme positions. The raid and other high-suppression activities resulted in the arrests of influential members of the Shoreline based in Oakwood. The arrest of these individuals created room for those Shoreline members who had moved over from Mar Vista and could then exert a greater voice in the group's affairs. Because the subpoena was issued in response to charges of arson that had taken place in Oakwood in the aftermath of the 1992 civil unrest, almost all of the individuals named in the subpoena resided in Oakwood or were associated with the Oakwood-based Shoreline. However, Shoreline members from Mar Vista tended to be more aggressive in their actions since they had been involved in intense battles over turf with members of the Culver City Boys for more than a year before being firebombed and driven out of the Mar Vista Gardens housing project. In contrast, the Shoreline and the V-13 members based in Oakwood had relatively amicable relations, which became strained after the turf battles in Mar Vista and were aggravated with the relocation of Mar Vista Shoreline members to Venice.

In other words, the arrest of Oakwood-based Shoreline members altered the composition of those remaining active on the streets. Residents knowledgeable about the internal dynamics of the Shoreline observed that these arrests contributed to the prominence of certain individuals from the Mar Vista Shoreline within the organization, shifting the internal balance of

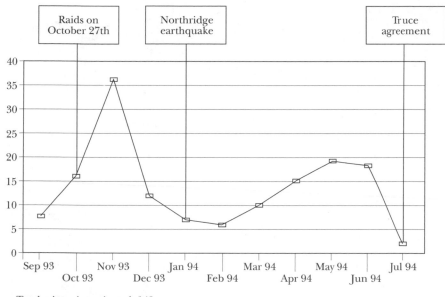

Total crimes investigated: 149

Source: Los Angeles Police Department, Operations-West Bureau CRASH (Community Resources Against Street Hoodlums)

Figure 6.1 Crimes investigated by LAPD Operations-West Bureau CRASH, September 1993– July 1994

power toward greater use of violence. Because high-suppression approaches do not consider these finer distinctions and dynamics, law enforcement officers did not anticipate the "boomerang effect" that their operations would have.

Figure 6.1 charts the number of reported gang-related incidents associated with the war. As chronicled in the previous chapter, conflicts began brewing earlier in 1993 in both the Mar Vista Gardens and Oakwood. The conflicts in the two locations began to dovetail in the summer and early fall of 1993. In September, Operations-West Bureau (OWB) CRASH had been called in to investigate five cases of attempted murder and three cases of aggravated assault.[19] It was also in September that Benjamin Ochoa was killed. The conflict began to escalate in October with the murders of Anthony Bibbs and John Anthony Kelley, the latter suspected as retaliation for Bibbs, both on 10 October 1993. For the entirety of September, OWB CRASH investigated a total of five cases of aggravated assault, eight cases of attempted murder, and one case of attack with a deadly weapon upon a police officer.[20]

In late October, the LAPD implemented the major search and seizure operation, as described earlier. This was followed by the greatest number of attacks and the greatest number of murders in a single month. In November, six people were murdered, including two women, Sienna Antwine and Cleo

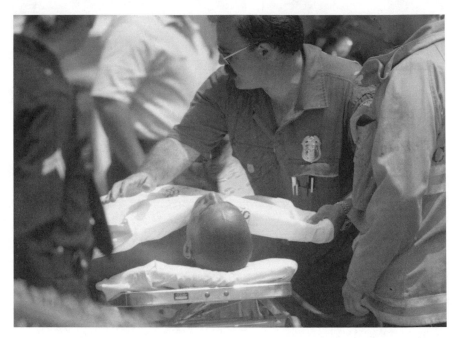

2. Victim on gurney getting medical assistance after being hit by gunfire in a drive-by shooting, April 27, 1994. Courtesy of Santa Monica Historical Society Museum/Outlook Collection.

Young, neither of whom were members of any of the gangs involved but were apparently in the proximity of other male victims who were either killed or injured. In addition to the six murders, OWB CRASH also recorded twenty-three cases of aggravated assault and seven cases of attempted murder.[21] These incidents occurred on fourteen different days and include only those cases reported to the police department. Thus, rather than decreased violence, the search and seizure operation was followed by the highest level of violence of the entire period.

The fighting subsided during the Christmas holidays. A major earthquake known as the "Northridge quake" hit the Los Angeles basin in January 1994. This quake left major structural damage, primarily in the San Fernando Valley, and kept families occupied with the aftermath. But damage also extended to the westside, including the Venice area. Federal Emergency Management Agency (FEMA) agents combed the affected areas, and numerous families applied for emergency assistance to repair their homes. The earthquake and its aftermath extended the holiday pause to the violence. But the fighting began to increase again in February and continued to escalate through June, when the truce was reached.

3. Friends mourn the death of eighteen-year-old Sienna Antwine, who was killed on November 18, 1993. Courtesy of Santa Monica Historical Society Museum/Outlook Collection.

High Suppression and Police-Community Relations

It is impossible to make any sweeping generalizations about the overall state of police-community relations at that time, since it varied widely by population segment, time, and circumstance. The tenor of relations also varied by individual police officer, some of whom enjoyed fairly cooperative relations across the many segments. Even among tightly knit social networks, there were wide variations in attitude toward law enforcement officers. And many judgments about fairness and social justice were contingent on many factors. For example, many African American residents interviewed expressed a willingness to cooperate more closely with law enforcement officers to curb criminal activities, but their willingness was tempered by certain conditions, such as: (1) greater alternatives for arrested youths to turn their lives around, (2) an attitude of respect among officers toward members of the African American community, and (3) antidiscriminatory reforms in the establishment and enforcement of criminal laws to ensure fairer enforcement and punishment. Many expressed sadness about the deteriorating social effects of drugs and violence on friends and relations and did not see much hope for turning the situation around. The "broken windows" approach of heavily enforcing minor infractions such as towing away cars with broken taillights was often seen as making life harder and more burdensome for those who were struggling the hardest to survive, let alone trying to help others within the neighborhood.

While police-community relations were complex and varied, it was clear that among African American residents, high-suppression activities such as the search and seizure operation placed greater strain on already tense relations. There was a fairly widespread belief among African American residents of all ages, occupations, and political attitudes that many of the police actions during this period were carried out with marked unconcern over the affected families. The result was further mistrust and resentment on the part of many African American residents toward law enforcement officers.

Narrative accounts about the treatment of family members in their homes during the raids circulated widely in their social networks, creating more anger in the community toward police actions. Interviews revealed two major complaints about the raids. One was the perceived disrespect on the part of police officers toward the families and a feeling among some of the affected families that the police had wrongly searched some of the homes. In regard to the latter complaint, incorrect information on suspects is not uncommon. Information on suspects entered into databases, or files become obsolete and are not regularly updated. Also, suspected youths who are questioned or held by police do not always give their correct address and instead give those of friends or relatives. Only several of the fifteen suspects named in the subpoena were found on this search.

A number of residents whose homes were searched joined together to file a lawsuit against the city. One of the attorneys assisting with investigations who spoke with many of the families who were connected to the lawsuit described his impressions of the operation:

> It seems to have upset too many innocent people. In one house a kid was sick. The family said the baby can't come outside, but stands outside for one hour. One very old man was treated extremely rudely and roughly. He was 75 years old, very old and very sick, but was dragged out of the house. Many not involved were handcuffed and treated badly in the presence of their children. A lot of people were forced out of their home wearing very little. It was extremely embarrassing. It was humiliating, deliberately humiliating.[22]

From the perspective of police trained in the militaristic style of the LAPD at that time, however, this particular set of raids was much less intrusive than on previous occasions, such as those under Operation Hammer. Operation Hammer was a very controversial anti-gang program launched in 1988 in which police conducted often large-scale sweeps and search and seizure operations to arrest those thought to be involved in illegal gang activity. This operation resulted in tens of thousands of arrests, primarily of young African American and Latino men. On one night, officers in Operation Hammer were reported to have arrested 1,453 people, of whom 1,350 were released with no charges filed.[23] Officers in this more recent operation, however, were instructed to avoid the legal problems resulting from Operation Hammer. In this raid, police officers videotaped the interior of the Shoreline homes for the purpose of avoiding costly lawsuits that had rendered large fines against the LAPD in previous cases.

Reframing the Problem and Realigning Publics

The intentions behind people's actions often have little resemblance to the way those on the receiving end interpret those actions. Peter Hall's insights on the "encoding" and "decoding" of meanings underscores the fact that these are separate processes among different people for whom the meanings of specific symbols and actions differ. For whatever the intent, law enforcement actions under the firefighter approach were interpreted as "biased targeting" and had the effect of increasing the salience of racial identity boundaries among African Americans—identities to which gang members and affiliates appealed in an effort to garner community support. The "gentrification conspiracy" narrative preempted greater cooperation between subscribers to the theory and the police, while simultaneously drawing together Shoreline members and residents concerned about gentrification into a common perception of a shared fate.

But neither are the meanings of symbols or actions set in stone. Individuals and groups actively attempt to win the support of others to their cause with narratives as a way of expanding the public within which they may congregate. Some Shoreline affiliates began to exploit the widespread acceptance of the conspiracy theory for their own defense. Explaining police activity within the frame of the gentrification narrative not only dampened an initial willingness among African Americans to work with police (especially with several African American officers who were trying more creative ways of working together with residents to solve the problem), but it also made it more difficult for individuals to initiate greater dialogue across color lines for fear of being perceived as "joining the grand conspiracy."

As police activities alienated some of the residents, gang members tried to win their allegiance by attributing new meanings to their own actions as well as to the actions of others. Some Shoreline members promoted the idea that they were "protecting the community" from Latinos and the police who sided with them. Distrust and resentment toward the LAPD based on residents' experiences and on what they had heard from others gave currency to the idea that the gangs offered a protection that police were not providing. One resident shared an exchange with Shoreline members: "There was a lot of blacks that was in Oakwood that had gotten shot. They were in Oakwood. But then when [other gang members] start hearing about their homies being shot, then a lot of them came back from the Valley and different other places to help them defend Oakwood area. And the black gangs had said to me, 'If we weren't here, you would be dead because the police wasn't here to protect you.' And that is very true. The police wasn't here as protection."[24] A much more ambitious effort to rally African American residents to back up the Shoreline and their defenders was initiated by Timothy Crayton under the name of the "Venice Pathfinders." A group of young to middle-aged African American men who lived or worked in Oakwood and who were from different walks of life had begun to meet in late spring 1994 to discuss strategies for intervention. Crayton, though present in that group, acted on his own initiative, distributing two different leaflets calling for support in the fight of "Black men" against victimization by the police and Latino gangs. One leaflet was directed toward African Americans in Oakwood, while the other was addressed to patrons of businesses in the surrounding retail and commercial strips. The leaflet distributed to Oakwood residents urged neighbors to "Stop Snitching" and stated, "When You See Black Men Carrying Guns Through Your Yard, *Support Him,*—Give Him A Hand Full Of Bullets! *Our Youths Are Out There Risking Their Lives To Protect You Older Folks From Mexican Bullets!*" The second leaflet distributed in the adjacent commercial district, headlined, "*Warning: Unsafe Area*" and warned "White Customers Shopping In This Section Of Venice May Be Shot Dead By Mexican Gangs—Without Notice" (see figure 6.2). The intent of these leaflets was to gain support from within the neighborhood for the Shoreline as well as to redirect public attention to Latino gang members who he believed were being favored by police.[25] Soon after the distribution of these leaflets, Crayton was arrested on parole violations, charges that he protested.

It is difficult to assess the full extent to which the larger population accepted this framing of the problem and how it, in turn, shaped the behaviors of those exposed to these arguments. As to the leaflets themselves, though they appeared to have had a limited impact on the immediate community, it did capture the attention of certain city and county officials. While it was soon understood that the leaflets were being created and distributed at the initiative of one individual, the leaflet did have the effect of raising awareness among public and elected officials across the county of the gravity of the situation.

Some Latino elected officials, who were a growing force in local and state government, took special notice, given the large proportion of their electoral support that was based on the growing strength of the "Latino vote." While Crayton's intention was to get law enforcement to pay more attention to Latino gangs, it may have had a greater effect among various government officials, particularly Latino elected officials, to the seriousness of the gang conflict and the particular activities of the Shoreline. This is not to say that Latino elected officials only acted to defend racially defined interests, only that the intended effects of actions on the part of gang associates and their concerned friends did not always result in the desired outcome. Though the leaflet may

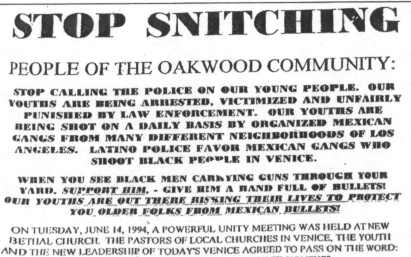

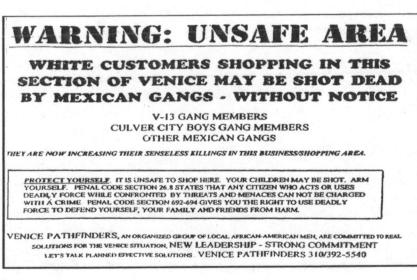

Figure 6.2 Leaflets

have been intended to bring about greater suppression of Latino gangs and to enhance the support of the Shoreline among local residents, this was not the actual outcome. Crayton's effort did not generate any stockpile of bullets. But it did reinforce the gentrification narrative and the idea of "gang protection" of African American residents by the Shoreline.

All of this led to subtle shifts in the prevailing alignments. This had grave implications for the range of future scenarios that would most likely unfold. Among many African American residents, the meta-narrative of "gentrification" enhanced the quite common perception of racial bias on the part of police officers, regardless of the police's actual intentions. The more pervasive the belief that the police were conspiring to rid the neighborhood not only of gang members but of the African American community as a whole, the greater salience that race had for that population. The more that race was perceived as a marker for victimization, the more racially polarized the population became and the more difficult it became to mobilize residents to intervene between the warring parties. As police practices fed into the gentrification narrative, the salience of boundaries between gang members and everyone else receded, while racial and, secondarily, class boundaries became heightened in relative relief.

The shift in the relative salience of race and class had several effects. First, it signified a stronger alliance among those African Americans who felt threatened by the prospect of gentrification. Currency in the idea that the Shoreline served as "protection" for African American residents created an environment in which it became difficult for some to voice opposition to gang activities. The more imminent the gentrification threat seemed, the more those who shared the fear banded together—gang and non-gang alike. This placed greater pressures on those who continued to openly express their opposition to continued violence. This phenomenon was greater for youths than for adults. Second, many of those who perceived the police as unjustly siding with Latinos expressed increased resentment and bitterness toward their Latino neighbors, resulting in even greater social distancing and polarization. This reinforced a social atmosphere in which it was more difficult to initiate cross-racial dialogue despite the presence of individuals for whom the salience of race was not prominent. Third, as the Shoreline came to believe that police were siding with Latino gangs to eliminate the Shoreline, their actions seemed to grow more extreme. Racial divisions and antagonisms only grew deeper, with prospects for peace far from view.

Thus, the gang war had morphed into a conflict that was perceived by a growing number of residents as creeping beyond the parameters of gang members; it was overflowing to conform to the boundaries of racial identification. As the targets of violence were falling beyond the borders of actual gang members, it reinforced fears that race was becoming a primary attribute marking victims, inconsistently but often combined with markers of gender, age, and attire. The barrage of events signaled iterations in which the language of race began to dominate the discourses and actions among direct combatants and among the expanding audience as well. Despite gallant efforts to halt the divisive momentum, cleavages grew where social ties had once held strong. Animosities grew between many Latino and African American residents and between police and affected residents. Those who struggled to create a "high ground" of peace and racial unity were doing so against the gravitational pull of a downward current, strengthened not only from the outpourings of the gang battle but also from the efforts to suppress it.

The Paradox of Police Powers

By spring 1994, after almost six months of violence, it had become clear to many that, short of a drastic increase in resources, declaration of martial law, or the sudden arrival of the National Guard, the current allocation of police and other law enforcement officers could not control the violence. Even with beefed-up patrols in the single square mile of Oakwood, shootings were still taking place. LAPD Lieutenant John Weaver expressed his frustration with what he described as evidence of the deliberateness of the shooters:

> Now the Oakwood area is only two square miles. . . . Probably on that night, [there are] ten cars—that's twenty officers. The metropolitan division is down there. CRASH was down there. The Oakwood Task Force was down there, and any Pacific units. There were four different police entities that had units in that area that evening, and you had two murders occur. Over the next six months there is this enormous number of police officers dedicated to this small area. They continue to do the shootings and killings, you know, literally, literally under the noses of the police officers.[26]

Not only did the violence continue, it spread over a larger geographic area. The initial series of incidents were centered in Mar Vista Gardens and in Oakwood. As the war progressed—as Weaver mentioned—incidents took place in a larger area between the two originating points (see map 6.1).

This raises a peculiar irony of moral panics. The panic over the problem of crime fueled the political momentum that gave law enforcement and criminal justice agencies in the United States far greater powers. But the actual ability of such physical forms of social control to quell violence does not approach what the general public is generally made to believe it is. The fallacy of the moral panic lay in an illusory presentation of power. Uniformed officials know their limited capabilities very well, but they must uphold the image of power in order to maximize their authority. Yet the more they boast about their brute authority, the less power they in actuality have, since the potency of their powers is heavily dependent on their ability to garner community cooperation to reveal information necessary to preempt and investigate

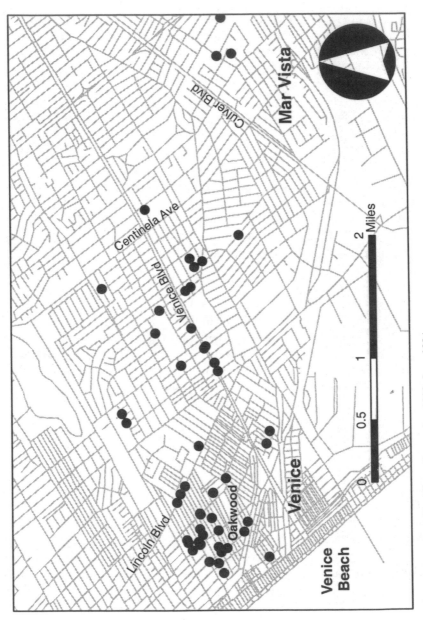

Map 6.1 Location of incidents, September 1993–June 1994

crimes. The stronger the popular belief in the power of police to stop crime, the more disillusioned, confused, and even suspicious people can become if crime is not stopped with such great infusions of law enforcement resources to an area.

The case of the police response to the gang war in Venice demonstrated the limited power of a strictly physical demonstration of force. No one understood the limited powers of the police more than the police officers themselves. As they drove their patrol cars through the neighborhood, they would hear shots fired on a street corner minutes after leaving it. Their inability to control the streets began to undermine their own authority. Asked what the entire experience teaches us for the future, one officer said with some exasperation, "You can't expect the police department to really have control over a neighborhood and what goes on there," without help from the community, which "pretty much takes care of their own problems."[27]

Mythologizing the power of the police had the effect of undermining their own legitimacy. Publicity promoting the need for increased allocations to law enforcement agencies—power and resources to investigate, enforce, penalize, and incarcerate—may have led to the successful passage of major crime reform legislation, but it also had the side effect of increasing expectations of law enforcement effectiveness. An unprecedented amount of police resources was allocated to this one neighborhood—yet the violence continued. Promotion of the belief that the police can control crime primarily by increasing their forces led to a rise in the expectation that the violence would be quelled. When the police failed to stop the violence, faith in police power was shaken, and theories of police conspiracy were fanned even more. As one religious leader described the feeling among his predominately Latino congregation, "A lot of people were feeling a sense of anger and a sense of hopelessness, like no one really cares and they just as soon let us kill one another."[28]

The paradox of police powers was this: the more resources that police claimed they needed to control violence, the more resources the public placed in their hands to do a job that was impossible to do—at least with added resources alone—leaving many residents more distrustful of police once their failure to quell violence became clear—and effective policing was heavily dependent on precisely trust and cooperation between police and residents.

Residents complained that they saw LAPD officers sitting in their cars or driving around the neighborhood while shootings were taking place just a few blocks away. For some, this was interpreted as deliberate neglect. One resident shared her interpretation of the same type of scenario that a police officer described earlier: "It was just that incidences happened, they arrived on the scene too quick. . . . One [police car] went down the street around the corner, then this person gets killed. I mean, how are you not catching [these people]? You arrive on the scene right after it happened. Each time, an incident [happens and] you're arriving right on the scene. You're right around the corner. You just park down the street. . . . It was just obvious that something was going on or something."[29] For those who raised a similar line of questioning, it was difficult to understand how such incidents could carry on with so many officers in such close proximity, which raised suspicion about police intentions.

One well-circulated theory was that police wanted African American and Latino gangs to keep fighting among themselves. There were many anecdotal stories which, when all told and pieced together, gave this explanation a fuller image. One youth worker retold this story of police officers who allegedly made inflammatory comments to others whom he knew: "There was a Mexican guy who was friends with some black people. He said, 'Something wild just happened. I was up at the 7–11 and they [police officers] told me I had two hours to shoot some blacks. "Go kill you some niggers and we'll give you two hours to let you get home."' [Then, in another incident,] I heard Mexican police tell my brother, 'The Mexicans are up. They're ahead.' "[30] He explained that the same type of instigations were taking place on the other side and that many believed it was in the interest of police to have gang members kill each other off to save them the work of having to arrest people only to see them back on the streets soon thereafter.

From the point of view of many officers, much of the ineffectiveness had to do with low officer morale throughout the force, which had reached an all-time low, they felt. Frustration had long been stewing within the ranks of the LAPD over a number of issues, most significantly the citizen response to the Rodney King beating, some of the workforce and wage policy changes brought about by the appointment of new police chief Willie Williams, and the contentious union contract negotiations. It was only the previous year that the April 1992 acquittal of the LAPD officers on trial for the beating of Rodney King led to the largest civil unrest in recent U.S. history. Police officers assigned to the Oakwood area still felt the repercussions of the beating and its aftermath. Police officers expressed their frustration with the lack of support they received in the communities they policed. LAPD Detective Rogers shared his frustration with the outcome of the federal trial of the police beating of Rodney King:

> The police do not believe they have any support. The individual officer just looks at the Rodney King thing and [says], "By the grace of God, it could've been me. Who's to say that I wouldn't have hit that guy." . . . You know, and officers are still human beings. They go, "Wait a minute. I'm involved in a fight with a guy and I'm not to get emotionally involved?" So the officer loses his temper and for eleven seconds, he ends up spending ten years of his life in prison. Twenty years of incredible work, and eleven seconds puts him in prison. There's no balance there. . . . I think the officers, the actual policemen out there, feel that they're in a very hostile, not physically hostile, [but] very politically hostile environment that they have no protection in. . . . And they feel very isolated. And when you're isolated, you're not very brave about just

jumping in there, unless you're really stupid. They know what the right thing is to do, and they gotta push themselves to [do it]. So there's not the aggressive attitude you would've had a couple of years ago. It's just not there at all.[31]

Some patrol officers who felt they were doing the best job they could expressed frustration at the lack of recognition expressed toward those officers who repeatedly risked their lives in the line of duty. One patrol officer who worked in the Pacific Division for most of his career expressed his frustration at the "pounding" they received from the public:

> I could tell of at least three times officers went into vehicle pursuit chasing guys with AK-47s, foot pursuits of people with guns. [Police] intervened in dangerous situations. . . . When officers put their life on the line, it seems you never get acknowledged for those things. They like to give criticism and say that police don't care and police just escalated the gang war, when the opposite is the truth. If that was the truth, why were we going chasing people with guns? We don't take sides. . . . I guess you can tell it frustrates me. It's been that way and it's always going to be that way. I just accept it as part of the way it is. It still bugs me after fourteen years.[32]

Morale was also affected by the tensions within the ranks of the LAPD. Differences had grown between those who embraced the incoming police chief, who was advocating a community-oriented approach, and those whose loyalties lay with the ousted former chief of police Daryl Gates and his traditional brand of law enforcement. Some officers believed that the change in leadership from Gates to Williams betokened a "loss of aggressiveness." This frustrated those officers who were trained to believe that forceful policing was the superior method and were skeptical of a "community-oriented" approach. Chief Williams's approach emphasizing community-oriented policing was just beginning to win over some officers, but stiff resistance from within the force hampered its implementation. Resistance to change was also deeply ingrained and was evident in management and communication styles, personnel procedures, and a host of other areas related to the internal politics of the police department and its relationship to city hall. Nevertheless, the philosophical tension surrounding methods of policing was exhibited in the differentiated approaches that officers took to the streets.

So on the one hand, high-suppression plans were in place, but many officers were in a state of demoralization because they believed they did not have public support. And without public support, their powers were limited, since they were reliant on witnesses and others for leads, depositions, and other documentation in order to close investigations. Those officers who felt that they were performing to their highest potential believed that their efforts were not being recognized. At the same time, residents did begin to notice positive changes with new community-oriented policing and voiced a desire for greater police protection as the war continued, but at the same time they were skeptical because they believed that the police was exhibiting at best a lack of concern, and at worst behavior consistent with the larger conspiracy. Many residents preferred a community-oriented approach but were not sure of the department's commitment to sustaining it and keeping officers in the neighborhood for the length of time they believed it would take to build trust and meaningful working relations.

Some residents expressed a sympathy toward the odds that police officers face and the accompanying realization that police officers alone cannot curb the violence of the type seen in the Venice gang war. Those who responded in this way either believed that more law enforcement resources should be brought in or resigned themselves to the fact that the war would end on its own or due to attrition on the part of gang members themselves. This was in contrast to the belief that the police did indeed have the power to stop the violence but were not committed to doing so.

Regardless of opinions, the realization that traditional police approaches alone were not effective in slowing the violence created space for the consideration of other approaches. This other alternative would support the conditions for a gang truce from within. This approach required a more intimate understanding of the social dynamics of the participating gangs and the creation of trust among gang members. And it also demanded an understanding of the multiplicity of views, interests, internal politics, and institutional pressures among the parties involved—gangs, law enforcement agencies, and community organizations.

Though the gang war may have begun over turf, in its escalation the war came to symbolize much more. It involved the reputation of one's gang and the need to exact revenge for those who had been killed or injured. As the war progressed, the stakes were raised even higher, as acts of vengeance were no longer in the name of the gang but began to be expressed in terms of race. Boundaries in the line of battle had edged their way from a war between individuals to families to gangs and were headed precariously toward racial group boundaries. Prior to the truce struck in June 1994, there were rumors that other gangs might potentially join the fray to help defend their brethren. This scenario of wider "contagion" along racially connected gang boundaries would have pushed it further toward a greater racial divide. Before others joined in the battle, the boundaries had to be reshifted and delimited so that negotiations could meaningfully take place. To this we now turn.

Chapter 7

Mediators

Negotiation from Within

Despite the vigorous implementation of traditional high-suppression law enforcement approaches through most of the fall and winter months, the violence steadily continued. Except for the dip in the crime statistics during the Christmas holiday season and the January earthquake that immediately followed, the violence continued from the fall of 1993 through the spring of 1994.

Finally, in June 1994, representatives of the V-13 and the Venice Shoreline Crips met and negotiated a truce agreement, bringing the war between them to an end. A similar truce was not made between the Shoreline and the Culver City Boys, and conflict between them sporadically continued beyond the study period. Over the course of a ten-month period, seventeen people had been killed, and over fifty had been injured. And of those killed, less than a third were members of any of the three gangs involved.

The road to truce was a long and complicated one. While many groups, including law enforcement agencies as well as the gangs, claim credit for the peace that was struck, it would be erroneous to give sole recognition to any one group or individual. Many efforts were made over the war's duration. The residents who marched and held prayer vigils, the *veteranos* and OGs (Original Gangsters) who lobbied for resolution, the friends and relatives who refused offers to avenge their loved ones, mothers who pleaded with gangs for peace, community activists who worked to raise awareness of the broader impact of the war on the future survival of the neighborhood, community organizations that offered jobs and other alternatives to gang-involved youths, police officers who worked with members of the community to quell the violence, courageous individuals who dared to communicate across racial divides, gang representatives who stepped forward to negotiate the truce, and the probation officers who helped arrange the meeting—all of these and more were part of the peacemaking process. Some individuals may deserve more credit than others for the truce, but that is not for this author to judge.

Some say that the war would have died down eventually, arguing that economics, family, police, and other pressures along with the attrition in the number of active gang members would have inevitably forced the gangs to reckon with a losing predicament. Ultimately, one gang would have suffered defeat or all would have reached some form of settlement.

There are others who argue to the contrary. Some believed that the war would have continued to escalate. All three gangs—the V-13, the Culver City Boys, and the Shoreline—had alliances with other gangs throughout the region. One law enforcement agent central to the peacemaking process expressed concern that one of the gangs was already prepared to bring in "back-up" had the war not been settled at the time that it was. Given the increase in racial solidarity among black and Latino gangs, respectively, the recruitment of other gangs to each side was not unfathomable. The frequency and seriousness of race riots within the California state prisons was one indication that racialized street gang violence had the potential to escalate to greater proportions. The size and organization of street and prison gangs created the potential for the localized war to spread into some larger conflict, as 1,000 gangs and 150,000 gang members were estimated to reside in Los Angeles County during that period (Reiner 1992).

Regardless of conflicting opinions, one thing is clear: the path to a truce settlement involved the "deracialization" of conflict just as the escalation of conflict involved the racialization of it. Shifting the major line of cleavage from "race" back down to "gang" (and also to "class") led to two outcomes. One was a new definition of the terms of victory, away from a "racial" headcount of victims to a scoreboard that counted strictly active gang members. This redefinition allowed members of both gangs to uphold their reputations and claim victory. Second, the shift back to gang and class boundaries in effect reshuffled the situational salience of multiple identities, suppressing racial cleavages in relative relief. The shift from one line of cleavage to another did not erase past divisions, but it reframed the problem in such a manner that widened the latitude for peace negotiations. The shift also redirected the energies of gang members to their survival *as gang members* under law enforcement and community scrutiny. It also redirected the attention of the broader community within their sphere of influence to the survival *of their community*, defined more prominently along class boundaries, as in the old scheme of gentrification. This resurrection of old cleavages created new problems, which we will address, but it also allowed for greater interracial cooperation.

The road to the truce and the morphology of conflict de-escalation was a largely unscripted yet detailed process. A network of individuals committed to a process of mediation and settlement across multiple publics emerged. I refer to these networks of individuals as "transpublics"—individuals able to understand the world from the lens of multiple publics. Transpublics actively tried to reframe the problem and shift the configuration of alliances and cleavages in order to open a path for truce negotiations. Through two separate and distinct efforts, transpublics tried to combine disparate activities into a "carrot and stick" strategy that encouraged gang members to consider a negotiated settlement. Each of the two efforts took a network-based mediation approach, focused on identifying windows of opportunity for gang members to proceed with some peaceful form of conflict resolution. One effort was headed by a probation officer and the other by a council aide. For many, a negotiated peace settlement was a highly desirable route. As a negotiated settlement, a truce had a greater chance of sustainability compared to one imposed from an external entity, particularly if that entity could not maintain a constant level of enforcement. The effort by the council aide was thwarted, while the other eventually led to gang negotiations. But the preeminence of one effort over the other also had implications for the post-truce future.

Compounded Fragmentation

Compounded social fragmentation can make any problem too complex to handle, but it can also be a resource for building new alliances and for reconsidering new ways of seeing and acting. In this case, there were four planes of fragmentation. The first, of course, was the contestation between gangs over turf and reputation. The second was the increasing racial distancing and polarization in the community that the gang war caused. On top of this, however, were additional fractures of two types. One was along the emerging tensions between locally based organizations and agencies that mirrored tensions surrounding high-suppression police intervention. Many community groups and individuals sought an end to the violence, but few shared any cohesive strategy as to how it should be done. Fractures appeared, dividing groups based on the strategy one aligned oneself with in the various intervention efforts. There was also growing frustration among individuals acquainted with members of the gangs; these individuals began to voice public opposition to the continuing violence. This growing group of residents was becoming increasingly intolerant of the actions of their friends and relations. They joined a growing chorus of community voices publicly pleading for peace. This section describes these two latter layers of fragmentation.

Local Agencies and Police-Community Relations

As discussed in the previous chapter, relations became increasingly strained between the Los Angeles Police Department (LAPD) and the Oakwood residents who objected to their high-suppression tactics. Over time, whether and how closely one worked with the LAPD became a distinguishing marker among others in the delineation of publics. Instead of coming together to co-ordinate their strategies to end the war, some residents and agency personnel became embattled over what they should or could do about it. In arenas such as in public meetings or in police-sponsored community advisory board meetings, these differences over the police's handling of the situation often aggravated already sensitive racial fault lines.

On one hand, there were those who supported the use of high-suppression tactics under the firefighter approach and expressed growing frustration that law enforcement's response was not forceful or comprehensive enough. Some homeowners blamed the new captain whom they saw as taking too "soft" an approach. The presiding police captain of the Pacific Division, Captain Richard Legarra, had just assumed his position at the beginning of the war. He later updated the "Oakwood Plan" with the "Oakwood Safety Plan," which had a larger community-based policing component than the previous plan. Some viewed this change as abandoning the previous plan in favor of a more "lenient" one. There was a feeling among those committed to the original Oakwood Plan that if that plan had not been "dismantled," the gang war would not have escalated to the degree that it did.[1]

Others, in contrast, believed that the early stages of police response inappropriately applied principles of suppression and strongly welcomed a community-oriented approach. There were many African American residents who charged that the high-suppression tactics resulted in harassment and an "over-labeling" of black youths who were not involved in illegal gang activity. One Oakwood parent explained, "The gang label is like a jacket, and once they put the jacket on you, there's no way to take it off."[2] They believed law enforcement had an important role to play but that police officers were not helping the situation with their arms-brandishing approach. They believed that this approach only fostered gang solidarity among many youths and unnecessarily alienated many law-abiding residents.

Whether or not one supported police efforts became a source of tension among residents. The cooperation of several outspoken leaders of the Oakwood Property Owners Association with the LAPD created racial distance between white and African American residents, homeowners, and renters alike, rekindling earlier tensions described in chapter 3. The Oakwood Property Owners Association was perceived by the predominantly low-income and nonwhite Oakwood Homeowners and Tenants Association as representing pro-gentrification interests and as led by white homeowners who, they believed, closely collaborated with police. Racial group division between whites and nonwhites also surfaced within community organizations and social service agencies as a result of differences, especially in the vantage points and interpretive frames through which individuals understood the gang war and what should be done about it. As with resident-based organizations, the social service agencies that chose to work publicly with the LAPD tended to become alienated from those who had taken issue with LAPD's handling of the war.

These tensions could be seen in the controversy over the role of the LAPD's Oakwood Advisory Committee, an advisory group made up of community organizations and residents in the LAPD Pacific Division's jurisdiction. The composition of this committee was very similar to that of Oakwood United, a network of nonprofit community and service organizations based in Oakwood and the surrounding neighborhood. There were several major differences, however, between Oakwood United and the LAPD's Oakwood Advisory Committee. One obvious difference was that the latter was sponsored by the LAPD, which had selected the body's chairpersons, while Oakwood United was sponsored by a consortium of community organizations and elected its own board democratically. The LAPD-sponsored meetings were invitation-only; residents perceived as "disruptive" were not allowed to attend, while Oakwood United meetings were always open to the public. The fact that the topics of discussion in the LAPD's advisory committee closely duplicated those of Oakwood United raised questions as to the motives of the LAPD brass and created some distance between those who appeared to befriend the LAPD brass and those perceived to maintain a more independent stance. The structure and composition of the LAPD-sponsored Oakwood Advisory Committee mirrored the unequal relations between whites and nonwhites in a racially segmented hierarchy within many private and public institutions throughout the city, including those serving the affected neighborhoods. The LAPD's task force was chaired by a white female executive director of a health clinic located in Oakwood. Oakwood United was chaired by an African American male who was the head pastor of New Bethel Church, also located in Oakwood. The LAPD tried to settle the controversy over the delineation between the role of the LAPD committee and Oakwood United by distinguishing the geographical boundaries upon which they focused (LAPD's advisory committee would focus on a "broader geographic area"). However, the social distance stirred between organizations and individuals by LAPD's real or perceived relations with them nevertheless affected interorganizational relations. The point is that, ultimately, racial tensions surrounding the gang war and police interventions steeped into the circles of individuals who were trying to seek a resolution to the problem. Divisions among "problem solvers" crippled the ability of these coalition-type bodies to act in any concerted manner.

Community Voices against Violence

Meanwhile, a rainbow of vocal activists and community leaders began to express their opposition to the violence, building informal alliances across color lines and distinguishing themselves from the sphere of gang members and law enforcement agencies alike. Even those with close relations to gang members began to voice their frustration toward the continued violence. Murmurs of opposition grew stronger among all segments of the affected neighborhood. Pastor Marvis Davis of the New Bethel Church in Oakwood relayed the sentiments of many residents: "Children, mothers, relatives, longtime family were just saying, 'Enough is enough.' When it first got started, those are the gang rules. Somebody gets taken out, we go take somebody out. And after that tit for tat kept going on and on and on, eventually somebody gets tired and fed up, saying, 'Hey, this is enough.'"[3] Wives and girlfriends became frustrated and burdened with the extra responsibilities they incurred. Since it had become dangerous for the younger men to walk the streets, women ended up doing most of the errands, even chauffeuring partners and friends forced to hide themselves on the seat or in the trunks of their cars as they traveled in and out of the neighborhood.

Gang members, tired of being cooped up, were also becoming restless. And for those reliant on the street economy, the inability to sell their goods openly created an economic squeeze. As one observer described the situation: "Black people were getting tired of staying up in they house and having the girls get everything for them when they wanted a soda pop or whatever. And money was running thin. To go out there [to deal], you don't know if they were going to pull a gun out on you."[4]

Community residents and many community institutions organized activities to voice their desire for peace publicly. Several peace rallies were held in which more than 100 people marched the streets with placards and chants to make their views known to those involved in the war. In February 1994, several churches and community groups jointly organized a march through the streets of Oakwood. In May 1994, a Mother's Day rally was held at the Oakwood Recreation Center with various speakers calling for peace. One of those given acknowledgment was Rosie Lodge, mother of the slain African Ameri-

4. Youth from the Pearl White Theater in Oakwood perform at a "Community Jam Against Violence," February 11, 1994. Courtesy of Santa Monica Historical Society Museum/Outlook Collection.

5. Mothers Against Violence hold photos of their slain sons in their call for peace at a rally at the Oakwood Recreation Center, May 7, 1994. Courtesy of Santa Monica Historical Society Museum/Outlook Collection.

can man who had worked as an orderly at the UCLA Medical Center. In addition, voices from other parts of the city were pleading for a halt to the violence, including the Mothers of East Los Angeles on the opposite side of town.

Akerloff and Yellen (1994) argued that the willingness of local residents to cooperate with the police depended both on the behavior of the local gangs and on the legitimacy of the police in the community. They argued that there is a threshold of violence beyond which residents stop being willing to protect gangs and start being willing to cooperate with police. Clearly, the activities of the gangs had exceeded the threshold of tolerance. And while there was increasing frustration among residents with the ineffectiveness of police and with their application of suppression tactics, many residents also became more willing to engage in dialogue with police on these issues. On one occasion, a contingent of African American, Latino, and white residents filled a bus to attend a police commission hearing, where they demanded greater police protection from the violence of the war while also raising grievances that they hoped the LAPD would correct. These and other actions sent a direct message to gang members on all sides that the community around them had more than reached its limit. The more intolerant the community became, the less support and protection gangs knew they could receive in their confrontations with their opponents.

Mounting Pressures on Police and Gangs

Police and other law enforcement agencies were under increasing pressure from elected officials, residents, and local businesses to find more innovative ways to stop the violence. Complaints from residents about the alleged misbehavior of officers during the war drew scrutiny from high-ranking officers in the Pacific Division and even LAPD headquarters, as they looked into the policing practices of officers assigned to the Oakwood and Mar Vista areas. Moreover, contract negotiations between the police officers' union and the City of Los Angeles were taking place in early 1994. For the union, this created, on the one hand, pressure to show their effectiveness in suppressing crime and, on the other, pressure to demonstrate the need for more officers and pay increases. While the proliferation of crime bolstered their argument for institutional growth, their inability to quash the violence also weakened their claims of valuable performance. It was time for the LAPD to exhibit greater effectiveness.

One change in operations under the new police chief Willie Williams and his new appointee as head of the Pacific Division, Captain Richard Legarra, was an augmentation in community-oriented policing. This shift was most visible with the addition of one Latino male officer and one African American female officer assigned to community relations in the Oakwood neighborhood. The senior lead officer for the Oakwood patrols also increased community relations activities as an additional liaison to community organizations. In addition, other rank-and-file officers received further training in community-oriented policing.

The V-13 and the Shoreline also faced increasing pressures, particularly because law enforcement agencies were beginning to hone in on their movements and also because of the rising body count. Many gang members were getting injured or arrested or were placed under law enforcement scrutiny or surveillance. FBI agents were highly visible. Gang members arrested for suspicion of criminal acts were tracked to ensure thorough investigation and the maximum penalty if convicted. The implementation of the "three strikes" provision of the crime bill (described in chapter 4) began to take effect, creating a chilled atmosphere for those considering criminal acts. Increased patrols had put a damper on the drive-through narcotics trade, hurting the local underground economy that not only supported dealers but their friends and families as well. Increased patrols placed additional restrictions on their outdoor movement, which over time grew quite tiresome. These pressures were felt more heavily by members of the Shoreline because of the geographical concentration of their activities in Oakwood and the concentration of law enforcement on their operations.

This convergence of factors—compounding fragmentation over the war and what to do about it, increasing public protest against the violence, the mounting pressure on police and gangs alike—created both opportunities and challenges to find an endgame to the conflict. Multiple crisscrossing lines

6. Los Angeles Police Department deploys a new bike patrol in Oakwood, March 18, 1994. Courtesy of Santa Monica Historical Society Museum/Outlook Collection.

of fragmentation also represented potential outlines for the realignment of publics. Just as race grew to be a major cleavage over the course of the conflict, fractures in formative groupings presented opportunities for more active reorganization in the discursive as well as physical contests over the meaning of the war and the choices to be made. New constellations of groups might be formed such that race would no longer be the prominent trajectory of conflict. If the scale and trajectory could be reduced back down to the boundary of gang, for instance, community-wide polarization could be eased and gangs could address the conflict free of much of the symbolic accoutrements that it had amassed. In this context, "transpublics" wanting an end to the violence made targeted appeals to gang leadership, rank-and-file gang members, law enforcement officials, political leaders, residents, and service agency employees across the fractured landscape to mobilize support for their respective strategies to reframe the problem.

Transpublics and a Network-Based Mediation Approach

Among the fragmented tiles, a new mosaic gradually appeared that outlined an alternative to the high-suppression approach. This alternative entailed a different problematic, a different set of goals, a different set of skills, and a different approach toward gang members themselves. From the viewpoint of many individuals crossing racial, organizational, and institutional boundaries, the major problem was not the gangs per se but the illegal and destructive *behavior* of gang-involved youths as well as the *social conditions* that led to those activities. The objective was not to excise gang members from the neighborhoods wholesale but to redirect their behavior by channeling them into activities that would lead to a more hopeful future and drawing on the resources within the neighborhood. This approach demanded collaborative partnerships between agencies and relied heavily on community support.

Several concerted efforts were made to leverage, in an informal way, the fragmented efforts of various law enforcement agencies and community-based organizations to urge a settlement. Those who collaborated in this approach did not bank their hopes on any law of attrition, since they saw the capability of each of the gangs to call for backup resources. They believed that the best solution was one reached among the participants themselves, ending the conflict "from the inside out." They acknowledged that individuals could "shoot and hide" despite circling patrol cars, with some recalling scenes of guerrilla warfare during the Vietnam War. Their immediate objective was to find a way to open a path so that gang representatives would and could enter into truce negotiations and find common ground for a settlement.

This mediation approach was not a tightly coordinated strategy but was comprised of a series of attempts by two loose networks—a neighborhood-based network that included residents and individuals from various community organizations and a separate law enforcement–based one. The parallel efforts by each network were not coordinated or directly related to each other. In fact, some individuals in one network distrusted some individuals in the other. The neighborhood-based network was comprised of young male adults from the neighborhood, primarily but not exclusively African American men familiar with the players on the street and other members of the community linked, either by virtue of their profession or other prior experience, to "mainstream" institutions and organizations. It included former gang members, several older gang affiliates, several youth service workers, several social service agency workers, and several residents with close ties to members of the Shoreline. One individual who initiated a mediation-oriented strategy was Dermont Givens who worked as an aide to the area's Councilwoman Ruth Galanter. This network formed over the course of interaction as individuals informally shared their assessments of the situation and ideas for intervention. Though Givens' strategy was eventually halted with the termination of his employment as council aide, it represents one adaptation of the "mediator" approach.

The second network, based on law enforcement personnel, was comprised of several individuals in the probation and police departments and in the Los Angeles County District Attorney's Office. One of the enforcement agents

connected to this informal network was an African American probation officer in his mid- to late thirties by the name of Brad Carson. He was the probation officer assigned to Venice and had many of the Shoreline and the V-13
on his caseload. Though kept at arm's length by many residents connected to
gang members since he was known to revoke probationary privileges upon
violation of legal conditions, his day-to-day duties offered him much greater
dialogue with gang members and their relations compared to other law enforcement agencies such as the police and the courts. But by maintaining dialogue with gang members and informal networks within the community, he
was also looked upon with suspicion by some of his fellow law enforcement
colleagues. His relationships with gang members were seen by some police officers as going against the grain of the "tough on crime" movement that
sought as a primary goal to apprehend and incarcerate. Some of his peers perceived any mediation approach as "negotiating with the enemy," particularly
the mediation approach used by the community-based network. Nevertheless,
for those who believed in the potential of mediation, concern over that perception was decidedly secondary.

Both of these networks of individuals attempted to package various intervention efforts under an umbrella strategy that counterposed "carrots and
sticks" made up of both incentives and deterrents. It conceptually coupled efforts of community-based organizations that offered opportunities (such as
jobs, education, training, and substance abuse programs) as incentives or
"carrots" together with law enforcement actions (such as the threat of increased penalties, the revocation of probation and parole, court injunctions,
and increased surveillance) as deterrents or "sticks." They worked to package
these disparate incentives and disincentives together into some semblance of
a strategy, identifying "windows of opportunity" to leverage the powers of each
in delicate tandem toward peace.

Each of the two loosely knit efforts used different variations on the carrot
and stick incentives and deterrents. The law enforcement–based efforts
placed greater emphasis on the stick while the community-based efforts
placed greater emphasis on the carrot. Despite these differences, which are
nevertheless significant, a common denominator was a commitment to the
belief that an internally brokered resolution to the conflict was the best way
to end the fighting. The carrot and stick approach was also appealing to those
who felt strongly that sustained peace could only be maintained by the resolve
of gangs themselves. Also, many of those who subscribed to this approach
were committed to giving youths a chance to choose a different path for themselves, with hopeful and realistic alternatives from which to choose.

A central component to each of these two efforts was the reframing of the
problem. Two different themes were promoted in the reframing effort. One
theme was to "save the neighborhood," and the other was to "save yourselves."
The two networks engaged members of the gangs in these respective discur-

sive contests in order to open a path to the negotiating table. Reframing was accompanied by a corresponding reshuffling in the salience of identity boundaries, which, in effect, shifted the line of cleavage away from race.

Reframing the Problem

As the previous two chapters have shown, the major line of cleavage among the conflict participants and residents who formed multiple publics had shifted over time. By the war's midpoint, race had gained relative prominence among other lines of division, as discussed earlier, mainly the boundaries of family, class, and gang. The efforts of transpublics to reframe the situation and reshift salient lines of cleavage away from race helped open avenues for dialogue and eventual settlement.

The two networks, however, took quite different approaches and promoted two very different narratives in their attempt to persuade gang members to cease the fighting. The neighborhood-based network framed the problem as an issue of poor versus rich, attempting to shift the major cleavage from race back to class, harkening back to the problem of gentrification. They tried to reframe the problem from a "race war" to a "struggle to maintain Oakwood as a community where poor people could live." This narrative conceptually placed African Americans and Latinos in the same boat along class status categories, situating the salience of "class" above that of "race." The call was to "save the neighborhood" from further dispersal of their neighbors in the name of gentrification. In contrast, the law enforcement–based network promoted narratives that raised the salience of "gang" identification over that of "race." Storied scenarios posed a choice to gang members: utter destruction (through the violence or incarceration) or survival through mediated settlement. The theme of this narrative call was to "save yourselves."

Dermont Givens, the aide to Councilwoman Ruth Galanter, was a visible proponent of a carrot and stick strategy among the neighborhood-based network while county probation officer Brad Carson spearheaded the law enforcement–based strategy. Both were African American men in their mid- to late thirties. One of the major differences in their strategies was that Givens emphasized increasing the benefits of making peace, while Carson emphasized increasing the costs of continuing the war. This difference was a function of the occupations of the two men as well as the techniques of power and the resources available to them. But it was also based on their assessments of what was pragmatic or possible given the constellation of publics.

"Save the Neighborhood"

Givens worked with various individuals in the neighborhood-based network. Among them was Darryl Goode, the president of the Santa Monica chapter of the NAACP. Along with a group of residents, they worked to get residents and gang members to see the problem as one of community survival for African Americans and Latinos in the face of gentrification, redirecting the trajectory of conflict along class divisions. Goode and chapter vice president Melvyn Hayward stressed that African American residents in Oakwood historically had greater political clout than other constituencies in Venice under the tenure of former mayor Tom Bradley's administration and the liberal coalition that had long dominated local politics. They argued that the decline of the African American community in Oakwood would threaten its livelihood as a low-income, affordable neighborhood for all. As Goode explained: "What we were trying to tell the Shoreline guys and some of the Latinos is if the African American community is gone, blacks *and* Latinos will be gone. African Americans were targeted. If enough move out, there's no place where people could go. Latinos aren't targeted—but are vulnerable."[5] The logic was that since African Americans had gained some political leverage in the Westside, the decline of African American residents would also mean the decline of political influence. This political decline would, they argued, mean the demise of all low-income residents, blacks, Latinos, and white equally.

Within this narrative, there were some who actively promoted the theory of conspiracy between police and developers. This explanation for continued violence theorized that police and developers wanted to drive poor residents out by *letting the gang war continue.* This not only reshifted salience from racial lines to class lines, but it also reinforced the cleavage between low-income residents and the police.

Though he did not promote this idea himself, Givens pursued a strategy to use the gang war and the army of law enforcement personnel assigned to the war as an opportunity to establish policies and programs that could address the broader problems of gang-related violence and the marginalization of young black and Latino men. Givens was brought onto Councilwoman Galanter's staff in August 1993, after the first incidents in January but before the sharp escalation in November. He was assigned to the Oakwood section of the council district. He spent much of the first several months getting to know residents, business owners, and staff members of various community organizations and agencies. He appeared to be received well by a cross section of the community, from more conservative property owners to gang members.

Givens believed in a "carrot *before* stick" approach. His general strategy was to give gang members a chance to make a transition to "legit" institutions and lifestyles *before* any heavy suppression operation would be used against them. He distinguished his approach from past carrot and stick practices: "It's always been the stick. And then when it's time for the carrot, 'Oh we're out of funds. We don't do this and that,' you know. So for me to maintain some credibility and just to be morally correct knowing this, there had to be something there for the gang members to say, 'Okay, we can buy into this. We're going to get something first.'"[6] Givens tried to develop incentives based on the desires of gang members who wanted to take "positive" steps in their lives. Gang members expressed two desires to him in this regard. One was to have mentors who could give them guidance and training to survive in the "legit" world. Their other desire was to create opportunities to exit the cycle of the criminal justice system. This cycle often began with suspension from public school. Repeated suspensions or violations of specific codes often led to expulsion. A high proportion of those expelled would begin to hang out on the streets and some would join local gangs. They, along with those mistaken for gang members, were often stopped by police in areas targeted for gang suppression activities such as Oakwood. Field investigation cards were filled out for apprehended youths on a fairly routine basis to gather information about suspected gang members and their whereabouts, regardless of the ability of police officers to confirm gang membership. Many were placed in local and national gang databases. When LAPD officers arrested suspected gang members, their files were tagged and processed by special gang investigators and prosecutors. For those convicted of felonies, it became very difficult to find employment once released, as few employers were willing to hire those with prior felony records. Once in the criminal justice system, prison culture as well as the treatment of those with prior convictions reinforced relations and behaviors that made it difficult to leave the system.

Givens claimed that he and various law enforcement agents with whom he worked to some extent agreed on a plan to cull the lists of names in various gang databases as one opportunity for individuals to exit this cycle.[7] He elaborated on the plan, which was designed to give greater responsibility to gang members and local residents and community organizations to work in partnership to address the more basic problems leading to illegal gang activity and gang violence:

> Let the community decide and tell law enforcement who should be on that list. And if there were any people who, definitely, nobody had ever heard of . . . get those people off the list. Then there were the marginal people. And at that point, several community people who lived in the community, worked in the community, whoever, would have to go and talk to that person, and they would make a decision. The community, like three or four people would say, "Okay. Well, you're on this list. You're a gang member. Now either you can stay on this list, or we will work with you. What is it that you want?" They can say, "Get me off that damn list so I can live my life, and I will go into a program." And there would actually be, like, mentors in the community that would be assigned to this person that he could talk to and whatever. So this person would know it's these people in the community that have your life in your hands. And if they say, "We give up," that's it.[8]

Culling the list and moving toward a consultative approach to maintaining the list was one example of a "carrot" that would be used to entice gang members to halt the violence and redirect their energies into mentoring programs along with a host of other options.

Due to controversy over the details of the plan, however, these efforts were never implemented. In the spring of 1994, Councilwoman Galanter terminated Givens from his position, believing that he was going beyond the parameters of his assigned duties and was acting on his individual agenda based on political beliefs that she did not necessarily share.[9]

"Save Yourselves"

While Givens worked with local residents and law enforcement agents, Brad Carson from the county probation office was independently making similar attempts to nudge gang members toward a settlement. Carson was a member of the gang unit of the county probation office, and his caseload included members of the warring gangs. His job was to get to know the youths and their backgrounds in order to counsel and refer them to the appropriate programs, where they could gain training, employment, and social services. As a probation officer, he had the power and responsibility to apprehend those caught violating the conditions of their probation; this gave him limited leverage in influencing the actions of probationers. Like police officers, probation officers had a steady, long-term presence in the neighborhood, but their relationship to gang members was very different from that of most police officers due to the nature of their responsibilities and their institutional mission and objectives.

While Givens's strategy placed emphasis on carrots before sticks, Carson's tack placed more emphasis on the stick, largely as a function of his position as a probation officer and the techniques of power available to him. He did not pursue Givens's efforts to convince law enforcement agencies to remove formerly identified gang members from gang databases. Rather, Carson harvested "carrots" primarily from ongoing efforts by community-based and private sector organizations that offered opportunities and services to gang members, their families, and others deemed "at risk."

Carson and other law enforcement officers were taking a slightly different tack at reframing the war, shifting emphasis from "race" back to "gang" identity boundaries, appealing to their sense of survival as gangs and gang members. One step in reframing the war was an effort to tip the perceived scale of costs and benefits. Tipping that scale could create space for dialogue and reflection among those involved in the war. In the one-on-one talks, Carson tried to get Shoreline and V-13 probationers to take stock of the situation and more carefully weigh the costs and benefits as members of their respective gangs. He explained:

> Basically, I would ask them: Why are they having this war? What are they gaining from it? What are they losing from it, you know? What do they have to

prove? They're not making any money. All their family members are mad at them. They're getting shot on a daily basis, they're going to jail on a daily basis, and they have nothing to gain. They were losing. All they had to do was look out the window and see that they're losing. Basically they were frightened, fighting over pride, you know what I'm sayin'? They ain't gaining nothing.[10]

To tip the perceived balance of costs and benefits in the direction of fewer benefits and heavier costs, Carson joined forces with the District Attorney's Office and the City Attorney's Office to introduce the threat of gang abatement. There were earlier rumors that an injunction would be filed, imposing heavy restrictions on the movement and the activities of identified gang members. Indeed, the County District Attorney's Hardcore Gang Unit had been preparing an injunction against the activities of the three participating gangs. They had gathered testimony and evidentiary materials and prepared numerous documents that could then be filed in court to allow special laws to be imposed on the three gangs. Such an injunction had been used in an effort to remove gang activity on Blythe Street in the northern section of Los Angeles County. A spokesperson for the Hardcore Gang Unit of the Los Angeles County District Attorney's Office explained some of the features of the possible injunction against the Culver City Boys, the Shoreline Crips, and the V-13: "We were going to say they couldn't carry beepers. They couldn't wear gang colors. They couldn't be on certain street corners where the dope was sold anymore. They couldn't carry telephones. They couldn't carry graffiti equipment. There would be a curfew both for juveniles and adults. . . . They could not solicit people."[11] This was a highly controversial policy that would under normal circumstances have been strongly opposed by residents and civil liberty groups. But the violence was reaching such proportions that the level of desperation in favor of ending the violence would have silenced much of the opposition.

Carson conveyed this information along with his assessment of the political climate to those involved:

> Then I would tell them why they were going to lose 'cause law enforcement was going to come in and wipe them out. And all they'd have to show for it was either they'd be dead or have a long prison term. And then I would tell them that we were coming with the gang abatement program. And I said, you know, "Summer's coming around the corner and you know how law enforcement and LAPD in general doesn't play that around the summer." And all the tourists are going to come, and it's going to affect the money, the economy. And when it affects the economy, they're going to come after you.[12]

Perceptions among gang members that law enforcement was ready to clamp down on all three organizations *evenly and indiscriminately* contributed to the salience of gang boundaries relative to racial and other identity boundaries.

These appeals were made to their sense of survival as members of their respective gangs, shifting emphasis away from the racial cleavage between African Americans and Latinos.

While Carson conveyed law enforcement plans, he also offered carrots, incentives to gang members and associates who were willing to redirect their energies by directing many of them to community-based agencies. Several community-based organizations and businesses worked very hard to find alternatives for gang-involved youths, parolees, probationers, and ex-offenders. Several jobs programs were established that targeted recruitment of gang affiliates and offered employment to gang members, probationers, and those considered "at risk." The Venice Community Housing Corporation, an affordable nonprofit housing development organization, established a job training program in the construction and rehabilitation of affordable housing in Oakwood. Oakwood United, a consortium of community organizations and social service agencies, set up an economic development project distributing water-saving toilets. This project was set up for the purpose of employing local residents, with emphasis on gang-involved youths. The Franklin Mint Corporation made a noble effort to employ gang members at a new facility they had opened in Venice. This was one of the most celebrated efforts on the part of the private sector in addressing the problem of unemployment among gang members. Other organizations provided activities for youths and social services for families affected by the violence. The Pearl White Theater offered a wide range of recreational and cultural activities for youths in the neigh-

7. Members of the Body of Christ Church in Oakwood march for peace, April 30, 1994. Courtesy of Santa Monica Historical Society Museum/Outlook Collection.

borhood. The Community Service Organization along with other social service agencies offered assistance to the families of victims. The Venice Skills Center encouraged youths to participate in their education and training programs. Churches offered spiritual counsel and offered comfort and support to victims and their families. These programs offered potential leverage to reach those who could influence the actions of those directly involved in the war.

Paving a Road for Settlement

Packaging the various efforts by law enforcement agents, concerned citizens, businesses, and community organizations by themselves, however, did not necessarily translate to an end to the violence. There was a discrete set of processes that unfolded within the Shoreline and the V-13 that allowed their representatives to enter into truce negotiations. Among these internal processes, three elements were essential: (a) taking pause to weigh the costs/benefit ratio of continuing the war among participants, (b) reframing the war internally and reshifting lines of cleavage within the gangs in terms that would allow them to negotiate with one another, and (c) facilitating the logistics for dialogue among the members of the adversarial groups.

Weighing the Options

In the midst of a gang war, participants did not have the habit of regularly measuring the costs and benefits of each action taken. Lives were lost and people were injured or driven from their homes, generating intense emotions ranging from vengeance and rage to sadness and fear. In the heat of such passions, the fighting generated its own momentum apart from "rationally" calculated responses. Hits were met with retaliation, commonly under the auspices of one of the gangs and sometimes at the initiation of an individual member or affiliate.

Perhaps more important than the specific carrot and stick proposals themselves was the opening of dialogue with participating gang members to assess the risks and benefits of continuing the war. In the heat of battle, plans for the next round of retaliation often took precedent over a more thoughtful consideration of overall costs and benefits. Carson used his position as a probation officer to pull members of the V-13 and the Shoreline on his caseload aside for one-on-one discussions. He explained:

> I talked to them for hours, one on one, right here in the office. It's totally different than out there on the streets, out there when they're in a group. One on one, and they let their guards down, too. They come in here and talk about their problems. They talk about all the stress and all the pressure. This is like

a safe environment for them. And they just drop, you know, their guard. We would just sit down and talk, and we would just rationalize. You know, 'cause out there they weren't rational. Out there they were set on survival mode, they were almost like in a war zone. They *were* in a war zone. When they come in here and they get to relax for just a minute and they get a little bit of stress off of them, you know, it affected them. It was easier to have a rapport with them.[13]

Veteranos, OGs, community leaders, girlfriends, family members, and other affected parties also pressed war participants for answers to questions: "How far does this have to go?" "Who is really losing and winning in this war?" "When will you stop fighting?" Cumulatively, the pressure and questioning had the effect of urging participants to reevaluate the costs and benefits of continuing. One youth worker who resided in Venice shared the moment when he realized the perverse costs and benefits to residents of the neighborhood. He explained: "I was sittin' cooped in the house because of the violence when it hit me. These white guys were all out there joggin' in their jogging suits, riding their bikes, like nothin' was happenin'. And I asked myself, *Why are we stuck inside while they're playin' outside?* The price of houses were dropping, but none of us had the cash to buy them and outside developers were scoopin' 'em up. It made me think, *Who's really making out in this war?*"[14] He and others shared these thoughts as they tried to call attention to the costs and benefits of the battle, appealing to the sense of loyalty to the community and the sense of self-preservation as a neighborhood held by the Shoreline and the V-13 alike.

Some of the younger and more active members of the V-13 and the Shoreline also began to reconsider the costs of the war. As a V-13 who supported the truce explained, "I got tired of them killing these innocent guys. If they killed all V-13, it may have been a different story. [But] maybe it'll be your aunt or uncle who gets killed."[15] This sentiment was shared by one Shoreline, who echoed: "I mean, too many loved ones lost. You know. Who wins? You know. I mean, who actually wins? We don't win, you know. They don't win. All they doing is losing lives. We losing lives. I guess we losing our freedom. They losing their freedom."[16]

Particularly for those in leadership positions, the burdens and responsibilities of facing the friends, neighbors, and relatives of those who had lost loved ones began to wear on some of them. A sister of one of the Shoreline explained:

I mean, for a person to be given the status of being a leader of one of these gangs, whenever somebody innocent was shot or killed, you know, that person would have to deal with that because they've been given this authority to be the leader. You know what I'm saying? And that was not easy for these kids. I mean, speaking to both the Latino leader and the black leader . . . that was one of the things that bothered them the most, was the fact that somebody would be stupid enough to shoot somebody that didn't have nothing to do with this and then they would have to go to the funeral and look in the face of those parents. That was eating these guys up.[17]

Controversy grew within the ranks of participating gangs over whether or not to continue the war. On one hand, each side had a limited amount of resources in the way of money, guns, and manpower, and it was not clear how long such conflict could be sustained. At the same time, each had potential access to additional resources in the way of support from other gangs and the issue of sustaining the battle was not insurmountable. Nevertheless, the question of whether or not the gains from sustaining the war would be worth the costs was raised in all corners. For those in the gangs who wanted an end to the war, the challenge was to persuade their associates to want the same.

Reframing from Within the Gangs

There was a lot of speculation about the decision to end the war. Some believed the war was taking too great a toll on the drug trade. Others credited law enforcement for placing pressure on gangs in the form of arrests and threats of pending injunctions. Some suspected that threats between the warring gangs to increase the stakes of the war may have served as an incentive to stop the fighting before it escalated further. Some claimed that a critical mass of gang members had problems with the victimization of non–gang members such that they became reluctant participants willing to seek an end to the fighting. Which of these and possible other factors made the difference is difficult to confirm. It was most likely a combination of factors that converged at a specific juncture, creating a window of opportunity to end the violence. Regardless of the weight of the various factors, gang members supportive of a truce faced the task of convincing their fellow members that negotiations to reach a settlement was the best step to take.

These individuals appealed to their memberships in slightly different ways. The Shoreline was in a somewhat more defensive position, as their ranks were less organized and they felt greater pressure from law enforcement. For members who grew up in Oakwood, the gentrification conspiracy frame promoted by many of their relations provided a compelling reason to seek a resolution. The fact that Shoreline members from Venice were so closely intertwined within the long-established social networks among African American residents gave those residents and transpublics among them some influence in reframing the situation. That the gang war threatened the survival of this deep-rooted community did move key gang members to consider the ramifications of their actions, as explained to them by friends and relatives. As mentioned in chapter 3, Oakwood was the only location where African Americans were allowed to live before racial segregation was made illegal; Oakwood had special significance due to the perpetuation of that legacy. Central to the identity and collective memory for many African American residents was a history of resistance against removal and relocation that had more recently taken the form of neighborhood gentrification. The African American population had been in decline starting in the 1970s, and the survival of their historic community was part of their collective conscience.[18]

A reframing of the situation within the narrative of gentrification served to pit real estate speculators, landlords, and the police on one side and low-income and minority residents on the other. The gentrification narrative explained police ineffectiveness as deliberate attempts by the police to let the war continue so that the gang members would eliminate themselves from the area. Opposition to the police was equated to the preservation of the neighborhood against gentrification. To oppose the police was to protect the community. For members of the Shoreline, protecting the community under those circumstances and protecting their ranks as a gang were both compatible with a peace settlement.

For members of the V-13, reframing the predicament in terms of the survival of their "historic community" did not have the same resonance. Oakwood did not have the same meaning as a historic or residential center for the local Latino or Chicano community. In fact, only a few families with affiliations to the V-13 actually lived within the boundaries of Oakwood, as members resided in various of Venice's neighborhoods. What was of greater concern, however, was their reputation and honor in the eyes of their rivals as well as of their allies.

A critical moment arrived after several members of the V-13 came to feel that it was time to end the war. Their challenge, however, was to convince the remaining members that a truce was the best way to end it. This was no small challenge, because the gang's membership exceeded several hundred and contained numerous cliques or social circles. As a war defined along racial lines, the V-13 could be seen as losing the war. Latinos suffered more deaths and injuries in terms of the number of victims. However, of those killed, only a few were recognized members of the V-13. Reframing the war from one tallied along boundaries of race to one tallied according to gang membership would not induce the V-13 to concede defeat.

Though more casualties were suffered by Latino victims, the actual number of gang members killed on each side was very close in number and totaled less than a third of all deaths. By reframing the conflict from one measured by a racial body count to the number of gang members lost, both sides were able to "save face." This reframing was very important, particularly for the V-13, whose concern for honor was paramount in their deliberations. This reframing of the evaluation from a racial to a gang conflict was far from automatic. Specific individuals had to take the initiative to convince others that it was in their interest to forge a truce. "It was reputation and what you have at stake that gave certain individuals respect and influence," as one associate explained.[19] Normally, one individual has limited influence, since there are many social circles within a large gang. But one of those who commanded respect at that time was able to successfully reframe the conflict to make way for truce negotiations: "[A V-13 member] said to the group, 'Listen, that's [number of people] they got. One of these days it'll be one of us. We're winning. They killed [number of people] members. That doesn't make us look bad. We could decide [to negotiate] now, or it will go on forever. . . . There's no need to go on. We're winning the war. If it goes on, our people will get locked up with life.' It was a matter of a good speaker getting them to think differently."[20] As for other Latino victims killed in the war, the V-13 associate described how the speaker conceded to his fellow V-13 members: "[the Shorelines] got the last shot: the two killed at Venice High School. But we didn't even know these guys."[21]

Threats and rumors of raising the body count on the part of the Shoreline also figured into the deliberations of the V-13. One resident with friendship ties with both gangs shared her description of some of the dialogue between the Shoreline and V-13, stating that one of the things that led to the truce was "the gangs meeting with each other and saying, 'We need to stop. Too many innocent people is getting killed,' [or] 'When you kill somebody, we're going to take five of yours out.' And they didn't want that no more, so they stopped."[22] Both the V-13 and the Shoreline moved away from scorekeeping according to a racial identification of victims and shifted attention to their survival as members of their gang and as members of a larger community of families and residents, respectively. Under the circumstances described at the beginning of this chapter, this reframing and relative shift in salient group boundaries opened opportunities for formal negotiations between them.

Transpublic Facilitators

Dialogue was not opened without some groundwork and coordination among individual gang members and several facilitators who assisted in arranging a meeting. There were individuals within the V-13 and the Shoreline who wanted to see an end to the shootings for the various reasons mentioned above. It was necessary, however, for this set of individuals to meet and also to convince their organizations that a truce was not only desirable but possible to enforce. As one Shoreline member explained: "Well, the meeting came with just a couple of people going that wanted it stopped on that side that never really wanted it to happen on that side, plus this side. It took those people to get together and then actually pull certain other people in on each side so the meetings could get bigger."[23]

Brad Carson, the probation officer who handled the caseload of Venice gang affiliates, was able to see the desire to end the war among a set of individuals as a "window of opportunity" and helped to arrange a meeting between key representatives of the two gangs. While some believed that the meeting would have taken place regardless of Carson's efforts, others felt that had he not arranged the meeting at that point, there might have been even greater violence, after which there would have been no such opportunities. Regardless, it was significant that there were go-betweens through which arrangements for face-to-face negotiations under terms agreeable to both gangs could be made.

Only certain individuals had the influence, interest, and charisma to carry forward such negotiations on the part of each gang. Carson, along with a fellow probation officer Jim Galipeau, who had a good reputation with the Shoreline, made logistical arrangements for a meeting between two representatives of each gang who had the requisite "juice," or pull. On 13 June 1994, Galipeau transported the Shoreline representatives while Carson brought the V-13 representatives to an undisclosed location. The representatives met privately for over an hour after being searched for weapons by both probation officers. As part of the negotiations, the two gangs established mechanisms to enforce the truce, including communications between gangs and internal sanctions against members violating the terms of the truce.[24] At the end of the meeting, a truce was reached and the violence came to an abrupt halt.

Carson credits the V-13 and Shoreline members who negotiated the truce for putting a halt to the war. Carson's involvement, however, is significant, as it represents a particular approach taken by a law enforcement officer in the context of the dominant policy environment of gang suppression. He understood from his conversations with gang members that they shared common concerns of "family pressure, fighting over nothing, seeing their homies get shot or taken to jail, and getting long prison terms with nothing to gain."[25] As a transpublic, he was able to communicate these concerns across gang boundaries in order to help identify common ground. He explained: "I was going back and forth, you know, getting their point of view and then getting the other point of view, and then relating that to each other through me. I would say, 'Well, this is what the Shorelines think, and this is what they feel,' and I knew it was directly related to what they were talking about, and it was a common ground so they had a common experience."[26] Knowledge on the part of each gang that the other was feeling the same about the situation helped to pave way for dialogue between them.

Many of the older and former gang members—*veteranos* and OGs—were also urging peace efforts based on the damaging impact the war was having on the survival of their community more broadly defined. Probation officer Carson also credited them and described: "[The V-13s] had their own OGs, and they were always saying the same thing: 'This is stupid. We need to have peace. We need to talk.' And then on the other side, people were saying the same thing and some other Gs particularly were very, very influential as far as trying to settle things down."[27]

Carson had also come to understand that neither gang would initiate dialogue for fear of losing face. He believed that they needed a "neutral" mediator to arrange a forum for dialogue so that neither side would have to cop to initiating it. As he put it:

> They needed a middleman, an objective middleman, nonpartisan, with no interest or nothing really to gain, and that could take the heat from both sides. They needed a way out, and that's where I came in, you know, where the two sides can come together without either side saying that they made the first move. 'Cause if you make the first move in that game, you lose. They hadn't talked since September 26th of 1993 and it's now June the 13th, 1994. So the first one to the table, the first one that says something, the first one that blinks loses, in their minds. I was like that middleman, that cap that could bridge it over without either one of them saying that they did anything. Without either one of them saying that, you know, they made a move for peace or cease-fire.[28]

Because he had built a certain level of trust among certain individuals, he was able to make the arrangements for a meeting once both gangs had come to a decision to attempt a settlement.

Trust for Truce

As with peace settlements between countries at war, developing a system to enforce the truce is a major challenge. One of the concerns of the V-13 was the organizational structure of the Shoreline. The V-13 enforced fairly strict discipline on their members and felt more confident that they could maintain their end of the bargain. The Shorelines, however, were organized such that individual members had greater independence. A V-13 associate explained his concern: "The Shorelines are loose. No internal organization. No one plays the role of speaker. No one could put people in their place. From our experience, that causes a problem on V-13. If they have a problem with V-13, we come to know how to control our people. How do you communicate with people who can't [internally] get the message across?"[29] Part of the difficulty in enacting the truce was the initial lack of trust that remained even after the agreement was made. As one Shoreline described, the truce was "eased into." He said, "It took a 'put the guns down' system, or not put them down, but if you see me and I see you, let's not just straight start shooting. See if you can drive by and just watch me." At the beginning, the truce was "real shaky, 'cause you don't know if this man is going to start shooting at you. You don't want nobody to get the drop on you first, so it was like a Catch-22 type thing."[30]

Over time, the truce became more stable; eventually, members of the Shoreline and the V-13 within Oakwood began to interact under terms of peace. The Shoreline member continued to explain the peace-building process: "The Oakwood community was still on edge, but they'd be over there playing their sports. We'd be playing ours. They'd be having their little, what-

8. Members of the Victory Outreach ministry from the South Bay pray before a Keep the Peace rally in Oakwood, September 20, 1994. Courtesy of Santa Monica Historical Society Museum / Outlook Collection.

ever, picnics. We'd be having ours. You know. And then it eased into it to where, we might not have spoke and then people started, 'What's up?' 'What's up?' And you know. They went to play us softball and, you know, then they start with the little positive type war. You know what I'm saying?"[31] There were several skirmishes that took place fairly soon after the truce, but they were quickly put to rest, and mechanisms were established to ensure better enforcement of their agreement. Fighting did not completely end, but, as one observer put it, "There's peace, but there's still fighting. The difference is now there's no killing without thinking."[32]

Residents and gang members helped to maintain peace over the months that followed. Events were organized by community organizations to involve the youths in positive activities, including sports and recreational activities. A Pop Warner football team that had gone defunct was reactivated. The Pearl White Theater summer program featured conflict mediation training for youths. Others organized events specifically focused on supporting the truce. On 14 February 1995, a community celebration entitled "Bridge the Gap" was sponsored to demonstrate community support for the truce and to make a call to various organizations for the need to work together to address the remaining problems faced by all residents in the neighborhood, such as unemployment and education. Residents, gang representatives, police, social service organizations, and city officials were among the over 150 persons who attended the dinner celebration. Recognition was given to several of the individuals responsible for forging the truce. The event represented a message to all parties involved that residents in the community of Oakwood and surrounding areas wanted an end to the violence and supported all those who worked for peace.

Retrospective Narratives and the Reification of Power

Foucault (1977) described Jeremy Bentham's nineteenth-century designs for a "panopticon" to illustrate the social force of surveillance and the importance of perceptions of power in social control. Bentham's panopticon was a multisided prison building in which a guard tower located in the center was surrounded by a single layer of see-through prison cells. Guards in the guard tower would be able observe each prisoner in each cell, but the prisoners would not be able see the guards in the tower who were shielded from sight. The power of the guards did not reside in their ability to monitor the cells but rather in the inmates' *perception* that the guards might potentially be watching at all times. The power of the guards did not lie in their numbers, since it did not matter if anyone was in the tower. Instead, it was the knowledge (or perception) that the guards might be in the tower that would exert control over the behavior of inmates. In other words, if one perceives an entity to exert power, then that entity does, in fact, exert power—not by direct control itself but rather by etching in people's minds a certain belief. Promoting a belief, in essence, is a technique of power. Promoting a belief that one can exert power helps to ensure it. Thus, claiming credit for a settlement is serious business. For one's ability to maintain the perception of power determines how much one can sustain it. If one group can claim credit for bringing peace to a neighborhood, then it protects its mask of authority, regardless of who was directly responsible for the truce itself.

Everyone involved, from law enforcement officials to gang representatives, claimed credit for ending the war. The probation officer gave the major credit to those Shoreline and V-13 members who took the step to negotiate the truce, adding that had he not arranged the meeting for the particular day it took place, the war could very well have escalated and spread to other parts of the city.

The police claimed that their increased presence hampered gang members' mobility and ability to deal drugs, putting social and economic pressure on them to end the fighting. One detective put it this way: "The violence stopped. That was the main objective, and that we accomplished. . . . There's so many police that they've disrupted the narcotics trade there to the point that it was almost nonexistent. Economically it was hurting everybody, so therefore they came to an agreement, and so now they can get back to dealing drugs and life is back to normal."[33]

City Hall and the District Attorney's Office claimed that had they not prepared an injunction against the three gangs, there would not have been the threat that the councilwoman's aide and the probation officer were able to use in their respective carrot and stick strategies. Givens, the councilwoman's aide, is certain that the carrot and stick strategy he forged with other agencies would not only have put an end to the war but would also have been effective in the long term to reintegrate gang members into mainstream social, economic, and political institutions. Without a more comprehensive intervention that would allow gang members to make meaningful inroads into the legal job market, he argued, illegal gang activities would continue even with a truce in place. Since his plans dissolved with his job termination, there were no opportunities to test his theory.

Gang members denied that law enforcement actions played any major part in their decision to come to a truce and claimed that the major impetus was their realization that too many people were dying and therefore that little would be gained from continued warfare.

The different viewpoints described above are shaped by the respective lenses, experiences, and interests of each group. Even if some did agree with another's point of view, they may not have admitted it. For the legends surrounding the war are sources of power, which are guarded just as much as the positions and interests they protect.

Chapter 8

Transforming Racial Conflict

It is difficult to capture the full range of viewpoints and experiences contained in this tragic Los Angeles episode. What I have done is attempt a synthesis of the more distinct and publicly articulated stances among the participants and observers of the "gang war" in order to examine the complex dynamics of contemporary urban conflict. In particular, this narrative of the gang war attempts to highlight the divergences in viewpoints among different groups and individuals and "replay" major events to show how differing meanings, norms, and interpretations contributed to the escalation of conflict within a given policy and social environment. By reflecting upon the series of events, we may begin to grasp the importance of understanding social conflict from multiple positionalities, for a deeper understanding not only of the dynamics of conflict but also of the consequences of intervention when read from different standpoints. This may enable us to seek more effective solutions to urban violence in the future.

A central feature of conflict in a world of multiple publics is the slipperiness of its substance and form. Once initiated, a conflict becomes a site for groups and individuals to continually contest its meaning and redirect its trajectory. Views as to the object of contestation, the motive of contestants, and the meaning of actions can often collide with one another. What one may intend to accomplish in an action may become lost in the chaos of the engagement that follows. Actions can lead to unintended consequences or send unintended messages. Snippets of reality in the flurry of conflict can be assembled by different groups to create grand pictures that show no resemblance to one another. Narratives frame these snapshots of reality as groups compete to win the uncommitted to their point of view. If knowledge is power, discursive contests to win over hearts and minds are one of the keys to securing it.

The case study of Venice illustrates a conflict that unfolded, slip-sliding along several trajectories over its evolution—from individual to family to gang to race and then back to gang boundaries, often teetering along several interdependent tracks at once. As the conflict grew racially charged, tensions escalated and enveloped a wider portion of the population, particularly as fear and suspicion of racial targeting spread throughout the neighborhood. While the escalation of conflict may appear somewhat haphazard, one can pinpoint key moments in time when explicitly drawn racial meanings were infused into the fray. One can follow, as I have tried to do, the iterations in which racial constructs were elevated in the meaning-making process and in the clarification of oppositional boundaries. But it is to highlight the fact that the prominence of race in delineating the boundaries of conflict ebbed and flowed relative to other lines of division. The boomerang effects of police suppression activities, the sensationalist reporting in the print media, the rumored threats of racial targeting, and the pattern of victimization through the course of the conflict elevated the meaning of race and spurred racial polarization within the broader community. Conversely, the efforts by many to deracialize the conflict contributed to its de-escalation.

In each of the iterative steps in the escalation and de-escalation of the conflict, there were simultaneous processes. One was a constant struggle among key individuals and organizations to define or redefine the problem. Law enforcement agencies viewed the primary problem as one of "predators" driven by the quest for territory and turf, with clear distinctions made in the perceived nature and characteristics of African American and Latino gangs. Their main objective was to apprehend, remove, and isolate as many gang members from the neighborhood as possible. Meanwhile, gang members in Oakwood initially managed to contain the conflict between several individuals as a family affair, cordoning it off from full-scale gang involvement. But that soon changed when conflicts originating in Mar Vista dovetailed with events in Oakwood and an attack on a Shoreline member was interpreted as a declaration of war between the Shoreline and the V-13. From there, the public competition to define the conflict began its upward trajectory. Police actions that initially focused more heavily on the Shoreline were promoted by Shoreline and others sympathetic to their plight as favoritism toward their Latino adversaries, framing the conflict as "Black versus Brown *and* Blue." A few individuals began a short-lived public mobilization effort, distributing leaflets asking residents to donate bullets to the Shoreline since it was "protecting residents from Mexicans." The V-13 maintained that it was fighting a gang battle, pointing to the Shoreline as raising the stakes of violence with the "race card." Shorelines suspected prison-based gangs steeped in a rising atmosphere of ethnic nationalism as a major force behind local confrontations. Meanwhile, media headlines definitively declared, "Deadly Gang War Turns to Race War." In protesting this depiction, some argued that the ordeal was fueled by developers and a handful of police officers as part of a larger conspiracy to drive out low-income residents from the last affordable seaside enclave remaining in the region. They saw the problem as one of economic poverty and social marginalization in the face of gentrification and the widening gap between rich and poor. The cacophony of positions clamored in competition for an audience that would join them in their efforts to reach their respective aims.

Parallel to this discursive contest over the defined problematic was a simultaneous realignment of individuals in a changing constellation of publics. Each problematic implied a set of allies, enemies, and desired outcomes. Constituencies regrouped as individuals gravitated from one position to another. Persuasive arguments were crafted to win sympathy and support to a particular side. Police appealed to residents for support to "eliminate predators." The Shoreline appealed to its Oakwood neighbors, whom they were "protecting from the Mexicans." Some also joined various community spokespersons in an appeal to stop the violence "to save the community from gentrification." Ministers appealed to their congregations to support peace "for the sake of God." A rainbow of protesters marched for peace in a more overarching moral appeal to "stop the violence." By the end, gang members appealed to their fellow associates, arguing that it was time to settle since, by their account—reframing the problem in terms of the number of victims counted by gang membership rather than by racial identification—they "were winning" while the costs of war were mounting, not only for themselves but also for others around them.

Arguments were embedded in narratives that appealed to the many people in the neighborhood yearning to make sense of what was going on around them and to gain clarity as to what actions they themselves should take. As has been shown, shards of evidence were selectively pieced together to make each case. Some of these narrative-based arguments were embraced and others rejected, depending on a number of factors, such as how compelling a problematic was in view of one's experience and vantage point, the perceived implications of a position, and the credibility of the promoter. If explanatory arguments were too disconnected from existing frames of reference, the narrative would not hold water for that group or individual. But if those narratives could convincingly explain the unfolding sequence of reality frames, the conversion of subscribers could swing the social momentum in a given direction. At the height of the conflict, narratives positioning race as an explanatory variable gained currency for a good many residents who were desperately trying to comprehend the motives and targets of the two sides and the scope of the conflict. At the same time, conscious efforts were made to disengage race as a justificatory or score-keeping construct in the war. While race remained a salient division for many, its prominence receded relative to gang boundaries on the road to truce.

Public constituencies were not discrete groups and, in fact, often overlapped in expected and unexpected ways. Some who believed that the police had conspired with developers to let the violence continue were also willing

to work with police officers, making finer distinctions among individual officers, some of whom they came to trust. There were also many who sympathized with the Shoreline as they accused the police of unfairly favoring
Latino gangs but who also marched for peace alongside their Latino neighbors. And as described in chapter 4, there were many instances in which gang
members, residents, and government agents reached out across social and institutional boundaries in gestures of cross-racial support and cooperation.
Whereas the racial divides grew wider as the conflict developed, the formation of publics traversing those major divides could also be seen. Oftentimes,
allegiances were shared only privately out of fear of repercussion. But many
others publicly took steps to counter the prevailing winds of polarization.
Thus, within the general tide of racial polarization, there remained crisscrossing allegiances and relationships that were expressed on a case-by-case
basis.

One irony in the dynamics of conflict was that for those familiar with the
intricate details of the events that unfolded, simplistic categories of division
were less compelling, as opposing poles in the conflict were shaded with many
hues of gray. Those further away from the conflict, whether spatially or rela-
tionally, often tended to emphasize the racial dimension to a greater degree
than those in closer range. This was due to the fact that the further distance
one was from the epicenter, the more the picture was simplified through the
filtering of the media or social networks through which accounts of events
were necessarily relayed. When the local newspaper declared the conflict a
"race war," for example, residents closer to the events were more skeptical
than those in the surrounding area who relied on the media as a major source
of information. Those closer to events and in more direct reception of discursive contests to define the problem were often more resistant to side with
more extreme and simplistic positions. Under these conditions, socially polarizing narratives were compelling to a broad spectrum of publics, given the
shorthand nature of stories. This tendency to abide by a more polarizing
stance in times of uncertainty was likely greater in the crossfire of violence
where concern for physical safety can drive individuals to the most risk-avoid-
ing position.

In the introductory chapter, I posed a number of questions that I believed
could be answered more insightfully if we were to examine conflict according
to its morphology. I defined the morphology of conflict as the incremental
transformations in the boundaries and scope of conflict, the objects under
contest, and the defined interests among those stakeholders involved in
processes of conflict escalation or resolution. Morphing describes the iterative and seemingly seamless transformation of conflict defined along one set
of salient boundaries and issues of contestation to an altered set. I suggested
that this approach would be useful to illuminate the fluid and complex dynamics of contemporary urban racial conflict.

At the outset, this approach highlights a particular set of questions: How do changing definitions of the problem affect shifts in salient group boundaries in conflict? How do differences in interpretation shape the character of conflict? How do groups construct oppositional identities in which racial boundaries become the most salient? How do the meanings of race and the boundaries of division in the conflict transform? How can we identify differences within racial and ethnic groups among those who promote conflict and those who promote cooperation? What are the variables that heighten or diminish the salience of race relative to other social boundaries in the course of conflict? And how can residents and public and private sector agencies intervene in such a way that their actions, rather than exacerbating racial antagonisms, enable collaborative problem-solving and fruitful deliberation? The previous account of events along with the following discussion is an attempt to begin addressing these questions. The next challenge is to examine the iterations in the morphology of conflict to gain insight into what we can do as concerned citizens, policymakers, and practitioners to address such quagmires better.

Examining the Iterations in the Morphology of Conflict

Transformations in the Problematic

Examining discursive contests over the definition of the problem and over the meaning of actions or events can reveal how various publics see a conflict. These problem definitions include a set of explanations that weave together empirical evidence, myth, and rumor in narratives that explain the "who, what, when, where, and why" of a problem. Understanding how different publics problematize a situation is extremely valuable, since how people define and assess a problem or conflict setting has much to do with how they will respond in a given situation. All too often, those who try to intervene in conflict fail to understand these problematics from multiple positions. Instead, they assume that most people "see the same reality," only to be perplexed by the varied and unexpected responses to their actions.

In cases of urban violence where rumors fill the air, gaining a "reality view" among multiple publics is complicated by the wash of hearsay and by the elusiveness of verifiable evidence. Because information, whether witnessed or rumored, often travels through informal social networks, different groups make their assessments based on different sets of "facts." Furthermore, the same pieces of evidence often mean different things to different groups based on differences in experiential and historical contexts. It is not uncommon for one group of individuals to have a different assessment of a given situation than another group. Oftentimes, one group may not be able to make sense of why another group may view the situation in the way they do.

In other situations, groups or individuals engage in intense debates over the assessment of a situation and the meaning of actions and events. These forums of debate, whether in public meetings or the privacy of a home, can bring together insights from a wider range of sources and perspectives. In some instances, people engaged in these dialogues may transform their own ideas, including their definition of the problem. An important question is why some assessments gain more currency than others. From an examination of the case study, the degree to which a particular view of the problem is embraced by the broader population depends upon the credibility of the proponents of an explanation, the credibility of their following, and the coherence and weight of the evidence as they relate to one's lived experience. Fear can also heighten a defensive impulse to adopt an explanation that reduces one's exposure to possible danger.

In the Venice case, for example, there was a period during which members of the Shoreline and their associates were trying to determine the intentions of the V-13 and assess their relationship with it following the murder of Anthony Bibbs. Prior to the murder, members of the V-13 and the Shoreline had enjoyed a relatively amicable relationship that spanned decades, recently negotiating the bounds of a skirmish as a family affair and not a problem between the gangs. But after the murder of Bibbs, there was a flurry of speculation among those close to Bibbs. Members of the Shoreline and others in their social circles pieced together various bits of evidence to lead many of them to conclude that the murder was probably a deliberate act of aggression by the V-13 as part of the Mexican Mafia's move to take over the regional drug trade. Acknowledgment that Bibbs was known to deal narcotics as well as date Latino women lent a certain potential meaning to the murder. Though it was not known who the assailant was, the murder was read as a message from the V-13 and the Mexican Mafia that they were challenging the Shoreline's share of the drug trade and their "mixing" with Latino women. Whether or not that was the intended message of the perpetrator was not confirmed before retaliatory action was taken. And when members of the V-13 perceived those retaliatory acts as attacks against them by the Shoreline, they responded in turn. What may have been formerly defined as a family affair escalated squarely into a gang confrontation. A similar process unfolded in the racialization of gang conflict, as will be discussed.

Problematics are defined within a historical context that includes the nested relationships that have existed in a particular place. The conflict between the gangs was nested in the history of Oakwood, where African Americans had for generations struggled to maintain a social and cultural center and preserve the community as a place where low-income residents could live. In the face of gentrification, which had begun several decades earlier, tensions had arisen between low-income residents and more wealthy newcomers. This context shaped the perceptions of the unfolding gang conflict, as Shoreline associates and many African American residents came to believe that the police were conspiring with developers to allow the gang war to continue so that African American and low-income residents would be driven away, making way for the completion of the gentrification process.

The recent social history of Venice shaped interpretations of police actions and cooperation with them by members of the local property owners association, led by those identified with gentrification efforts. Stories about individual property owners and their relationships with certain police officers circulated as part of the body of evidence supporting the theory of conspiracy. Additional stories surrounding the Latino police captain and his allegiance to his fellow Latinos fanned suspicions of racial bias and collaboration within the administrative ranks of the police department. When police raided the homes only of African American residents, the discursive groundwork had already been laid for those who would piece together evidence to advocate a conspiratorial explanation of the problem.

The adoption of this general problematic by members of the Shoreline contributed to the severance of communication lines between Shoreline and V-13 associates. Adoption of the theory of conspiracy among many residents, African American and otherwise, also generated greater distrust toward law enforcement officials and suspected officers. If there were any opportunities to clarify or discuss the problem between members of the V-13 and Shoreline associates or to initiate more cooperative efforts with police, the hardening of this particular problematic among residents prevented any such initiatives among those who subscribed to the theory.

Discursive contests over the nature of a problem are often influenced by entities *external* to the conflict, which help to shape public perceptions or create incentive structures that nudge conflict toward one trajectory over another. For example, many of the articles and headlines published in the local daily paper, *The Outlook,* had both effects. Its descriptions defined the conflict more squarely as a racial conflict and created an incentive for retaliation along racial boundaries by highlighting the racial identification of victims over gang identifications in their reporting. Gang members read the newspaper reports that routinely mentioned the racial identification of victims and suspects as a public scoreboard regardless of the intentions of the editors. It was only after a series of meetings initiated by residents that the editorial staff modified their reporting practices. Likewise, gang members reported stories of a two-column list of victims posted in the police station where suspects and witnesses were taken, also reading them as public tallies. Together with a LAPD incident hotline that initially included the racial identification of perpetrators and victims, two influential institutions—the media and the police—unwittingly (some argue purposefully) contributed to the heightened salience of race within the battle. Again, residents' demands to downplay or omit the racial identities of victims and perpetrators signified an effort to downplay the construct of race as a marker in broadcasting the conflict.

Problem definitions play a critical role in that they "condition" the interpretation of unfolding events as well as temper the reactions to them. When the local daily proclaimed, "Deadly Gang War Turns to Race War," African American and Latino residents who were nowhere near the epicenter of conflict began to distance themselves from one another, not knowing the extent to which they might become a victim of racial violence and not knowing who exactly the perpetrators may be. Parks, sidewalks, and other public places in and around the neighborhood quickly became empty. Students felt an atmosphere of suspicion and distrust in schools. Racial antagonisms grew with the perception that the violence was racially motivated. As described in chapter 4, responding to an attack as if it was a race war could easily turn it into one. Thus, the acceptance of the problematic that the gang war was turning into a race war had the effect of conditioning social behavior in such a way as to hasten its advent.

Problem definitions also condition the strategies and styles of intervention by government agencies and community organizations. The Oakwood Plan represented a clearly articulated problematic from the standpoint of a group of police officers stationed at that time in the Pacific Division. This problematic included descriptions of the Oakwood neighborhood and its residents. Written police assessments stating that the vast majority of African American families were tied through intermarriage to the Shoreline, for example, introduced the probability of an attitudinal bias against all African American families. Particularly for the many officers who were not familiar with Venice or neighborhoods similar to it, such generalized descriptions tended to blur important distinctions within the population. Simplified assessments that overlooked important distinctions between individuals often led to the unnecessary alienation of those who could play a role in collaborative efforts towards peace. By categorizing African Americans as suspect through "guilt of association," many felt unfairly "labeled." Instead of winning the trust and cooperation of the residents who desired an end to the violence, the police alienated many of them by acting on the assumptions embedded in training materials and internal plans.

As Stone (1997) and others have shown, problematics also serve an instrumental function to further the agenda of a particular group by promoting a viewpoint to mobilize support or to justify actions. In the realm of government policy, problematics underpinning the "War on Drugs" and "War on Gangs" were used to justify the increase in law enforcement powers used against suspected gang members (Reinarman and Levine 1997). On the other hand, at the community level, the conspiracy theory was used by one vocal resident to rally African American support for the Shoreline among residents. The Culver City Boys, meanwhile, justified their attacks against the Shoreline in Mar Vista Gardens in part by constructing a problematic that posed the Shoreline as getting "more than their fair share" of the drug market in Mar Vista Gardens. And many community organizations and activists emphasized the problem of disempowerment and poverty to advocate for more programs and services to steer youths and young adults away from violent behavior instead of relying so heavily on the power of suppression.

Attention to the substance of problematics among multiple publics provides a way to understand a conflict from the lens of disparate groups who respond to their surroundings based on a particular interpretation of events. Problematics are not static but are instead publicly contested and can transform over the duration of a conflict. Transformations can signal shifts in primary lines of division as well as in the composition and constellation of publics. These dynamics of conflict offer windows of opportunity to find effective and appropriate interventions to end violent clashes. In selecting the most appropriate intervention, however, many policymakers and practitioners fail to understand the multiplicity of frames. As Shön and Rein (1994) argued, policymakers "must overcome the blindness induced by their own ways of framing the policy situation in order to see that multiple policy frames represent a nexus of legitimate values in conflict" (187). I would add that even if one does not see another's value set as being "legitimate," it is important to acknowledge the existence of different values and interpretations just the same.

Oppositional Identities and Shifting Lines of Division

Problematics often delineate a perceived "ingroup" from an "outgroup," distinguishing the "self" in relationship to "the other," or, in a conflict situation, "allies vs. enemies." The constellation of alliances between groups and individuals tends to shift with changes in definitions and circumstances. Since problematics often attribute interests and motives that separate friend from foe and ally from adversary, they also indicate the tenor of future interactions, whether based on trust, suspicion, competition, shared fate, or strategic alliance. These relationships are primed in unfolding events as well as in the discourse surrounding those events. Identities can assume an oppositional form through the course of group interaction. Examining the iterative process of oppositional group formation in the racialization of the gang war reveals several useful insights.

This and other cases of urban racial conflict have shown that lines of division are often more fluid than publicized accounts of racial conflict portray. Usually there are crisscrossing alliances or social ties that individuals maintain across racial or any other type of group boundary. Parents, for example, may traverse cleavages of class or race. Conversely, class or religious differences may temper shared racial identities. Friendships across gang boundaries or divisions within gangs may represent potential lines of alliance or division, respectively. As one Venice resident shared, members of the V-13 and the Shoreline were known to "watch each other's back" when under attack by an outside rival gang. Even at the height of the gang war, some of the former gang members were able to maintain open lines of communication based on long-standing relationships that did not just evaporate as the conflict escalated.

Out of this fluidity often emerge windows of opportunity to build upon the maintenance or regeneration of the crosscutting ties. In reflecting upon the war after the truce was stuck, one affiliate of the Shoreline acknowledged a common plight underlying the fight over territory—that "neither of us *own* this land." Likewise, as in any organization, internal tensions between different "sets" and leaders within each respective gang were not uncommon. Thus, individuals may identify with multiple and crisscrossing social and organizational networks within a conflict setting; the primary lines of cleavage may subsequently shift over time, depending on the situational salience of identity group boundaries, which lends more malleability to conflicts than one may perceive unless one is attentive to more subtle patterns of relations.

But what are the factors that engender an oppositional identity and antipathy along racial lines within a social landscape crosshatched by many identity boundaries? This question is similar to a more general question once posed by John Agnew (1989, 42): how do the social constructions of parties to a conflict generate objectified conditions that are seen by the parties as mutually exclusive practices, interests, stakes, and goals? At one point, members of the two Venice gangs living in Oakwood shared ties of friendship and loyalty to the neighborhood that went back several generations. But in a relatively short time, the two gangs were engaged in violent clashes.

It appears that individual friendships were overshadowed by the weight of larger organizational objectives and strategies. As groups consolidated their forces, voices of mediation or negotiated settlement were lost in the increasing tumult of combat and competition. As Tajfel noted, systems of social categorization may allow for the justification of actions against "outgroups"—whose individual members are seen with decreasing variability—by "ingroups"—whose members behave with greater uniformity. Under these circumstances, one's social identity may become more salient than one's personal identity (Tajfel 1981, 1982). As real and perceived gang objectives attained primacy over individual relationships in driving intergroup dynamics and as group decisions increasingly affected individual actions, interpersonal relations between individual members of the two gangs choked under the weight of group imperatives. And as race became a major feature of intergroup conflict, mobilization along racial cleavages worked to suppress many interpersonal ties across color lines even further, affecting relations beyond the boundaries of gang membership.

The degree to which identities are defined as oppositional affects the permeability of boundaries. As observed in many other conflicts, the greater the degree to which individuals define their groups *in opposition to others,* the less likely it becomes for individuals to interact across group boundaries. Group loyalty, peer scrutiny, and, in some cases, group sanctions put an end to many cross-racial exchanges that had existed prior to the gang war. By examining the morphology of conflict, we can identify the iterative steps in the hardening of oppositional boundaries. The oppositional character that began initially as most salient along gang boundaries became increasingly racial, elevating the salience of race not only among gang members but also within the broader population.

At the same time, the gang war is a reminder that systems of social categorization are not impermeable and that crosscutting boundaries create a more complex mosaic within the social landscape, where ties are maintained or broken. A deeper understanding of the ever-changing mosaic can be instructive in problem-solving. Established social categorization theories in social psychology insightfully identify tendencies in conflict dynamics that bind affinity groups. But the process of defining those boundaries among crosscutting dimensions of difference is one that is constantly under negotiation, as is the attribution of meanings to those categories. There are often feelings of ambivalence about the conflict, even among members of opposing groups, as it is not as easy to "objectify the other" when there are deep relationships. In one extreme case, for example, two brothers of mixed racial ancestry who were members of the opposing gangs lived under the same roof, abiding by the house rules laid down by their parents, while at the same time navigating the dictates of their respective gangs. One can hardly imagine the complexity of the spoken and unspoken negotiations, both emotionally and behaviorally, interpersonally and organizationally. In diverse metropolitan areas where individuals maintain multiple identities and varied affiliations, the process of individual and group negotiation over the meaning of those identities in relation to others is continually tested and contested. While some scholars argue that individuals maintain a relatively stable "core sense of self" (Northrup 1989) that contributes to the intractability of conflict, there is much more to know about the factors that affect the relative salience of multiple identities and the relative strength of bonds across various affiliations, such as the nuclear family and gang, in this particular example.

The case study also illustrates that the power or "kinetic charge" of race as a line of division is partially contingent on its centrality in other arenas of conflict. Using the metaphor of earthquakes and seismic fault lines, one can envision a tremor along one social fault line that sends strong reverberations along adjacent fault lines. Likewise, a tremor along one fault line can draw additional energy from adjacent fault lines. In the case of the gang war, racial antagonisms along multiple fault lines tended to energize one another. Racial tensions did indeed exist among segments of the population in other areas prior to the gang war surrounding increased competition for jobs, housing, and services, as explained in chapter 3. As the gang conflict became conflated with preexisting racial divisions, the gang war drew energies from preexisting racial fault lines—and vice versa. Racial animosities that already resided within the neighborhood as well as those generated within the prison system were drawn into the flames of gang conflict. Simultaneously, events surrounding the gang conflict fueled tangential arenas of racial tension. The conflation of gang and racial boundaries pushed the scope of tensions beyond the boundaries of the gangs along racial cleavages within the broader population, tapping latent resentment that may have accrued in other venues.

In addition, government interventions perceived to favor one group over another in racially charged conflicts can severely aggravate racial conflicts by hardening oppositional identities and by tipping the perceived or real balance of power. Horowitz (1985) observed that when government institutions are perceived to favor one group over another, the disfavored group often redoubles its efforts to gain recognition and redemption, resulting in intensified conflict. The desire for group worth and legitimacy is one explanation why conflicts can be intensified by actions on the part of the state in its role as grand arbiter of precious psychological goods (see also Esman 1990 and Ryan 1990). Tensions created by real or perceived state favoritism can also be further exacerbated through political mobilization where advocates and political entrepreneurs can rally ethnic groups under the banner of neglect and injustice. Similar findings have been made in psychological studies of intergroup behavior where favoritism exhibited on the part of an authority figure brewed antagonisms between two competing groups (Brewer and Kramer 1985). This gang war revealed a phenomenon consistent with earlier studies, as law enforcement actions were viewed by the Shoreline as favoring Latino gangs, prompting the Shoreline to intensify the level of conflict. In this case, however, the effects of state intervention on group worth and legitimacy seemed secondary to its effects on perceived power relations, which would have not only psychological but also physical, social, and economic consequences for each of the warring parties, particularly the group that felt disfavored.

Interpretive Lenses in Intergroup Dynamics

The most difficult challenge for those interested in the peaceful resolution of conflict is to understand how the dissonance between interpretive lenses functions to complicate conflict dynamics. The interpretation of events and actions is as critical as the events or acts themselves, as their meanings are often read in unintended ways. While seldom the main source of conflict alone, the misreading of others' actions can exacerbate conflicts at critical moments and in serious ways (Agnew 1989). Some of the ways in which differences in interpretive lenses may complicate conflict include imputing false motives to or misplacing blame for an act, attaching unintended messages to an act, and implying relationships or inferring causal links that may not exist. Hall (1980) alerted us to the discontinuity that can occur between the encoding and decoding of messages. In conflict settings, these discontinuities can generate unnecessary aggression or circumvent opportunities for resolution.

In examining the morphology of conflict in the gang war, one source of misinterpretation had to do with differences in organizational culture. When one group assumes that other groups abide by a similar set of cultural norms or operate within a similar organizational culture when there are actually substantial differences, it is easy for actions to be misread. For example, when V-13 members attacked several men who were affiliated with the Shoreline in their younger days, V-13 members viewed those attacks as a direct hit against the Shoreline. Members of the Shoreline who had come to respect those victims' independence from their organization, on the other hand, viewed these attacks as reaching beyond the boundaries of the gang and into the larger community, marked by the salience of race and territory. As described in chapter 4, differences in organizational culture between the Shoreline and the V-13 could explain differences between the V-13's view and the Shorelines' interpretations, since the permanency of affiliation and tightness of organization was greater for the V-13 than it was for their counterpart.

A second source of misreading had to do with the ambiguity of the acts themselves, especially acts of violence in which there were many questions that remained unresolved, leaving room for a great amount of speculation. With little exchange other than physical shows of force, ambiguities abounded, such as the exact identities of the perpetrators, their specific motives, and the reasons for the selection of a particular target. When communication lines between combatants are severed, individuals in groups come to their own conclusions as to the meaning of those events. Whether an act was intended as merely a warning or as an outright declaration of war, whether it was perpetrated by an opposing gang or a third party, whether the victim was specifically targeted or a case of mistaken identity—such questions were often left unsettled.

Events with such a high degree of ambiguity are also ripe for manipulation by those in pursuit of a clear agenda. In the midst of uncertainty, individuals within groups can persuade others to see those events in a way that furthers their own objectives or raises their leadership authority. Absent any easy way to verify an explanation, persuasive and charismatic individuals can heavily influence public perceptions, drawing on fears along with a gendered sense of pride or "manhood" expressed in terms of "protection of territory" or "reputation." Deliberation and reflection can be hazardous luxuries in the spinning vortex of events whose pull can draw groups into a narrow funnel of life-and-death encounters. In the frenzy that accompanies intense skirmishes under these conditions, the more resolute-sounding, extreme-leaning, physically bold positions often win out, pushing the momentum of violence upwards.

Not only are the meanings of events commonly misread, but so too are the "representative scales" of specific acts. Interactions in the midst of conflict often take place on an interpersonal level. But it is not always clear whether an act of aggression is meant to represent an affront by a larger group with whom an individual is affiliated or whether those exchanges are exclusive to a particular set of individuals. Intergroup conflicts are complicated when an individual acts independently against members of a rival group—but the rival group interprets the act as conducted *on behalf of* the entire group, rather than by a sole individual. When this occurs, the scale of the act is misread—the act is seen as representing a much larger group than was actually behind it. Blame for an act is attributed to a whole group rather than an individual who may have acted alone, out of anger, resentment, or some other motive. In the Venice case, it appeared that several of the attacks against Latinos were perpetrated by individuals acting independently of the Shoreline. But in the void of communications between the groups, these tended to be interpreted as attacks by the Shoreline as an organization and avenged in turn, regardless of any organizational backing an individual may or may not have received. Similarly, actions of individual police officers were often read as signifying the position and approach of the department as a whole. Many acts of police misconduct or apathy among individual officers were often read as signifying apathy and conspiracy by the department more generally, generating distrust of officers who had nothing to do with those engaged in misconduct or, more pointedly, were not in any way affiliated with developers or land speculators.

This phenomenon was consistent with the observations of social psychologists in experimental studies; they found that when there is greater social distance between groups, actions on the part of a few members can be read to represent an action by the group as a whole (Tajfel 1981, 1982). They also observed that the degree of internal group cohesion and the degree to which groups view each other as internally homogeneous affect the intensity of intergroup conflicts. The Venice case also illustrates, however, that it is through the interpretive process that attributions or misattributions are made, rather than necessarily through any innate propensity to homogenize the "other." Social distancing functions to allow greater variation in the interpretation of events, since communication between embattled groups is usually diminished. Various factors can combine to misread the scale and source of the attack.

Likewise, other factors may contribute to its clarification, such as the establishment and maintenance of informal social networks through which information can be conveyed. For example, it was at a high mark in the conflict that communication between gangs, through veteranos and OGs as well as through certain probation officers, was made possible, allowing messages to be relayed and clarifications to be made, which in turn led to tide-turning events. The maintenance of crosscutting networks can partially counter the functions of social distancing to minimize distortions in the reading of actions and tendencies consistent with "homogenizing the other."

Finally, power differentials affected the extent to which some interpretations were promulgated over others. Not all individuals or publics possess the same techniques to shape interpretive lenses, to promote a particular reading of events, or to clarify misinterpretations between groups. Media organizations have a developed infrastructure to propagate or reproduce certain viewpoints among its viewers. Government officials enjoy an aura of legitimacy that allows their voices to be featured in media reports and to be given standing among agencies they oversee. In Venice, media organizations captured various points of view, ranging from residents to law enforcement officers, with official positions given much greater coverage. At the same time, gang members, residents, members of the clergy, and others promoted their particular readings of the situation through the use of leaflets, public gatherings, sponsored events, discussions in informal social networks, testimonials, and the power of the pulpit to communicate to the audiences within their reach. Differences in the level and techniques of power combined with the disconnectedness of interpretive lenses only hampered constructive communication in the absence of more effective forums for exchange and dialogue.

Points of Intervention and the Role of "Transpublics"

So what, if anything, could have been done in this situation to bring a quicker end to the conflict, sparing lives and avoiding unnecessary hardship? As in any conflict, there is no "silver bullet" or simple remedy. Nor can one construct an altered scenario with a high degree of certainty in the outcome. But an examination of the morphology of conflict reveals various "trigger points" that could have been sidestepped or disabled as well as other points of intervention that could have been identified. More important, by making it a habit to understand conflicts from multiple positionalities, it might have been possible to minimize the role of unintended consequences and to take advantage of windows of opportunity more quickly. While it may not have been possible to prevent conflict, the conflict might have been more effectively addressed by leveraging opportunities for de-escalation. Moreover, opportunities to develop cooperative, community-wide strategies might have been more effectively used to secure a more sustained peace.

One dynamic evident in the Venice gang war is a constant tension between the pull toward separation and the push toward cooperation. There were hands reaching across the social divide even as physical conflicts ensued. Many individuals expressed a great deal of ambivalence, sharing friendships and family ties across conflicting parties. Levels of antagonism varied from person to person and fluctuated over time. Efforts to find mediated solutions waxed and waned relative to the intensity of conflict. The currents moving in the direction of conflict were characterized by the articulation of exclusivist ideology, commitment to the gang and its territorial objectives, feelings of desperation, latent or overt racial antagonism, and the lack of connections outside immediate gang boundaries. Conversely, the articulation of more humanistic philosophies along with meaningful interpersonal relationships across many social circles—racial, religious, gang, institutional, among others—characterized many of those actively working toward a peaceful resolution.

One of the critical aspects of intervention was the ability to strengthen the relationships and voices that could converge to secure peace. All too often, high-suppression law enforcement operations alienated rather than gained the trust of segments of the population who, though they may have had ties to gang members and their affiliates, also wanted to see an end to the violence. Gang members are part of community networks, informal social and familial networks as well as organizational networks. High-suppression operations tend to be extremely blunt instruments, casting a very broad net without discriminating between individuals caught within it. Consequently, they often resulted in alienating a good number of people who could potentially play a constructive role in community problem-solving efforts. In this case, it led to the arrest of those among the Shoreline thought to have been more "reasonable," leaving the project of ending the war to more extreme elements. The failure to understand multiple perspectives and the tendency to lump people into very broad categories exacerbated the problem.

There is a pragmatic conclusion that one can draw from these insights: by combining the vantage points of multiple publics, practitioners can better foresee "trigger points" as well as "intervention opportunities" that can contribute to the escalation or de-escalation of conflict. More precise and effective strategies can be developed by understanding the strategic choices facing participants, given varying assessments of the problem or situation, existing interests and incentives, the potential responses to alternative interventions, and the substance of public and private discourses that point to potential trajectories of conflict.

Had the goal of ending the violence been sought with an understanding of the situation from multiple vantage points (assuming a shared immediate goal among those who would see themselves as problem-solvers of stopping the violence), some things might have been done differently. It is possible that news reporting practices could have avoided the unnecessary racialization of the conflict. It is possible that the police hotline could have been formatted differently so as not to serve as a racial scoreboard. It is possible that public demonstrations of support for peace could have been more quickly organized and more broadly supported, had civic structures and lines of communication been maintained. It is possible that law enforcement agencies could have taken a more critically balanced, community-oriented approach at the initiation of their operations in light of public suspicions of racial bias and conspiracy. It is possible that institutional sites of racial antagonisms, such as many of the state prisons, could have instituted reforms to stop actively reinforcing the ongoing racial divisions taking place on the streets. It is possible that more "carrots" could have been made available to accompany the "sticks" to provide problem-solvers a wider array of tools with which to work. It is possible that healthier partnerships uniting community-based organizations and government agencies could have been developed, based on mutual respect and a high regard for the value of local knowledge. A more collaborative approach might have consummated sooner, had these partnerships been more solidly established. And others might have been earlier able to identify and act on windows of opportunity.

There were venues that brought different publics together that could have served as forums to identify points of intervention. One was Oakwood United, as described in earlier chapters. Oakwood United represented the broadest collection of community and government representatives who gathered on any regular basis to address the problem. But the obstacles posed by differing problematics, oppositional identities, and differences in interpretive lenses and techniques of power made it difficult at that time to build the trust and cooperation necessary to pave a road to peace. Especially in a harsh policy environment that tended to cast innovations as compromises, the search for collaborative solutions was quite constrained. Givens's proposal, for example, received very little attention, quickly dismissed by most law enforcement representatives favoring the zero-tolerance paradigm that dominated any consideration of alternative intervention strategies as "negotiating with the enemy." Though the proposal was unlikely to gain the consensus necessary for implementation, more thoughtful consideration of its elements and approaches may have informed the group as to potential avenues for sustained solutions. The development of a shared understanding of the changing situation based on the viewpoint of multiple publics might have produced innovative intervention strategies that could have prevented short- and long-term consequences that were counterproductive to the attainment of sustained peace.

In the absence of any collective body to deliberate assessments and ideas from diverse standpoints, "transpublics" play an even more critical role. I defined "transpublics" as those who are able to traverse multiple publics and gain a deeper understanding of the contrasting lenses, pictures, motives, concerns, objectives, and incentives that are at play at any given moment in time. Perhaps it is no coincidence that, at least among government and law enforcement personnel, it was a probation officer who was able to identify a window of opportunity and helped secure the setting for negotiations to occur. A probation officer, by occupational role, is in one of the most advantageous positions to understand the situation from multiple vantage points. They are in direct contact with participating gang members, their families and associates, and the wide range of practitioners from public institutions and private agencies that have some relation to those affected or involved in the conflict, such as teachers, counselors, social workers, police officers, and gang intervention workers. They are in a position to understand the complex circumstances of an array of groups and individuals—their viewpoints, constraints, powers, motives, commitments, and modes of operation. This allows them to make decisions that take into account all of the "reality frames" that may be operating in a given social dynamic. Open lines of communication with disparate publics also afford them better opportunities to bring groups together for dialogue or to mediate between them. Most importantly, transpublics who can understand the world through the lens of different constituencies can better identify windows of opportunity and points of intervention toward the resolution or de-escalation of conflict.

Rethinking Approaches to Racialized Conflict and Gang Violence

One of the lessons of this book is the need to evaluate critically how we come to understand problems such as racialized youth gang violence and devise strategies to address them *from the standpoint of multiple publics*—with the input and participation of residents, community groups, civic and business organizations, and members of other public and private institutions that reside or work in neighborhoods experiencing violence and racial tensions as well as participants in the conflicts themselves. I defined publics in this usage as formal or informal groups that emerge based on the salience of a certain set of identities *vis-à-vis* a given situation. "Identity bundles" distinguish publics that can be seen to share a common lens through which they interpret, analyze, and give meaning to events. Most of the time, we refer to "the public" as if it were a monolithic entity when in fact we really have multiple publics who see the world in very different ways.

Examining the many "realities" through the eyes of multiple publics can reveal "parallel universes" where the same phenomena are experienced at different planes of understanding. The challenge is to design interventions that are appropriate given different frames of interpretation and points of leverage and eventually to develop processes that can gather disparate groups together to forge a set of common goals and sustain cooperative partnerships critical to effective problem-solving. If problem-solvers can come to understand a situation from many disparate vantage points, agree on at least the main short-term goals, and develop a constructive dialogue and working relationship that can increase trust, then collaborative efforts have a greater chance of reaching collectively desired outcomes. In this way, collaboratively forged solutions can avoid unintended consequences and achieve identified outcomes with a heightened rate of success.

This challenge is akin to many players trying to solve a Rubik's Cube, with each player having a view of only one side of the cube and pursuing a competing strategy to tackle the problem as he or she sees it. The way to solve the dilemma is either to travel to different positions or to communicate between positions in order for all players to gain a fuller picture of the puzzle and to devise a more fully informed strategy to solve the puzzle.

One of the tragedies of the Venice case was that though there were many very concerned people who wanted to do something constructive about the problem, they saw the problems from such different angles and acted on the basis of that point of view, only to find that their actions often had totally unexpected or unanticipated consequences. Different people tried different things, often counter to what someone else was trying to do; in many cases, such confounded efforts only worsened the problem.

Law enforcement agencies often operate under an institutional culture that further complicates this puzzle-solving. A reality of secretive and hierarchical organizations, such as many tradition-bound police departments where community-oriented policing is the exception rather than the norm, is that institutional practices often keep officers at a remove from knowledgeable or influential members of communities, whether because of defined protocols, the lack of adequate resources, traditional *modus operandi*, selection and training of officers, unchecked officer misconduct, rotational schedules, or organizational philosophy. The lack of a full and well-rounded understanding of communities and the lack of more cooperative working relationships with community-based organizations and institutions severely limits the vantage point from which they develop and implement intervention strategies. This results in patrol officers and administrators who are often constrained by a unidimensional understanding of the communities in which they work.

At the same time, there is a growing consensus that collaborative problem-solving through meaningful partnerships between diverse sectors of the community and government agencies can lead to more successful and sustainable results (Hagedorn 1991). The movement toward community-oriented policing is one example of a shift in government agencies that would allow officers to work in tandem with residents, workers, and business owners who experience community problems on a daily, more intimate basis. Collaborative problem-solving in a world of multiple publics is critical for addressing problems such as racial tensions and gang violence.

Challenges and Opportunities in an Era of "Zero Tolerance"

The racialized gang war in Venice reached its highest intensity in 1993–94 at the very time the nation recorded the highest levels of violent crime in its recent history. From the study period, which ended in 1995, to the dawn of the new millennium, rates of violent crime declined to their lowest levels since before 1988, with the most dramatic decreases among young offenders (Blumstein and Wallman 2000; Butts and Travis 2002; Travis and Waul 2002; Rennison and Rand 2003). There is no single explanation for this decline. Scholars cite numerous factors that may explain the downward trend, such as shifting demographics, the late-1990s economic growth, the decline in crack cocaine, a changing youth culture more wary of violence, and the possible effects of policies such as stricter gun control, community policing, and increased imprisonment (Blumstein and Wallman 2000; Travis and Waul 2002).

It is unclear, however, how long this decline will continue. After six consecutive years of decreasing crime rates, there was slight upturn, beginning with a 0.3 percent rise in 2000. Travis and Waul (2002) noted that homicide rates in nine of the nation's largest cities showed a slowdown in declines in some along with a rise of up to 38 percent in others.[1] The city of Los Angeles experienced an upward trend after a three-year decline from 1996 to 1999, with a 143 percent increase in gang-related murders from 1999 to 2000 (McCarthy 2001). At the county level, there was also an increase in homicides, with a notable 25 percent rise in 2002 driven mainly by gang-related cases (Winton 2003).[2] Many practitioners and researchers attribute the increase in Los Angeles to the demoralization of the LAPD coinciding with the release of prisoners who had been incarcerated in the earlier part of the decade. Any rise in violent crime in large metropolitan areas is particularly troubling, since trends in big cities have foretold the future for the nation overall; they were the first to experience the rise in the mid-1980s and the first to drop in the mid-1990s (Travis and Waul 2002).

One of the major challenges to addressing gang violence and racialized conflict stems from the large increase in the rate of juvenile and adult incarceration and the lack of reintegrative, rehabilitative, and restorative programs for prisoners who are being released, which at the beginning of the new millennium was happening at an unprecedented rate. One of the legacies of the zero-tolerance era is the large number of individuals who circulate through the criminal justice system with diminished opportunities for employment in the formal labor market upon release. An increased chance of a prison sentence after arrest for nearly every type of crime helped to drive incarceration rates to their highest levels in history (Lagan 1991). Absolute levels and rates of increase in imprisonment within the United States dwarf that of all industrialized nations to such an extent that it is fair to characterize it as a distinctly American phenomenon (Tonry 1999). By 2003, the United States had the highest incarceration rate in the world, with 714 prisoners per 100,000 population held in state and federal prisons and in local jails. Juvenile and adult incarceration loomed particularly high in California, a state that had consistently topped the list of state custody rankings.[3]

Researchers and practitioners have expressed concern that the high rates of imprisonment may have simply postponed the emergence of a more serious problem steeped in our burgeoning prison system. Joan Petersilia (2000) outlined the political, economic, and social consequences of the large number of prisoners who were returning to distressed communities upon release, noting that "the numbers of returning offenders dwarf anything known before, the needs of released inmates are greater, and corrections has retained few rehabilitation programs" (1). In 1999 alone, 600,000 inmates were released from state and federal prisons and secure juvenile facilities across the nation. At about that same time, an estimated 100,000 gang members were incarcerated and gang members were being released at a rate of about 3,000 per month, according to the California Department of Corrections.

It is widely acknowledged that prisons do little to prepare inmates for successful reintegration upon their release. Only a small fraction of those in need of substance abuse treatment receive it while incarcerated (Byrne et al. 1998, cited in Petersilia 2000).[4] Nearly one in five inmates in U.S. prisons suffer from some form of mental illness, and mental health services for prisoners are scant (Ditton 1999, cited in Petersilia 2000).[5] And as many as 60 percent of former inmates fail to find stable employment in the legal labor market within a year after release (Petersilia 2000). Felony records preclude many from gaining decent employment, especially in recessionary times and given persistent discrimination in the labor market against those with a criminal record.

Imprisonment in the absence of programs to expand inmates' abilities to succeed in the legal workforce and to address mental and physical health issues may contribute to the rise of more violent forms of crime. The rising rates of recidivism among ex-offenders and parolees remains an unattended problem. In 1998, more than half of all parolees in the United States were rearrested during the calendar year. The proportion of readmissions as a percentage of all admissions rose from 17 percent in 1980 to 35 percent in 1998 (Beck and Mumola 1999 and Snell 1995, cited in Petersilia 2000). A study published by the U.S. Department of Justice tracking prisoners released from state prisons in 1994 found that more than two-thirds (67.5 percent) of those released were arrested for a new crime within the first three years, nearly half (46.9 percent) were reconvicted for a new crime, and over half (51.8 percent) eventually returned to prison (Langan and Levin 2002).[6] With 95 percent of all state prisoners released by the end of their sentence to their communities, the challenge of re-entry is one of the most critical issues that will affect gang violence and racial tensions (and crime more generally) in the future. With the lack of restorative and rehabilitative programs that could ensure a more successful transition from prison to the workforce, to educational opportunities, or to cognitive and behavioral changes, the rate of recidivism may continue to rise.

In states such as California where prisons and juvenile detention facilities have become breeding grounds for racial and gang conflicts, the high rates of incarceration and recidivism will have even more disastrous long-term consequences if the system is not reformed. The inability of correctional authorities to manage these tensions has led to scores of fatal conflicts. While prisons are operated under the formal supervision of prison administrations and guards, in many facilities leadership networks among prison gangs dictate many of the daily routines, such as the use of phones or physical space, as well as the functioning of markets in the underground drug trade (Montgomery 2005). Competition over territory, both within and beyond prison walls, feeds social conflict. Given the centrality of race in defining gang membership, competition and conflict are highly racialized. Circulation of youths and young adults through the prison system imprints a gang identity that underscores race as a major line of demarcation differentiating ally from enemy. The shortcomings of the prison system, including overcrowding, unchecked misconduct among prison guards, and a lack of proper training, add heat to the pressure cooker of division and enmity.

Researchers have found no clear evidence that imprisonment and harsher sentencing under the mantra of zero tolerance leads to a long-term decrease in crime rates.[7] In fact, many argue that the increasing number of prisoners and the lack of restorative, rehabilitative, or enrichment programs have left former inmates in more desperate straits. Arditti and McClintock (2001) suggest that the war on drugs has likely increased the number and intensity of harms to drug offenders and their families, including at-risk developmental pathways for children, uncertain quality of familial care, family dissolution, and weakened communities. The increased prosecution of adolescents in the adult criminal justice system has also had harmful effects on youths and their families.[8] Mandatory minimum sentences for even small amounts of illegal drugs have also contributed to the increase in women's imprisonment, resulting in the separation of children from their mothers. The transfer of juveniles to adult court and possible incarceration in adult prisons appears to retard rather than promote juvenile offenders' accountability and development of competencies (Redding 1999). Other consequences include physical harm to youths detained in adult facilities, increased stress, and greater marginalization of family members (Schindler and Arditti 2001).

Others add that zero-tolerance policies and high rates of incarceration may actually be exacerbating the crime problem, with unintended consequences such as the recruitment of younger adolescents to replace those arrested, a diminished deterrence effect of incarceration for those with some experience of prison life, and an increase in broken families and social disorder in severely affected communities (Tonry 1995; Clear 1996; Hagan 1996; Moore 1996; Ayers, Dohrn, and Ayers 2002). Zero-tolerance policies in schools have left many youths with slim options to continue to receive a decent education and, in fact, have led to an increase in expulsion rates. By expelling students without providing hopeful alternatives, vulnerable youths are at higher risk of involvement in harmful activities (Verdugo 2002), including gang involvement.

The policies and practices of the zero-tolerance era have had particularly profound consequences on communities of color where incarceration rates are disproportionately high, particularly among African Americans and Latinos. The problem of disproportionate minority confinement has been well documented (Tonry 1995; Hsia and Hamparian 1998; Hamparian and Leiber 1997; Devine, Coolbaugh, and Jenkins 1998; Brownsberger 2000). In 1983, minority youths comprised 53 percent of the detention population (Hsia and

Hamparian 1998). By 1995, minority youths constituted 32 percent of the youth population but 68 percent of the juvenile population in secure detention. At the end of 2002, 10.4 percent of African American males aged 25 to 29 were in prison, compared to 2.4 percent of Hispanic males and 1.2 percent of white male cohorts, with even more under other forms of law enforcement supervision (Harrison and Beck 2004). The level of turmoil caused by both gang violence and the negative effects of high-suppression zero-tolerance policies and practices have weakened the ability of many distressed communities to participate as partners in collaborative problem-solving efforts, especially as urban poverty continues to worsen.

Despite the dangers of maintaining a zero-tolerance approach and the lack of evidence supporting the effectiveness of suppression approaches (Klein 1995; Spergel 1995), many federal agencies and national political leaders maintain their support. At the same time, however, state and local efforts to reform criminal justice policies and practices have grown, across the entire political spectrum. The cost of imprisonment is an added burden to growing budget and trade deficits fueled by the economic recession, tax cuts, increases in entitlement spending, and rising military expenditures, which ballooned with the war on terrorism in the early 2000s. Meanwhile, the cost of alternatives, such as drug treatment for minor substance abuse cases, decreased despite showing greater promise. Reform advocates began to support the view that the drug problem should be considered a health problem rather than strictly as a crime problem, with a growing number of states passing legislation that would redirect drug offenders to treatment programs rather than to prisons.[9]

In the field of law enforcement, there has been a slow but steady shift toward community-based collaborative approaches to reducing youth and gang violence. Scores of specific recommendations have been made about the police, courts, corrections, probation, and parole as well as a range of educational, rehabilitative, and restorative programs.[10] A common theme among reform advocates is the importance of multi-modal collaborative approaches that address the cognitive, behavioral, and physiological needs of youthful offenders, preferably in community settings (Corbett and Petersilia 1994). A forum of criminal justice experts assembled by the Urban Institute in 2000 identified four promising strategies to crime that also pertain to the specific problem of youth violence: (1) capitalizing on community strengths to increase neighborhood resilience to address problems related to crime; (2) coordinating community efforts to analyze crime problems; (3) expanding and improving correctional programs to integrate ex-offenders as contributing members of their communities; and (4) promoting innovations in policing, including community policing, police accountability, and training (Travis and Waul 2002).

Community models for gang intervention have been developed and implemented that stress systematic, comprehensive, collaborative approaches based on shared knowledge of local communities (Spergel et al. 1994; Spergel 1995). And practitioners have experimented with new methods to support offenders in seeking atonement, reconciling severed relationships, regaining self-esteem, redefining one's role in society, and taking advantage of opportunities and privileges that enable individuals to participate as full citizens in all aspects of social, economic, and cultural life. Much of the success of these efforts depends on the ability of programs to learn from its participants' collective experiences, to access the necessary resources and assistance, and to adapt to changing demands and circumstances.

Implications for Planning, Policymaking, and Collaborative Problem-solving

A phenomenon that continues to muffle reasoned deliberation in the search for sound solutions is the revival of moral panics. The projection of gangs and drugs as a major cause of the nation's ills by political figures, lobbies, and the media framed a policy discourse promoting zero-tolerance, highly punitive policies as the favored alternative among decision-makers over the past several decades (McCorkle 2002). Politicians and pundits have exploited the "tough on crime" campaign and the patriotic symbolism that it has gained as a ticket to electoral victory across the nation. According to Tonry (1999), the unprecedented increase in incarceration rates arose partly from American moralism and partly from the structure of an American government vulnerable to moral panics and long-term cycles of tolerance and intolerance. The growing power of prison lobbies continues to influence decision-makers to institute policies that further the perpetuation of the prison system.[11] Moral panics sway public opinion in the service of political and economic agendas that only fuel the pendulum swing between harsh and lenient punishments, with neither extreme providing favorable outcomes.[12] Innovative methods that veer away from zero-tolerance "broken windows" approaches risk being labeled "soft on crime." The tendency to juxtapose approaches in this dichotomous way poses a grave challenge to the fuller consideration of innovative reforms.

Issues of gang violence and criminal justice policy continue to swirl in controversy, as people see and experience those issues from very different vantage points and from competing philosophical foundations. In diverse societies such as the United States, where economic, cultural, social, political, and other differences create "worlds apart," collaborative problem-solving is difficult but critical for a fuller understanding of problems and the formulation of successful solutions. Given wide contrasts in life opportunities and indicators of community and family well-being, people from different walks of life can provide a spectrum of insights at every stage of the planning and policy process—from problem definition and policy or program design to implementation and evaluation. A "360–degree" perspective, while complicated by conflicting viewpoints, offers the most complete picture from which effective solutions can be envisioned and enacted.

Lessons gleaned from the Venice gang war echo the widely acknowledged need for more holistic, re-integrative, community-oriented approaches to address gang violence and racial tensions. Community-based partnerships can help practitioners resist the strong tendency of traditional approaches to overlook the finer distinctions among different segments of the targeted and affected populations. Instead of categorizing whole communities indiscriminately and alienating important constituencies, community-based approaches allow one to peel away at the problem to understand its many layers and intricacies. Instead of treating people as "guilty by association," collaborative partnerships can differentiate distinct segments of the affected population and support various efforts among those wanting to solve the problem. Instead of rushing youths and young adults to the harshest form of punishment, an adequate array of effective programs can lead to long-term change in behavior, outlook, competencies, and opportunities. Instead of such heavy reliance on suppression tactics, which cannot be maintained over a long period of time, multi-modal, community-based solutions can promise greater success and sustainability given adequate assistance and support. And instead of fragmented approaches in which different agencies and organizations work at cross-purposes, community-based collaborations can combine and coordinate efforts based on collectively defined goals and strategies informed by the wisdom of multiple publics.

One of the most critical challenges in the business of "planning for peace" is building genuine partnerships that allow for the differences in vantage points. In racialized conflict, differences often manifest in competing claims of justice and competing definitions of fairness. In the Venice gang war, there was a myriad of justice and injustice claims. These claims and counterclaims were as fractious as the violence itself. Some protested their loss of property value as the violence escalated. Others claimed injustice at their loss of freedom to walk the streets safely. Others filed complaints of police harassment, while some lobbied for the right to adequate police protection. Some believed that penalties for criminal actions were unjustly lenient, while others believed it unjust that young minority males faced such a high degree of discrimination that gang involvement became an attractive option. Those who viewed police as conspiring with developers to grab their property claimed abuse of police powers and violation of their civil rights. Many protested the killing of "innocent" people as one of the greatest injustices of the war. Those who disagreed on one set of justice claims did not necessarily disagree on others. A debilitating problem, however, was that disagreement on one justice claim would often prevent discussion or collaboration around points of potential agreement.

Problems like the one featured in this book fit the description of "intractable conflicts." "Intractable conflicts" are defined, in part, by the inability of individuals to reason together to reach mutually agreeable solutions due to conflicting interests, goals, and perceptions of reality (Frohock 1989; Kriesberg, Northrup, and Thorson 1989). Conflicts become particularly intractable when they involve a core sense of identity (Northrup 1989). They are characterized by different rationalities or systems of thought, a multiplicity of issues, a changing dynamic of conflict, and, frequently, a lack of desire for parties to resolve disagreements through peaceful negotiation. At the same time, it demonstrates the role of "reframing" conflict as one possible means to achieve at least a short-term resolution to an immediate problem.

But if there is anything constructive we can learn from this episode in Venice's history, it is the critical role of collaborative problem-solving at the community and institutional levels with deliberative processes that include viewpoints across the spectrum of actors and stakeholders. An inclusive approach is the one most likely to ensure that any remedy is built on a well-grounded foundation of knowledge and understanding based on multiple standpoints. Equally important is the political will to reconsider traditional assumptions, rethink new approaches, and reallocate resources in order to invest adequately in the health and development of people and communities that have been historically marginalized or disadvantaged. Without the civic engagement of communities and more hopeful but realistic prospects for realizing positive change, the challenges likely remain insurmountable. Improving the role of government as an enabler of collaboratively designed solutions to collectively defined problems is one of the most challenging tasks in the new millennium. The possibilities for communities, agencies, and institutions to engage in fruitful deliberations to shape policies, programs, and practices in order to enact meaningful and effective solutions offer the greatest promise in overcoming the many challenges we have discussed.

The ability to create inclusive settings for a fuller deliberation of policies and practices among multiple publics in the face of intractable conflicts has profound implications for governance in a multicultural plurality. In her appeal for deliberative democracy, Iris Marion Young (2000) writes, "democratic discussion and decision-making is better theorized as a process in which differentiated social groups should attend to the particular situation of others and be willing to work out just solutions to their conflicts and collective problems from across their situated positions" (7). She also urges us to use difference as a resource in democratic deliberation rather than allowing differences to cripple communication (Young 1995). This means tapping into different ways of knowing as well as different life conditions, privileges, and opportunities to gain a better insight into potential pathways. Our ability to see the world and empathize from the standpoint of different groups, resolve problems arising from differentiated positions, and chart a path for the collective well-being of all will determine the meaning of "multiculturalism" in the United States. Like a limited view through a stationary telescope, single-minded approaches to decision-making will fail to identify the entire horizon and see important details of the social landscape from different angles. In an age of waning confidence in civic democracy, the level of inclusion of diverse voices and vantage points in public policy will shape our ability to flourish as a multicultural plurality with a robust civil society or, more modestly, effectively attend to pressing problems such as gang violence and racial tensions.

Notes

Chapter 1. Urban Conflict in Multicultural Cities

1. This development is part of an evolution of racial conflict theory in the United States tracing back to the 1930s. It is difficult to provide a concise, comprehensive historiography of racial conflict theory largely because the scholarly plane is seriously separated by disciplinary canyons (Gittler 1995). Related to this, theoretical works also differ in their units of analyses, including micro-, meso-, and macro-level analyses. There is also a difference in the foci of study, with some of these theories focused on the *causes* of racial conflict while others focus on the dynamic *processes* involved in conflict. See Jennings (1992) for a discussion of contemporary urban racial conflicts in U.S. politics.

2. Martinez, Marilyn, "Deadly Venice Gang War Turns to Race War: Police See Violence in Venice Widening," *Venice-Marina News*, 25 November 1993.

3. Interview with Anonymous #17, 21 June 1995, Los Angeles.

4. Interview with Pearl White, 10 July 1995, Los Angeles.

5. It is useful to note that there is a theoretical tension across the disciplines that mirrors debates between what has been most commonly framed as postmodernism and positivism. While this debate has not always been sharply articulated in theoretical discussions on the topic of racial conflict in the United States, positivist approaches have tended to focus more on the material causes and institutional sources of conflict (Park 1950; Glazer and Moynihan 1963; Blauner 1972; Katznelson 1976; Bonacich 1980; Nagel and Olzak 1982; Oliver and Johnson 1984; Nielson 1985; Olzak and Nagel 1986; and Olzak 1992). Likewise, psychologists have tended to focus on both the cognitive and social psychological processes that contribute to intergroup relations, including racial and ethnic conflict (Tajfel 1982; Brewer 1997; Alexander and Levin 1998; Bettencourt and Bartholow 1998; Dovidio, Maruyama and Alexander 1998; Esses, Jackson, and Armstrong 1998; and Goodwin, Operario, and Fiske 1998). For reviews of psychological theories of intergroup relations, including explanations of conflict, see Tajfel (1982), Turner (1984), Brewer and Kramer (1985), Condor and Brown (1988), and Lakin (1995). Meanwhile, scholars taking poststructuralist approaches have tended to focus on the discursive processes and interpretive dynamics by which intergroup conflicts emerge (Waters 1985; Waters 1992; Saito 1993; Umemoto 1994; Park

1996; Romer et al. 1997; Kim 2000). See also Chang and Leong (1994) and Chang and Diaz-Veizades (1999) for analyses of racial conflict and cooperation in Los Angeles.

6. I refer to the definition of a gang as summarized by Curry and Decker (1998) that covers a fairly permanent group whose members share common symbols, modes of communication such as graffiti, protected turf boundaries, and involvement in criminal activity.

7. Figures released by the Los Angeles County Sheriff's Department. See also Katz (1993). Numbers of gang homicides from 1980 to 1998 accessed at Los Angeles County, Department of Health Services website at http://phps.dhs.co.la.ca.us/ivpp/subjects/intentional/homicide/ganghomi.htm (accessed 28 September 2003). Gang violence continued at high levels into the new millennium in many parts of Los Angeles, such as in the south and south central areas.

8. According to interviews with various police officers and gang intervention workers, reports of interracial gang violence increased in the late 1980s and early 1990s. In Long Beach, for example, Latino gangs found themselves in conflict with Cambodian gangs, while in Pomona, African American and Latino youth gangs battled. See also Umemoto and Mikami (1999).

9. Many have publicly voiced complaints that violence in minority communities has received inadequate government action and has generated disappointing levels of public outcry. The question of why gang violence in exclusively minority communities went on with less attention from government agencies and the media is a legitimate one. This question is only partially answered here and deserves fuller study.

10. Erving Goffman (1974), a pioneer in the development and application of frame analysis, proposed this method in recognition of three concerns: (1) any event can be described in terms that focus on either a wide swath or a narrow one; (2) in most situations, there are many things happening simultaneously; and (3) the retrospective characterization of the "same" event may differ widely.

11. Schön and Rein (1994) have applied the method of frame analysis to understand conflict between parties surrounding several policy controversies and suggest that we study public controversy as frame conflicts. Parties to policy controversies see issues, policies, and policy situations in different and competing ways that embody different systems of belief. They state that frames determine what counts as a fact and how one makes the normative leap from fact to prescriptions for action.

12. Among the fifty-eight people formally interviewed, approximately one-third were women and two-thirds men. Eleven were Latino, twenty-eight were African American, seventeen were European American, and one was Asian American. All were English-speaking and at least nine were bilingual in the Spanish language. Their age ranged from the early twenties to the early seventies. Approximately six fell between the ages of 18 to 29, thirteen age 50 and over, and the remaining were in their thirties and forties. Twenty-six of the fifty-eight were residents of Oakwood or Mar Vista, and at least three lived in HUD-subsidized housing units. Seventeen were parents with children who lived in the neighborhood. Seventeen worked full-time or part-time with a social service agency or school. They included counselors, teen workers, gang prevention workers, educators, child care providers, and community organizers. Sixteen were active members of community-based organizations, including resident organizations, neighborhood watch groups, youth groups, churches, historical associations, and the like. Four were members of the V-13 or the Venice Shoreline Crips. Eighteen worked with government agencies that responded to the outbreak of violence. Of those, thirteen were law enforcement personnel; of those thirteen, seven were officers or former officers with the Los Angeles Police Department.

Chapter 2. Understanding the Morphology of Conflict

1. The formation of racial meanings through political struggle has been the focus of numerous studies (see Dominguez 1986; Carmines and Stimson 1989; Edsall and Edsall 1991; and Omi and Winant 1994).
2. The gradual and incremental process of morphing can sometimes lead to more dramatic changes in the look and character of conflict. Small transformations can lead to more substantial changes in the boundaries of conflict, in the objects under contest, and in identified interests among the stakeholders involved. The momentum of conflict generated by the iterative process involving action and interpretation can lead to periodic leaps in the intensity and scope of conflict as well as to its resolution.
3. Olzak argues that while modernization may have served as a catalyst for ethnic mobilization in non-industrialized nations, in the industrialized United States, it was the breakdown of ethnic inequalities and racially ordered systems that intensified competition and sparked conflict. She cites migration and immigration, economic contraction, dispersion from niches, and increasing prosperity for disadvantaged ethnic groups as four processes instrumental in raising levels of ethnic and racial competition.
4. For reviews of psychological theories of intergroup relations, including explanations of conflict, see Tajfel (1982), Turner (1984), Brewer and Kramer (1985), Condor and Brown (1988), and Lakin (1995).
5. Existing theories tend to have a higher degree of predictability in some countries than in others. Even within a single nation-state, there is variance in the occurrence of conflict across groups, regions, and historical epochs. This would suggest that there are other factors, such as cultural norms, that would cause some groups to avoid conflict and other groups to pursue it. Alternatively, social meanings that can be read into a situation may differ between groups in that same predicament, which would lead to a varied set of responses, including but not necessarily limited to engagement in conflict.
6. Ethnicity does not represent a static category based on a constant of cultural characteristics; rather, it denotes a set of boundaries which are both structurally and socially constructed (Barth 1969; Despres 1975). The variability in the affirmation of ethnic identities, however, is situationally specific (Okamura 1981). For a review of social anthropological literature on "situational ethnicity," see Okamura (1981).
7. Identities have also been described in terms of their "ascribed" or "achieved" status and have been distinguished in terms of "voluntary" or "involuntary" formations of race and ethnicity. See Omi and Winant (1994).
8. For succinct accounts covering racial groups in the United States, see Takaki (1993).
9. Horowitz (1985) argues that rational choice–based competition theories alone cannot explain the types and intensity of ethnic conflict witnessed throughout many parts of the world. Horowitz's observations of ethnic conflict in non-industrialized nations correspond with Tajfel's experimental findings that groups often make decisions that will increase their *relative advantage* over another group, even if such a decision would result in a smaller *net gain* for their group overall. Horowitz posits that ethnic conflict emerges from the politics of group entitlement, which itself is a joint function of competition for a favorable evaluation of their group worth (moral) and struggle for group legitimacy in the realm of the political system. He believes that ethnic ties in many non-industrialized nations fulfill the needs of dependency and intimacy, similar to those filled by kinship ties, particularly in times of stress.
10. This approach to the study of shifting group boundaries recalls E. E. Schattschnei-

der's (1960) comments on shifting political boundaries according to the particular issue at stake. Individuals or groups realign on different sets of axes, depending on the nature of the issue and how it is defined. In the case of multiple publics, they emerge and reemerge along various combinations of identity group boundaries in reference to a defined situation or problem.

11. In defining publics, the question arises as to how one would make a judgment as to what level of salience to apply and how to measure salience. I use the concept not to imply that identity salience is quantitatively measurable but as a conceptual tool to analyze the discourses associated with conflict and to observe intergroup dynamics in social conflicts. Hypothetically, one could define a public based on a shared set of salient identities, only to find that there is differentiation within that public based on a second-tier set of salient identities. And one could then subdivide this group to the point of disintegration. The main utility of this definition of publics is to grasp the epistemic or interpretive lenses that are more closely tied to social identity than to interests or organizations per se. The application of publics as a concept is not formulaic. There may be many "tiers" of salience along which publics can be distinguished. I leave it to the investigator or practitioner to determine which tier or tiers are most useful to understanding the social dynamics at hand.

12. For example, Waters (1992) emphasizes the mode of incorporation into U.S. society (voluntary immigrants or nonvoluntary groups) as a major experiential factor shaping a group's interpretive lens.

13. For example, Waters's (1992) case study of four racially charged incidents of violence in New York City illustrates how racial incidents were interpreted in different ways. Umemoto's (1994) analysis of the news coverage of a shooting death of an African American girl by a Korean merchant in Los Angeles by two ethnic newspapers similarly found that the Korean and African American press revealed very different interpretations of the same events and outcomes. In policy controversies, Shön and Rein (1994) argue for "frame reflective practice" in acknowledgment of divergent interpretive frames through which facts can be selectively weighed, complicating public deliberations and leading to intractable conflicts. See also Anita Waters (1985), who employs this approach in her analysis of symbols and their meanings in a case study of Jamaican electoral politics.

14. Shön and Rein (1994) make it a point to distinguish three levels of specificity of action frames in order of increasing generality and abstraction: policy, institutional, and metacultural frames. First, a policy frame is the frame an institutional actor uses to construct the problem of a specific policy situation. Second, an institutional action frame is the more generic action frame from which institutional actors derive the policy frames they use to structure policy situations, with points of view, prevailing systems of beliefs, category schemes, images, routines, and styles. And third, metacultural frames are broad, culturally shared systems of belief, which are organized around generative metaphors and lie at the root of policy stories that shape both rhetorical and action frames.

15. Encoding and decoding refers to the production and consumption of a message wherein its meanings are overdetermined by a range of influences, including the medium used to communicate the message, the discursive context, and the different technologies used, such as that of "live news" coverage.

16. A Rubik's Cube is a six-sided cube. The cube is divided further into smaller sections, each side having been partitioned into three rows and three columns. In other words, the one single cube is partitioned into 27 smaller cubes (3 rows × 3 columns × 3 deep = 27 cubes). Each side of the whole cube displays nine squares. At its start setting, all

nine squares on any side of the cube are all of the same color. Each *side* of the cube (including its nine smaller squares) features a different color. The color scheme on each side of the cube can be changed with a simple twist at any of the cube's six partitions which dice the cube into its 27 sections (actually 26, as the center of the cube plays no role in the game). At the start of the puzzle, the cube has been randomly twisted and turned so that the nine squares on each side are filled with an array of different colors. The puzzle is solved when all of the nine squares on each side of the cube are returned to their original positions, with each side showing only one color. In order to solve the puzzle, it is necessary to have a view of all sides of the cube prior to each move and to be able to know how a turn of the cube would affect all six sides simultaneously. A quarter-turn might solve one side of the puzzle but represent a setback to another side, if not all of the other sides. One must be able to anticipate the effects of each turn on all of the sides of the cube in order to make progress. A move may cause a setback to some of the sides, but that would cause no alarm if the moves are planned in a sequence that eventually leads to solving all sides of the cube.

17. There is a plethora of literature critiquing liberal democracy in the fields of political science and sociology that speaks to the inequality of power among social groups within each of these realms. Economic class, race, and gender are some of the major variables along which power has historically been differentiated. The "black box" mediating democratic processes within state institutions, the role of money in politics, and the power of the media in cultural production are but a few of the problems addressed in critiques of the liberal state.

18. By government institutions, I include the individual agents, organizational entities, and the structure, rules, and norms that govern their behavior. This is a broad definition of the term *institution* as it has been defined by the literature on "new institutionalism" in political science. See March and Olsen (1984) for a discussion on "new institutionalism" in the roles of institutions in political life.

Chapter 3. The Geography of Multiple Publics in Venice

1. This metaphor was used by scholars at the Centre for Contemporary Cultural Studies in Birmingham as early as the 1970s.

2. Most scholars acknowledge that there are many ways to interpret history. Any historical account is shaped by the types of artifacts, documents, and oral and written accounts that are available and uncovered. It is also shaped by the interpretive lens of the scholar who ties fragments of the past together in a more synthetic narrative. While this chapter does not seek a fuller engagement in the historiographical debate surrounding epistemology and standpoint, it is important to be aware of the biases and limitations of historical recollection. I am not trained as a historian, but I attempt this historical "preface" as a social scientist with an appreciation for the theoretical and practical applications of historical inquiry for understanding how contemporary problems, especially as historical contests, both "material" and "discursive" in form, shape identity and social interpretation.

3. Several movement organizations, such as the August 29th Movement, had called for a Chicano "nation" geographically defined as the territory of Aztlán in their platform of Chicano "self-determination."

4. The U.S. Census listed 33 "Negroes" in 1910 and 102 in 1920.

5. The U.S. Bureau of the Census shows that 3,191 African Americans lived in census tracts 2732 and 2733 out of a total population of 8,228. Opposite to those two tracts

across Lincoln Boulevard, two African Americans were found to live in tracts 2737 and 2738 out of a total population there of 6,027 (1960 Census).

6. See also Fogelson (1967) for a history of political fragmentation in Los Angeles.

7. Interviews and informal discussions with Flora Chavez and Pearl White in fall 1994.

8. Interview with Robert Castile, 4 August 1994, Los Angeles.

9. Figures for median household income and median house value are approximations based on the figures for census tracks 2732 and 2733.

10. Several factors led to the growth of the African American population during the 1960s. One was the Watts uprising in 1965. A number of African American families who could afford to relocate moved to surrounding areas further away from the central city. Venice became one of many destinations for the out-migration of African Americans. Another impetus for population increase was the construction of Interstate Highway 10. The freeway was routed through another minority neighborhood north of Venice. Many were dislocated, some of whom moved to Venice. African Americans found a long-established community, which they joined when they made Venice their home. A rich network of African American social, political, and cultural organizations became concentrated in Oakwood.

11. Los Angeles Police Department officers interviewed by the author estimated the membership of the V-13, the Culver City Boys, and the Venice Shoreline Crips to be approximately 300 each, though they emphasized the difficulty of having an accurate count of members who are active at any given time.

12. See Vigil (2003) for a review of the causes and characteristics of urban gang violence. He presents the two major explanations of gang violence—the "subculture of violence" framework and the "routine activities" theory—and argues that neither alone is sufficient to explain youth participation in gang violence. He suggests a more holistic, interactive model he refers to as a "multiple marginality" approach that includes these concepts but also integrates macro- as well as micro-social processes, especially the street socialization of youths.

Chapter 4. Law Enforcement Policy and the Oakwood Plan

1. Nationally, it was estimated that there were approximately a half million persons who were members of gangs during the early to mid-1990s. Studies of gang membership included the National Assessment of Law Enforcement Anti-Gang Information Resources (Curry et al. 1992) and a later extension of that survey (Curry, Ball, and Decker 1996). Estimates varied somewhat. A few years later Klein (1995) estimated a minimum of 400,000 gang members while the National Youth Gang Center, established by the Office of Juvenile Justice and Delinquency Prevention, estimated over 600,000.

2. Klein (1993) explains that suppression approaches (including heightened surveillance, patrol saturation, area sweeps, special task forces, and targeted concentration of forces) have been developed in the context of four developments: (a) a growing acknowledgment that past treatment/rehabilitation approaches had been unsuccessful; (b) the growth in gang intelligence-gathering sophistication on the part of the police, which has reduced questionable arrests and increased gang detail officer morale; (c) the emergence of gangs in several hundred American cities and their expansion in size and violence in gang hubs such as Los Angeles, which has created pressures resulting in the legitimization of suppression approaches; and (d) supplemental anti-narcotics tactics (including "buy-busts," reverse stings, multi-jurisdictional task forces,

civil abatement procedures, and technical hardware developed for fast entry into crack houses) inspired by real and purported gang involvement in drug distribution. Some of the components of high suppression stem from federal legislation such as the RICO law and the 1993 Crime Bill. The RICO statutes increase enforcement of laws against interstate trafficking of illegal drugs and stolen goods. The RICO statutes have been used to prosecute gangs as criminal organizations and convict them on felony counts that require incarceration in federal prison for longer sentencing periods. The Crime Bill expands the death penalty to 52 additional offenses and includes the controversial "three strikes" provision which provides mandatory sentences of 25 years to life for the third felony. There are also several provisions aimed specifically at gang-related crime. One provision makes membership in certain types of gangs a criminal offense. Street crimes involving firearms are also considered a federal offense.

3. Klein (1993) outlined specific programs established in Los Angeles. They were:

   1. LAPD's Community Resources Against Street Hoodlums (CRASH) and Los Angeles Sheriff's Department LASD Operation Safe Streets (OSS)—The police and sheriff departments each have special officers who work in gang patrol units throughout the city and county respectively. CRASH stresses high visibility surveillance and suppression activities and conducting follow-up investigations of gang-related arrests. OSS places more emphasis on intelligence gathering and maintains a county-wide gang database.

   2. *Gang sweeps*—Operation Hammer is the most well known of the types of gang sweeps conducted by the LAPD. Most often conducted in the South Bureau (covering the South-Central area of Los Angeles), between 200 to 2,000 officers crack down in a particular area, with a typical sweep resulting in several hundred arrests for violations ranging from misdemeanors to more serious crimes.

   3. *Operation Hardcore*—The Hardcore Gang Unit of the District Attorney's office supervises a vertical prosecution program aimed at gang leaders and homicide suspects. Hardcore Deputy District Attorneys seek high conviction rates and maximum sentences for suspects identified as members of gangs.

   4. *Specialized probation and parole programs*—The Los Angeles County Probation Department and the California Youth Authority assign gang-identified probationers and parolees to specialized officers with reduced caseloads to allow for closer supervision.

   5. *Street Terrorism Enforcement Program* (STEP)—Enabled by the California state legislature, the STEP Act allows for more severe punishments for suspected gang members, on the condition that they be given formal notice of their suspected affiliation.

   6. *Civil gang abatement*—Civil statutes, including building codes, zoning rules, nuisance laws and rules of assembly are used by the Office of the City Attorney to harass and discourage gang and drug activity operating out of specific locations within city limits.

   7. *School-centered suppression programs*—In addition to prevention and education programs, the LAPD in conjunction with the Los Angeles Unified School District conducts regular undercover drug buys on campuses. Schools are also employing stricter expulsion policies, closed campuses, metal detectors, and armed security guards.

4. Interview with former Pacific Division Captain Janice L. Carlson, 16 June 1995, Los Angeles.

5. The 1993 update was written under the leadership of Captain Richard Legarra, who had been assigned commanding officer of the Pacific division earlier that year.

6. It is important to note that there was a change in leadership in the LAPD, which meant a gradual shift in approach during the period of the gang war. This change took place at the level of chief of the entire LAPD and of the commanding officer at the Pacific Division. However, the dominant approach through most of its duration was shaped by the Oakwood Plan. The LAPD is organized under various geographic divisions, such as the South Bureau, Wilshire Division, Hollywood, Downtown, Hollenbeck, and the Pacific Division. Each division has its own commanding officer, detectives, supporting officers, patrol supervisors, and beat patrol. Many have specialized units within the division focusing on narcotics, vice, gang-related crime, and so on. In the Pacific Division, which patrols the west Los Angeles area that includes Venice, there has been a special task force called the Oakwood Task Force within the division. Under the command of Captain Jan Carlson, the Pacific Division developed the Oakwood Plan, which was written and implemented in 1989. This provided a blueprint for LAPD policing practices in Oakwood until the outbreak of the gang war in 1993. Around the time the war began, Captain Carlson left the force and was replaced by Captain Richard Legarra, who worked to modify the policy used in Oakwood toward a more community-oriented approach. The new captain instituted an "Oakwood Safety Plan." This adjustment in approach took place over the duration of the war and was not fully implemented until the war was almost over. For some of the senior patrol officers in the Oakwood Task Force, there was little change in policing practices between the Carlson and Legarra periods. For other officers, it meant a shift in their approach toward greater community involvement with local residents.

7. For example, the Omnibus Crime Control and Safe Streets Act of 1968 and the Organized Crime Control Act of 1970 expanded law enforcement privileges and powers while weakening the legal rights of the accused previously granted in Supreme Court decisions. These decisions included *Miranda v. Arizona* (1966), which granted the right to remain silent outside of the presence of an attorney, and *Gideon v. Wainwright* (1963), which granted the right to legal counsel.

8. It authorized $8.9 billion to hire 100,000 police officers, $9.7 billion for prisons, and $6.1 billion for prevention programs (U.S. Department of Justice 1994). This increase in expenditures followed an already fivefold increase between 1972 and 1988 (Chambliss 1995). Federal and state expenditures increased between 1972 and 1988 from approximately $1.5 million to over $7 million and from approximately $3 million to $21.5 million, respectively. This increase is not adjusted for inflation (U.S. Department of Justice 1984, 1988, 1992a).

9. Incarceration rates steadily increased throughout the 1990s; by 1999, the number of sentenced inmates under state and federal jurisdiction was 476 prisoners per 100,000 population (U.S. Department of Justice 2004a).

10. In 1980, 1,842,100 persons were under correctional supervision in the United States, including 319,598 in prison. By 1994, this figure had increased to 5,148,100, including 990,147 in prison. The prison population increased almost threefold in only fourteen years.

11. By 1994, 8.9 percent of the African American adult population was under some form of correctional supervision, compared to 1.9 percent of the White population and 0.8 percent of others (U.S. Department of Justice 2004c). The incarceration rate among African Americans in U.S. jails was over 6.7 times that of non-Hispanic whites. And the incarceration rate among Hispanics was 2.8 times that of non-Hispanic whites while less than half that of African Americans (U.S. Department of Justice 2004d).

12. Various newspapers in California reported on incidents of violence in California correctional facilities. See, for example, Morain (1996).

13. In 2005, the Supreme Court ruled in *Johnson v. California* that that the state must end the practice of segregating prisoners by race, but this only happened after more than two decades of the unwritten policy and without other alternatives to address racial conflicts in the prisons.

14. The term was first coined by Stan Cohen and applied by Stuart Hall to explain the change in attitudes and political mood that swept British society in the 1960s. Hall argued that it was moral panic that characterized the response to a British mugging incident. While much was made of this one incident in the early 1970s, it was discussed in public forums as representative of a breakdown in the traditional norms and values of England. The incident was thematically framed within the context of the growing urban crisis, rising crime, the breakdown of law and order, the liberal conspiracy, the white backlash, and racial violence, and it was embellished by the mass media, politicians, and political pundits. Muggings became known as a "black" crime and associated with problems of immigration and the welfare state.

15. During the 1980s and early 1990s, the incarceration rates had risen, but this did not necessarily indicate an increase in criminal activity. Bogess and Bound (1993) found that the increase was mainly due to an increase in the rate of incarceration per arrest. Though many gained the impression from media reports that the increase in violent crime was perpetrated by racial minority males, the percentage of African Americans arrested for violent crimes during that period actually decreased slightly, from 47.5 percent to 44.8 percent, while the proportion of whites arrested for those same crimes increased slightly, from 50.4 percent to 53.6 percent (Torny 1995).

16. This figure is for those homicides in which the race of both victim and perpetrator were known (Hutson et al. 1995).

17. Prepared statement of Daniel M. Hartnett, Associate Director, Bureau of Alcohol, Tobacco, and Firearms. See U.S. House of Representatives (1992), 5.

18. Ibid., 43.

19. Ibid., 6.

20. Howell and Decker (1999) provide a succinct review of the literature on the connections linking youth gangs, drugs, and violence.

21. Researchers have differed in their assessments of the degree to which gangs are involved in organized drug distribution. Some describe gangs as relatively disciplined entrepreneurial organizations, while others observe weakly organized groups lacking the stability and organization to sustain major drug distribution operations. See, for example, Sanchez-Jankowski (1991) and Klein, Maxson, and Cunningham (1991).

22. They qualify this finding by noting that though law enforcement agencies reported only 9 percent of gangs as drug gangs by their definition, the actual size of those drug gangs was unknown.

23. There is a rich literature on the causes and characteristics of gang formation. Spergel and Curry (1993) categorize perceived causes, at least among surveyed practitioners, into four categories: (1) social system problems such as poverty and demographic change, (2) the failure of institutions such as families and schools, (3) individual or peer-level problems including substance abuse and psychological trauma, and (4) the effects of responses to gangs, such as by police, social service providers, or the media.

24. See Taylor (1990). He presents an evolutionary typology of gangs that progress from "scavenger" to "territorial" to "corporate." Corporatized gangs have developed into more organized entities that oversee legal and, more commonly, illegal economic activities.

25. The original Oakwood Plan written in 1989 was in operation prior to the outbreak of the conflict and in 1994 was revised and retitled, "Oakwood Community Safety Plan."

26. Interview with Michael Genelin, Office of the L.A. District Attorney, 1 June 1995, Los Angeles.
27. Los Angeles Police Department (1994).
28. Los Angeles Police Department (n.d.).
29. Listings included the Venice 13 (V-13), the Culver City Boys (CXC), the Sotels (S-13), La Via (VIA), and the West Side Locos (WSL), which were largely Latino in composition, and the Suicidal Tendencies, the Pozers, the Sex Jerks, and the King of Dukes, which were described as mixed-race gangs.
30. See Wilson and Kelling (1982) for a full explanation of the broken windows thesis.
31. Interview with LAPD Detective K.R., 21 November 1994, Los Angeles.
32. Smith, Black, and Campbell (1979) found that the juvenile justice system in the United States had 25 system functions (e.g., police station intake), 121 alternative decision choices (e.g., counsel and release), and 22 termination processes. A system chart of the L.A. County Probation Department alone revealed a total of 138 decision points. Stapleton and Needle (1982) noted that the variation in flow of clients into and through different decision points is related to officers' contrasting philosophical perspectives on justice (criminal responsibility vs. individual liberties).
33. Klein (1993) reviews the research on deterrence and concludes that conflicting results have been the hallmark of research. Several studies went against the deterrent hypothesis and a larger group of studies yielded no support for or no disproof of hypotheses, while another group claimed clear evidence in support of deterrence propositions.
34. Prepared statement of Daniel M. Hartnett, Associate Director, Bureau of Alcohol, Tobacco, and Firearms. See U.S. House of Representatives (1992), 5.
35. Gates and Jackson (1990), 20.
36. Ibid., 9 (emphasis in original).
37. Ibid., 34.
38. Interview with LAPD Detective K.R., 21 November 1994, Los Angeles.
39. Los Angeles Police Department (1990?).
40. A similar type of investigation of the Los Angeles Sheriff's Department (LASD) was conducted and produced the Kolt Report in 1992.
41. The New York Draft Riots in 1863 that began in protest of President Abraham Lincoln's conscription policy are considered by some to be the most serious civil unrest in U.S. history, with over 50,000 participants, at least 100 killed, more than 300 more injured, and $1.5 million in damages in riots lasting four days. Many African Americans were mobbed in violent attacks.
42. Independent Commission on the Los Angeles Police Department (1991), xix.
43. Ibid., 34.
44. Ibid., 69.
45. Mitchell, John L., "Officer-involved Shootings at 10–year High," The Los Angeles Times, 28 January 1993, B1, B4.
46. Interview with anonymous, 13 August 1994, Los Angeles, California.
47. Ibid.
48. Ibid.
49. Ibid.
50. Serrano (1992), A-1.
51. Ibid.
52. There is no consensus on the degree to which racial or ethnic bias explains the disproportionate representation of minority youths in the juvenile justice system.

Bridges, DeBurle, and Dutton (1991) reviewed 37 studies of racial difference in the juvenile courts and found that 14 studies observed no significant difference in the processing of youths by racial or ethnic group categories, while 23 studies reported significant differences. Separate studies by Blumstein (1982, 1993) and Langan (1991) concluded that much of the disproportionate rates of incarceration of African Americans can be explained by differential arrest patterns. Blumstein concludes that 80 percent of African American "overrepresentation" in prison can be explained by the differential arrest rates between racial groups. However, differential arrest rates do not fully explain the disproportionate incarceration rates. The aggregation of data hides more specific explanations. For example, it does not allow for the examination of sentencing differentials for black-on-white, white-on-white, white-on-black or black-on-black crimes (Torny 1995). In addition, Blumstein concludes that only half of the racial disproportionality in incarceration rates for drug offenses is not explained by higher arrest rates (Mauer and Huling 1995).

53. The Sentencing Project report warns that the data for Hispanics are "somewhat unreliable and should be interpreted with caution" due to the absence of data on ethnicity for California and Texas (Mauer and Huling 1995).

54. Rate based on a single-day count of juveniles held in California public facilities for delinquency offenses. See Office of Juvenile Justice and Delinquency Prevention (1991).

55. Austin (1995) compiled data from the U.S. Department of Justice (1989a) and the Office of Juvenile Justice and Delinquency Prevention (1991) to show that between 1985 to 1989, the number of children aged 10 to 17 in custody in California public juvenile facilities increased among African Americans (47.9 percent increase), Latinos (38.3 percent increase), and Asian Americans (192.7 percent increase), while the number decreased among whites (9.9 percent decline) and American Indians (12.6 percent decline). African American, Latino, and Asian American rates of youth custody were quickly rising during the late 1980s, with Asian American custody rising at the fastest rate.

56. The 1990 National Institute on Drug Abuse (NIDA) national household survey on drug abuse showed that self-reported drug use among blacks and whites were, respectively, 10 percent and 11.7 percent who ever used cocaine, 1.7 and 0.7 percent who ever used heroin, 31.7 and 34.2 who ever used marijuana, 3.0 and 9.7 percent who ever used hallucinogens and 76.6 and 85.2 percent who ever consumed alcohol (National Institute on Drug Abuse 1991).

57. Hatsukami and Fischman (1996) concluded that the physiological and psychoactive effects of cocaine are similar regardless of whether the substance is in the form of cocaine hydrochloride or crack cocaine.

58. On 14 June 1995, the Los Angeles Times reported the release of a California Department of Education report on dropout statistics that included rates for the Los Angeles Unified School District, where 18,500 students in grades 9 through 12 left school without graduating or enrolling in school elsewhere. See Colvin (1995).

59. Haggedorn (1998) and Huff (1989, 1990) note that oftentimes cities tend to move from denial to overreaction, both equally dangerous approaches to crime and its prevention.

60. Thomas (1992) argues that within the cycle of policy shifts, "delinquents" are defined as a subgroup within some larger problem group (e.g., paupers, neglected children). Ideas that "sell" in reform movements focus on the behaviors of the larger problem group and attempt to change their behavior, avoiding economic or structural issues

which may harm the rich and powerful. Reformers make unfair comparisons to past practices with an optimistic assessment of the new reform promising to "solve" the problem of delinquency.

Chapter 5. Racialization of a Gang War

1. The County of Los Angeles Commission on Human Relations was the main county agency that allocated personnel to work with communities that experienced racialized gang conflict and maintained documentation of this problem, particularly in cases involving gang-related incidents classified as hate crimes. See also Umemoto (1999).
2. Interview with Anonymous #23, 13 April 1995, Los Angeles.
3. Panelist Dr. Lorenzo Merritt as broadcast on KCRW public radio program in Santa Monica, "Which Way L.A?" hosted by Warren Olney, 15 February 1994.
4. Interview with Pearl White, 10 July 1995, Los Angeles.
5. Interviews with Anonymous #2, 22 September 1994 and 10 August 1995, Los Angeles.
6. Interview with Anonymous #29, December 1995, Los Angeles.
7. Ibid.
8. Interview with Anonymous #2, 22 September 1994 and 10 August 1995, Los Angeles.
9. Interview with Anonymous #14, n.d., Los Angeles.
10. Interview with Anonymous #23, 13 April 1995, Los Angeles.
11. Interview with Anonymous #29, December 1995, Los Angeles.
12. Interview with Anonymous #14, n.d., Los Angeles.
13. Interview with Anonymous #29, December 1995, Los Angeles.
14. Interview with Anonymous #15, 21 December 1995, Los Angeles.
15. Interview with Anonymous #23, 13 April 1995, Los Angeles.
16. The Copely newspapers that ran the *Outlook* distributed a free weekly paper under the bannerhead *Venice-Marina News* that reprinted many *Outlook* articles. *The Outlook* was subsequently the major local bearer of gang war coverage and strongly influenced perceptions of residents on the westside.
17. Based on public statements by Gene Weeks, founder of Positive Alternatives Choices Today (PACT). While in operation, PACT solicited subscriptions in the Venice area for *The Outlook* newspaper by involving youths in door-to-door sales with adults as part of their youth economic development program.
18. Marilyn Martinez, "Deadly Venice Gang War Turns to Race War," *Venice-Marina News,* 25 November 1993, A-1, reprinted from *The Outlook.*
19. Ibid.
20. It is important to note that the *Los Angeles Times,* however, did not give the events the intensive daily coverage that *The Outlook* provided.
21. Interview with Anonymous #17, 21 June 1995, Los Angeles.
22. Interview with Anonymous #23, 13 April 1995, Los Angeles.
23. Ibid.
24. *Veteranos* and OGs refer to the veteran gang members or "original" gang members who were often sought for advice among the younger set. Some were less active or non-active in gang activities.
25. Interview with Anonymous #17, 21 June 1995, Los Angeles.
26. Interview with Anonymous #31, 22 September 1995.
27. Interview with Anonymous #17, 21 June 1995, Los Angeles.
28. Ibid.
29. Interview with Anonymous #25, 29 June 1995, Los Angeles.

30. Interview with Anonymous #3 with family, 27 June 1994, Los Angeles.
31. Interview with Jimmy Powell, 30 October 1995, Los Angeles.
32. Ibid.
33. Interview with Anonymous #15 and 16, 21 December 1995, Los Angeles. While this may have been agreed upon and respected by the older gang members, it is important to note that not all of the younger set shared these same bonds.

Chapter 6. Firefighters: Suppression from Without

1. These terms are my own and were not those used by law enforcement officials or in any public discourse, as far as I know.
2. Interview with Michael Genelin, Office of the District Attorney, 1 June 1995, Los Angeles.
3. Interview with Councilwoman Ruth Galanter, n.d., Los Angeles.
4. Information regarding agency strategies was obtained from interviews with the following agency representatives: Michael Genelin, Los Angeles County, Office of the District Attorney, 1 June 1995, Los Angeles; Commander Richard Legarra, Los Angeles Police Department (Captain of the Pacific Division at the time), 10 May 1995, Los Angeles; Jule Bishop and Martin Vranicar Jr., Office of the City Attorney, 5 July 1995, Los Angeles; Lt. John Weaver and Det. Kevin Rogers, Los Angeles Police Department, Operations West Bureau CRASH, 21 November 1994, Los Angeles; Brad Carson, Office of Probation, Los Angeles County, 26 June 1995, Los Angeles; Councilwoman Ruth Galanter, n.d., Los Angeles.
5. Los Angeles Police Department, *The Oakwood Plan* (1989), 13.
6. There was some discrepancy regarding response time, as residents interviewed noted a delay in dispatching.
7. Interview with Lt. John Weaver and Det. Kevin Rogers, LAPD CRASH Unit, 21 November 1994, Los Angeles.
8. Los Angeles County Superior Court, mimeograph, 21 October 1993.
9. Los Angeles Police Department, mimeograph, n.d.
10. Interview with Anonymous #18, n.d., Los Angeles.
11. Ibid.
12. Interview with Anonymous #2, 22 September 1994, Los Angeles.
13. Interview with Lt. John Weaver and Det. Kevin Rogers, LAPD CRASH Unit, 21 November 1994, Los Angeles.
14. Interview with Michael Genelin, Office of the District Attorney, 1 June 1995, Los Angeles.
15. Ibid.
16. Interview with Anonymous #14, n.d., Los Angeles
17. Interview with Anonymous #15 and #16, 21 December 1995, Los Angeles.
18. Interview with Anonymous #29, December 1995, Los Angeles.
19. Operations-West Bureau CRASH, "Gang-Related Crimes Investigated by OWB CRASH," mimeograph, 22 November 1994.
20. Ibid.
21. Ibid.
22. Interview with Anonymous #32, n.d., Los Angeles.
23. See Shaw (1992), A-1.
24. Interview with Anonymous #18, n.d., Los Angeles.
25. Interview with Anonymous #33, 4 August and 15 September 1994, Los Angeles.

26. Interview with Lt. John Weaver, LAPD Operations West Bureau CRASH, 21 November 1994.
27. Interview with Lt. John Weaver and Det. Kevin Rogers, LAPD Operations West Bureau CRASH, 21 November 1994, Los Angeles.
28. Interview with Anonymous #10, n.d., Los Angeles
29. Interview with Anonymous #17, 21 June 1995, Los Angeles.
30. Interview with Anonymous #24, 30 October 1995, Los Angeles.
31. Interview with Officer Bill Snowden, 24 October 1995, Los Angeles.
32. Ibid.

Chapter 7. Mediators: Negotiation from Within

1. Interview with Anonymous #34, 23 June 1995, Los Angeles.
2. Interview with Anonymous #21, 8 June 1994, Los Angeles.
3. Interview with Pastor Marvis Davis, 12 and 27 October 1994, Los Angeles.
4. Interview with Anonymous #17, 21 June 1995, Los Angeles.
5. Interview with Darryl Goode, 14 November 1994, Santa Monica.
6. Interview with Dermont Givens, 13 December 1995, Los Angeles.
7. There were several databases that maintained names and information on individuals identified by law enforcement agencies as belonging to a street or prison gang. Locally, a database was maintained by the L.A. County Sheriff's Department. Nationally, a database called GREAT compiled information from local agencies for nationwide tracking of individuals and their activities.
8. Ibid.
9. Interview with Councilwoman Ruth Galanter, 21 December 1995, Los Angeles.
10. Interview with Brad Carson, 26 June 1995, Los Angeles.
11. Interview with Michael Genelin, 1 June 1995, Los Angeles.
12. Interview with Brad Carson, 26 June 1995, Los Angeles.
13. Ibid.
14. Interview with Anonymous #14, n.d., Los Angeles.
15. Interview with Anonymous #29, December 1995, Los Angeles.
16. Interview with Anonymous #16, 21 December 1995, Los Angeles.
17. Interview with Anonymous #2, 22 September 1994 and 10 August 1995, Los Angeles.
18. The degree to which the idea of this "history community" was inclusive of other low-income residents across racial boundaries, however, was uneven among individual members of the Shoreline.
19. Interview with Anonymous #29, December 1995, Los Angeles.
20. Ibid.
21. Ibid.
22. Interview with Anonymous #18, n.d., Los Angeles.
23. Interview with Anonymous #16, 21 December 1995, Los Angeles.
24. Truce considerations with the Culver City Boys were saved for a later time, which had not materialized as of this writing.
25. Interview with Brad Carson, 26 June 1995, Los Angeles.
26. Ibid.
27. Ibid.
28. Ibid.
29. Interview with Anonymous #29, December 1995, Los Angeles.

30. Interview with Anonymous #16, 21 December 1995, Los Angeles.
31. Ibid.
32. Interview with Anonymous #29, December 1995, Los Angeles.
33. Lt. John Weaver and Det. Kevin Rogers, Los Angeles Police Department, Operations West Bureau CRASH, 21 November 1994, Los Angeles.

Chapter 8. Transforming Racial Conflict

1. Increases in homicides in 2000–2001 occurred in Phoenix (38 percent), Houston (16 percent), Los Angeles (7 percent), Chicago (6 percent) and Dallas (4 percent).
2. In Los Angeles, the increase in violent gang-related crime took place when a demoralized LAPD force was seen as retreating in the face of further scandals involving the old gang units, or CRASH, as described in chapter 3. These units were dissolved by Chief Bernard Parks in 2000 and replaced by new units under more limited rules of engagement.
3. According to the Office of Juvenile Justice and Delinquency Prevention Annual Report issued by the U.S. Department of Justice, the number of juveniles held in public detention centers on any given day increased 74 percent between 1985 and 1995. This represents a 20 percent rise in juvenile arrest rates during that ten-year period (Office of Juvenile Justice and Delinquency Prevention 1998). In 1997, California had 498 delinquent offenders per 100,000 juveniles, while half of the states had rates that were less than 209 per 100,000 (Office of Juvenile Justice and Delinquency Prevention 2000b).
4. A 1998 Office of National Drug Control Policy report showed that 70 to 85 percent of state prisoners needed substance abuse treatment, but only 13 percent received it while incarcerated.
5. A 1999 U.S. Department of Justice report on Mental Health and Treatment of Inmates and Probationers showed that nearly one in five inmates in U.S. prisons reported having a mental illness.
6. The 272,111 offenders tracked had accumulated 4.1 million arrest charges before their most recent imprisonment and another 744,000 charges within three years of release. Langan and Levin warn that recidivism rates based on state and FBI criminal history repositories understate actual levels of recidivism due to the failure of police agencies, courts, and administrative staff to notify or record cases to the state or FBI repository.
7. One of the most recent studies by DeFina and Arvanites (2002) was consistent with prior studies using fixed-effects models revealing that imprisonment rates were not significantly related to crime in the majority of states. Skiba and Peterson (2000) also note that there is no clear evidence that zero-tolerance policies and procedures in schools increase school safety or improve student behavior.
8. The number of juvenile cases waived to criminal court rose 71 percent between 1985 and 1994 (Sickmund 1997).
9. Voters in Arizona and California, for example, passed resolutions redirecting thousands of drug offenders into treatment programs rather than prisons. Michigan, Connecticut, and North Dakota repealed mandatory-minimum sentences for minor drug possession offenses. Indiana and Louisiana repealed some of their statutory sentences. California, Washington, Oregon, Hawai'i, Alaska, and Nevada have legalized the use of marijuana for medical purposes. And while programs like needle exchange remain

controversial, many states have supported them after harm-reduction approaches proved effective in slowing the spread of hepatitis C and HIV as well as reaching drug users in need of treatment programs.

10. For reviews of effective programs focused on youth gangs and illegal gang behavior, see Spergel (1995), Klein (1995), and Howell (2000). See also Braga, Kennedy, and Tita (2002) and Thornberry et al. (2003) on gang violence and delinquency prevention; Catalano, Loeber, and McKinney (1999) on school and community interventions; Coolbaugh and Hansel (2000) on comprehensive strategies for serious, violent, and chronic juvenile offenders; Skiba and Peterson (2000) on school disciplinary procedures to reduce violence; Haft (2000) on the use of restorative justice approaches in schools; and Wasserman, Miller, and Cothern (2000) on the prevention of violent offending among youths.

11. Researchers have also found that prison capacity may influence incarceration levels (Dalessio and Stolzenberg 1995, 1997). As prison construction has also reached an unprecedented rate of increase, the additional capacity may have contributed to increased rates of incarceration. The rise of the prison industry has created a very powerful lobby in states like California and Texas that promotes its continued growth and expansion, thereby contributing to the continuing rise in imprisonment.

12. In December 2002, Los Angeles City officials led by Mayor James K. Hahn and LAPD Chief William Bratton once again declared their commitment to the "war on gangs," with Bratton referring to gang activity as "homeland terrorism" (Garvey and Winton, 2002). While they also acknowledged the need for community-oriented approaches, this type of political rhetoric serves to widen the gap between the research-based recommendations concerning gang-related problems and public sentiment informed by fear and ill-advised symbolism.

References

Adler, Patricia. 1969. *A History of the Venice Area: A Part of the Venice Community Plan Study.* Los Angeles: Department of City Planning.

Agnew, John. 1989. "Beyond Reason: Spatial and Temporal Sources of Ethnic Conflicts." In *Intractable Conflicts and Their Transformation*, ed. Louis Kriesberg, Terrell Northrup, and Stuart Thorson. Syracuse, NY: Syracuse University Press.

Akerlof, George, and Janet L. Yellen. 1994. "Gang Behavior, Law Enforcement, and Community Values." In *Values and Public Policy*, ed. Henry J. Aaron, Thomas E. Mann, and Timothy Taylor. Washington, D.C.: Brookings Institution Press, 173–209.

Alexander, Michele G., and Shana Levin. 1998. "Theoretical, Empirical, and Practical Approaches to Intergroup Conflict." *Journal of Social Issues* 54 (4): 629–39.

Anderson, Elijah. 1990. *Streetwise: Race, Class, and Change in an Urban Community.* Chicago: University of Chicago Press.

Arditti, J. A., and C. McClintock. 2001. "Drug Policy and Families: Casualties of the War." *Marriage and Family Review* 32 (3–4): 11–32.

Austin, James. 1995. "The Overrepresentation of Minority Youths in the California Juvenile Justice System: Perceptions and Realities." In *Minorities in Juvenile Justice*, ed. Kimberly Leonard, Carl Pope, and William Feyerherm. Newbury Park, CA: Sage Publications.

Ayers, William, Bernadine Dohrn, and Rick Ayers. 2002. *Zero Tolerance: Resisting the Drive for Punishment in Our Schools.* New York: New Press.

Baran, Paul A., and Paul M. Sweezy. 1966. *Monopoly Capital: An Essay on the American Economic and Social Order.* New York: Monthly Review Press.

Barth, Fredrik. 1956. "Ecological Relations of Ethnic Groups in Swat, North Pakistan." *American Anthropologist* 58: 1079–89.

———. 1969. *Ethnic Groups and Boundaries: The Social Organization of Culture Difference.* Oslo: Universitetsforlaget.

Beck, Allen, and Christopher Mumola. 1999. "Prisoners in 1998." Bulletin. Washington, D.C.: U.S. Department of Justice, Bureau of Justice Statistics. *NCJ* 175687:12.

Bennett, T., and Janet Woollacott. 1987. *Bond and Beyond: The Political Career of a Popular Hero.* New York: Methuen.

Benson, E. J., and D. I. Perrett. 1993. "Extracting Prototypical Facial Images from Exemplars." *Perception* 22: 257–62.

Bettencourt, B. Ann, and Bruce D. Bartholow. 1998. "The Importance of Status Legitimacy for Intergroup Attitudes among Numerical Minorities." *Journal of Social Issues* 54 (4): 759–75.

Blauner, Robert. 1972. *Racial Oppression in America*. New York: Harper and Row.

——. 1992. "Talking Past Each Other." *American Prospect* 3 (10): 55–64.

Block, C.R., A. Christakos, A. Jacob, and R. Przybylski. 1996. *Street Gangs and Crime: Patterns and Trends in Chicago*. Research Bulletin. Chicago: Illinois Criminal Justice Information Authority.

Blumer, Herbert. 1969. *Symbolic Interactionism: Perspective and Method*. Englewood Cliffs, NJ: Prentice-Hall.

Blumstein, Alfred. 1982. "On the Racial Disproportionality of United States' Prison Populations." *Journal of Criminal Law and Criminology* 73: 1259–81.

——. 1993. "Racial Disproportionality of U.S. Prison Populations Revisited." *University of Colorado Law Review* 64: 743–60.

Blumstein, Alfred, and Joel Wallman. 2000. *The Crime Drop in America*. New York: Cambridge University Press.

Bogess, Scott, and John Bound. 1993. "Did Criminal Activities Increase during the 1980s? Comparisons across Data Sources." Research Report No. 93–280. Ann Arbor, MI: Population Studies Center.

Bollens, Scott A. 1998. "Urban Policy in Ethnically Polarized Societies." *International Political Science Review* 19 (2): 187–215.

Bonacich, Edna. 1980. "Class Approaches to Ethnicity and Race." *Insurgent Sociologist* 10 (2): 9–23.

Braga, Anthony A., David M. Kennedy, and George E. Tita. 2002. *Gangs in America III*. Thousand Oaks, CA and London: Sage Publications.

Brewer, Marilyn B. 1997. "The Social Psychology of Intergroup Relations: Can Research Inform Practice?" *Journal of Social Issues* 53: 197–211.

Brewer, Marilyn B., and Roderick M. Kramer. 1985. "The Psychology of Intergroup Attitudes and Behavior." *Annual Review of Psychology* 36: 219–43.

Bridges, G. S., L. DeBurle, and T. Dutton. 1991. *Treatment of Minority Youth in the Juvenile Justice System*. Unpublished manuscript. University of Washington, Department of Sociology.

Brownsberger, W. N. 2000. "Race Matters: Disproportionality of Incarceration for Drug Dealing in Massachusetts." *Journal of Drug Issues* 30 (2): 345–74.

Butterfield, Fox. 1995. "Political Gains by Prison Guards." *The New York Times,* 7 November.

Butts, Jeffrey, and Jeremy Travis. 2002. *The Rise and Fall of American Youth Violence: 1980–2000*. Research Report. Washington, D.C.: Urban Institute, Justice Policy Center.

Byrne, Candice, Jonathan Faley, Lesley Flaim, Francisco Piuol, and Jill Schmidtlein. 1998. *Drug Treatment in the Criminal Justice System*. Washington, D.C.: Executive Office of the President, Office of National Drug Control Policy, *NCJ* 170012.

California Council on Criminal Justice. 1989. *State Task Force on Gangs and Drugs*. Sacramento, California.

Carmines, Edward G., and James A. Stimson. 1989. *Issue Evolution: Race and the Transformation of American Politics*. Princeton: Princeton University Press.

Catalano, R. F., R. Loeber, and K. C. McKinney. 1999. *School and Community Interventions To Prevent Serious and Violent Offending*. Bulletin. Washington, D.C.: U.S. Department of Justice, Office of Justice Programs, Office of Juvenile Justice and Delinquency Prevention.

Chambliss, William J. 1995 "Crime Control and Ethnic Minorities: Legitimizing Racial Oppression by Creating Moral Panics." In *Ethnicity, Race, and Crime: Perspectives Across Time and Place,* ed. Darnell F. Hawkins. New York: State University of New York Press.

Chang, Edward T., and Russell C. Leong, eds. 1994. *Los Angeles—Struggles toward Multi-*

ethnic Community: Asian American, African American, and Latino Perspectives. Seattle: University of Washington Press.

Chang, Edward T., and Jeannette Diaz-Veizades. 1999. *Ethnic Peace in the American City: Building Community in Los Angeles and Beyond*. New York: New York University Press.

Chin, Ko-lin. 1990. *Chinese Subculture and Criminality: Non-Traditional Crime Groups in America*. Westport, CT: Greenwood.

Chin, K., and J. Fagan. 1990. *The Impact of Crack on Drug and Crime Involvement*. Paper presented at the meeting of the American Society of Criminology, Baltimore, Maryland.

Clear, Todd. 1996. "Backfire: When Incarceration Increases Crime." In *The Unintended Consequences of Incarceration*, ed. K. Fulbright. New York: Vera Institute of Justice.

Cloward, Richard A., and Lloyd E. Ohlin. 1960. *Delinquency and Opportunity*. Glencoe, IL: Free Press.

Cohen, Albert K, and James F. Short Jr. 1958. "Research in Delinquent Subcultures." *Journal of Social Issues* 14 (3): 20–37.

Cohen, Stan. 1972. *Folk Devils and Moral Panic: The Creation of the Mods and Rockers*. London and New York: Routledge.

Coleman, James. 1957. *Community Conflict*. New York: Free Press.

Colvin, Richard Lee. 1995. "Dropout Rates Twice the State Average Education." *The Los Angeles Times*, 14 June.

Condor, Susan, and Rupert Brown. 1988. "Psychological Processes in Intergroup Conflict." In *The Social Psychology of Intergroup Conflict: Theory, Research, and Applications*, ed. Wolfgang Stroebe, Arie W. Kruglanski, Daniel Bar-Tal, and Miles Hewstone. Berlin: Springer Verlag.

Coolbaugh, K., and C. J. Hansel. 2000. *The Comprehensive Strategy: Lessons Learned from the Pilot Sites*. Bulletin. Washington, D.C.: U.S. Department of Justice, Office of Justice Programs, Office of Juvenile Justice and Delinquency Prevention.

Corbett, Ronal P. Jr., and Joan Petersilia. 1994. "What Works with Juvenile Offenders: A Synthesis of the Literature and Experience." *Federal Probation* 58 (4): 63–68.

Coser, Lewis. 1968. "Some Sociological Aspects of Conflict." In *International Encyclopedia of the Social Sciences*, ed. David L. Sills. New York: Free Press.

Cummings, Scott, and Daniel J. Monti. 1993. "Public Policy and Gangs: Social Sciences and the Urban Underclass." In *Gangs: The Origins and Impact of Contemporary Youth Gangs in the United States*, ed. Scott Cummings and Daniel J. Monti. Albany: State University of New York Press.

Cunningham, Lynn Craig. 1976. *Venice, California: From City to Suburb*. Doctoral dissertation, University of California at Los Angeles.

Currie, Elliot. 1998. *Crime and Punishment in America*. New York: Henry Holt.

Curry, G. David, Richard A. Ball, and Scott Decker. 1996. "Update on Gang Crime and Law Enforcement Record Keeping: Report of the 1994 NIJ Extended National Assessment Of Law Enforcement Anti-Gang Information Resources." Research Report. Washington, D.C.: U.S. Department of Justice.

Curry, G. David, Richard A. Ball, Robert J. Fox, and Darryl Stone. 1992. "National Assessment of Law Enforcement Anti-Gang Information Resources." Final Report. Washington, D.C.: U.S. Department of Justice.

Curry, G. David, and Scott Decker. 1998. *Confronting Gangs: Crime and Community*. Los Angeles: Roxbury.

Curry, G. D., and I. A. Spergel. 1992. "Gang Involvement and Delinquency among Hispanic and African-American Adolescent Males." *Journal of Research in Crime and Delinquency* 29: 273–91.

Dalessio, S. J., and L. Stolzenberg. 1995. "The Impact of Sentencing Guidelines on Jail Incarceration in Minnesota." *Criminology* 33 (2): 283–302.

———. 1997. "The Effect of Available Capacity on Jail Incarceration: An Empirical Test of Parkinson's Law." *Journal of Criminal Justice* 25 (4): 279–88.

De La Rosa, M., E. Y. Lambert, and B. Gropper, eds. 1990. *Drugs and Violence: Causes, Correlates, and Consequences.* NIDA Research Monograph No. 103. Rockville, MD: National Institute on Drug Abuse.

Decker, Scott. 1996. "Gangs and Violence: The Expressive Character of Collective Involvement." *Justice Quarterly* 11: 231–50.

DeFina, R. H., and T. M. Arvanites. 2002. "The Weak Effect of Imprisonment on Crime: 1971–1998." *Social Science Quarterly* 83 (3): 635–53.

Despres, Leo. 1975. *Ethnicity and Resource Competition in Plural Societies.* The Hague: Mouton.

Devine, Patricia, Kathleen Coolbaugh, and Susan Jenkins. 1998. "Disproportionate Minority Confinement: Lessons Learned from Five States." *Juvenile Justice Bulletin.* Washington, D.C.: U.S. Department of Justice, Office of Juvenile Justice and Delinquency Prevention.

Ditton, Paula M. 1999. *Mental Health and Treatment of Inmates and Probationers.* Washington, D.C.: U.S. Department of Justice, Bureau of Justice Statistics. *NCJ* 174463.

Dominguez, Virginia R. 1986. *White By Definition: Social Classification in Creole Louisiana.* New Brunswick, NJ: Rutgers University Press.

Donner, Frank. 1990. *Protectors of Privilege: Red Squads and Police Repression in Urban America.* Berkeley: University of California Press.

Dovidio, John F., Geoffrey Maruyama, and Michele G. Alexander. 1998. "A Social Psychology of National and International Group Relations." *Journal of Social Issues* 54 (4): 831–46.

Duchaine, Nina. 1979. *The Literature of Police Corruption.* Volume 2. New York: John Jay Press.

Edsall, Thomas Byrne, and Mary D. Edsall. 1991. *Chain Reaction: The Impact of Race, Rights, and Taxes on American Politics.* New York: W.W. Norton.

Erickson, T. H. 1993. *Ethnicity and Nationalism: Anthropological Perspectives.* London: Pluto Press.

Esman, Milton J. 1990. "Political and Psychological Factors in Ethnic Conflict." In *Conflict and Peacemaking in Multiethnic Societies,* ed. Joseph V. Montville. Lexington, MA: Lexington Books.

Esses, Victoria M., Lynne M. Jackson, and Tamara L. Armstrong. 1998. "Intergroup Competition and Attitudes toward Immigrants and Immigration: An Instrumental Model of Group Conflict." *Journal of Social Issues* 54 (4): 699–724.

Fagan, J. E. 1989. "The Social Organization of Drug Use and Drug Dealing among Urban Gangs." *Criminology* 27: 633–67.

———. 1996. "Gangs, Drugs, and Neighborhood Change." In *Gangs in America,* ed. C. Ronald Huff. Newbury Park, CA: Sage Publications.

Fagan, J., and K. Chin. 1989. "Initiation into Crack and Cocaine: A Tale of Two Epidemics." *Contemporary Drug Problems* 16: 579–618.

Felson, M. 1987. "Routine Activities and Crime Prevention in the Developing Metropolis." *Criminology* 25: 911–31.

Felson, M., and L. E. Cohen. 1980. "Human Ecology and Crime: A Routine Activities Approach. *Human Ecology* 4: 389–406.

Fleisher, Mark S., and Scott Decker. 2001. "Overview of the Challenge of Prison Gangs." *Corrections Management Quarterly* 5 (1): 1–9.

Fogelson, Robert M. 1967. *The Fragmented Metropolis: Los Angeles, 1850–1930.* Cambridge: Cambridge University Press.

Foucault, Michel. 1977. *Discipline and Punish: The Birth of the Prison.* Trans. Alan Sheridan. New York: Vintage Books. Originally published in 1975.

——. 1980. "Two Lectures." In *Power/Knowledge: Selected Interviews and Other Writings, 1972–1977*. New York: Pantheon.

Freer, Regina. 1994. "The Black-Korean Conflict." In *The Los Angeles Riots: Lessons for the Urban Future*, ed. Mark Baldesarre. Boulder, CO: Westview Press.

Frohock, Fred M. 1989. "Reasoning and Intractability." In *Intractable Conflicts and Their Transformation*, ed. Louis Kriesberg, Terrell Northrup, and Stuart Thorson. Syracuse, NY: Syracuse University Press.

Gamson, William A., and Andre Modigliani. 1989. "Media Discourse and Public Opinion on Nuclear Power: A Constructionist Model." *American Journal of Sociology* 95: 1–37.

Garvey, Megan, and Richard Winton. 2002. "City Declares War on Gangs." *The Los Angeles Times*, 4 December.

Gates, Daryl F., and Robert K. Jackson. 1990. "Gang Violence in L.A." *Police Chief* 20–22.

Genelin, Michael. 1993. "Gang Prosecutions: The Hardest Game in Town." In *The Gang Intervention Handbook*, ed. Arnold P. Goldstein and C. Ronald Huff. Champaign, IL: Research Press.

Glazer, Nathan, and Daniel A. Moynihan. 1963. *Beyond the Melting Pot*. Cambridge, MA: Harvard University Press.

Goffman, Erving. 1974. *Frame Analysis*. New York: Harper and Row.

Goldsmith, William W., and Edward J. Blakely. 1992. *Separate Societies: Poverty and Inequality in U.S. Cities*. Philadelphia: Temple University Press.

Goldstein, Arnold P., and C. Ronald Huff, eds. 1993. *The Gang Intervention Handbook*. Champaign, IL: Research Press.

Goldstein, P. J. 1985. "The Drugs/Violence Nexus: A Tripartite Conceptual Framework." *Journal of Drug Issues* 15: 493–506.

Goodwin, Stephanie A., Don Operario, and Susan T. Fiske. 1998. "Situational Power and Interpersonal Dominance Facilitate Bias and Inequality." *Journal of Social Issues* 54 (4): 677–98.

Gottfredson, Michael R., and Travis Hirschi. 1990. *A General Theory of Crime*. Stanford, CA: Stanford University Press.

Gregory, Derek, and John Urry, eds. 1985. *Social Relations and Spatial Structures*. New York: St. Martin's Press.

Haft, W. 2000. "More than Zero: The Cost of Zero Tolerance and the Case for Restorative Justice in Schools." *Denver University Law Review* 18 (4): 477–86.

Hagan, John. 1996. "The Next Generation: Children of Prisoners." In *The Unintended Consequences of Incarceration*, ed. K. Fulbright. New York: Vera Institute of Justice.

Hagedorn, John M. 1990. "Back in the Field Again: Gang Research in the Nineties." In *Gangs in America*, ed. C. Ronald Huff. Newbury Park, CA: Sage Publications.

——. 1991. "Gangs, Neighborhoods, and Public Policy." *Social Problems* 38 (4): 529–42.

——. 1998. "Gang Violence in the Post-industrial Era." In *Youth Violence: Crime and Justice*, ed. Michael Tonry and Mark H. Moore. Volume 24. Chicago: University of Chicago Press.

Hagedorn, John, with Perry Macon. 1988. *People and Folks: Gangs, Crime, and the Underclass in a Rustbelt City*. Chicago: Lake View Press.

Hall, Stuart. 1980. "Encoding/decoding." In *Culture, Media, Language: Working Papers in Cultural Studies*, ed. Centre for Contemporary Cultural Studies. London: Hutchinson.

Hall, Stuart, Chas Critcher, Tony Jefferson, John Clarke, and Brian Roberts. 1978. *Policing the Crisis: Mugging, the State, and Law and Order*. New York: Holmes and Meier.

Hamparian, D., and M. Leiber. 1997. *Disproportionate Confinement of Minority Juveniles in Secure Facilities: 1996 National Report*. Champaign, IL: Community Research Associates.

Harrison, Paige M., and Allen J. Beck. 2004. *Prisoners in 2003*. Bureau of Justice Statistics Bulletin. Washington, D.C.: U.S. Department of Justice, Office of Justice Programs.

Hatsukami, Dorothy K., and Marian W. Fischman. 1996. "Crack Cocaine and Cocaine Hydrochloride: Are the Differences Myth or Reality? *Journal of the American Medical Association* 276: 1580–88.

Hawkins, Darnell F., ed. 1995. *Ethnicity, Race, and Crime: Perspectives across Time and Place.* New York: State University of New York Press.

Hechter, M. 1975. *Internal Colonialism.* Berkeley, CA: University of California Press.

Hirschi, Travis, and Michael Gottfredson. 1983. "Age and the Explanation of Crime." *American Journal of Sociology* 89 (3): 552–84.

Hofman, John E. 1988. "Social Identity and Intergroup Conflict: An Israeli View." In *The Social Psychology of Intergroup Conflict: Theory, Research, and Applications,* ed. Wolfgang Stroebe, Arie W. Kruglanski, Daniel Bar-Tal, and Miles Hewstone. Berlin: Springer Verlag.

Horowitz, Donald L. 1983. "Racial Violence in the United States." In *Ethnic Pluralism and Public Policy: Achieving Equality in the United States and Britain,* ed. Nathan Glazer and Ken Young. London: Heinemann.

———. 1985. *Ethnic Groups in Conflict.* Berkeley: University of California Press.

Horowitz, Ruth. 1983. *Honor and the American Dream: Culture and Identity in a Chicano Community.* New Brunswick, NJ: Rutgers University Press.

Howell, James C. 2000. *Youth Gang Programs and Strategies.* Washington, D.C.: U.S. Department of Justice, Office of Juvenile Justice and Delinquency Prevention.

Howell, James C., and Scott H. Decker. 1999. "The Youth Gangs, Drugs, and Violence Connection." *OJJDP Juvenile Justice Bulletin.* Washington, D.C.: U.S. Department of Justice.

Hsia, H. M., and D. Hamparian. 1998. "Disproportionate Minority Confinement: 1997 Update." *Juvenile Justice Bulletin.* Washington, D.C.: U.S. Department of Justice, Office of Juvenile Justice and Delinquency Prevention.

Huff, C. Ronald. 1989. "Youth Gangs and Public Policy." *Crime and Delinquency* 35: 524–37.

———. 1996. "The Criminal Behavior of Gang Members and Nongang At-risk Youth." In *Gangs in America,* 2nd ed., ed. C. Ronald Huff. Thousand Oaks, CA: Sage Publications.

———, ed. 1990. *Gangs in America.* Newbury Park, CA: Sage Publications.

Huff, C. Ronald, and Wesley D. McBride. 1993. "Gangs and the Police." In *The Gang Intervention Handbook,* ed. Arnold P. Goldstein and C. Ronald Huff. Champaign, IL: Research Press.

Huff, C. Ronald, and Matthew Meyer. 1997. "Managing Prison Gangs and Other Security Threat Groups." *Corrections Management Quarterly* 1 (4): 10–18.

Hutson, H. R., D. Anglin, D. N. Kyriacou, J. Hart, and K. Spears. 1995. "The Epidemic of Gang-Related Homicides in Los Angeles County from 1979 through 1994." *JAMA* 274 (13): 1031–36.

Independent Commission on the Los Angeles Police Department. 1991. *Report of the Independent Commission on the Los Angeles Police Department.* Los Angeles, California.

Jackson, Pat, with Cary Rudman. 1993. "Moral Panic and the Response to Gangs in California." In *Gangs: The Origins and Impact of Contemporary Youth Gangs in the United States,* ed. S. Cummings and D. J. Monti. Albany: State University of New York Press.

Jackson, Peter. 1995. *Maps of Meaning.* London and New York: Routledge. First published in 1989.

Jackson, Robert K., and Wesley McBride. 1985. *Understanding Street Gangs.* Sacramento, CA: Custom Publishing.

Jacob, Herbert. 1984. *The Frustration of Policy: Responses to Crime by American Cities.* Boston: Little, Brown.

Jankowski, Martin Sanchez. 1991. *Island in the Street: Gangs and American Urban Society.* Berkeley: University of California Press.

Jennings, James. 1992. "New Urban Racial and Ethnic Conflicts in U.S. Politics." *Sage Race Relations Abstracts* 17(3).

Jennings, Keith, and Clarence Lusane. 1994. "The State and Future of Black/Latino Relations in Washington, D.C.: A Bridge in Need of Repair." In *Blacks, Latinos, and Asians in Urban America: Status and Prospects for Politics and Activism,* ed. James Jennings. Westport, CT: Praeger Publishers.

Katz, Jesse. 1991. "Gang Killings in L.A. County Top a Record 700." *The Los Angeles Times,* 8 December.

———. 1993a. "County's Yearly Gang Death Toll Reaches 800." *The Los Angeles Times,* 19 January.

———. 1993b. "Clashes between Latino, Black Gangs Increase." *The Los Angeles Times,* 26 December.

Katznelson, Ira. 1976. *Black Men, White Cities: Race, Politics, and Migration in the United States, 1900–30, and Britain, 1948–68.* Chicago: University of Chicago Press.

Kennedy, L. W., and S. W. Baron. 1993. "Routine Activities and a Subculture of Violence: A Study of Violence on the Street." *Journal of Research in Crime and Delinquency* 30 (1): 88–111.

Kim, Claire Jean. 2000. *Bitter Fruit: The Politics of Black-Korean Conflict in New York City.* New Haven, CT: Yale University Press.

Klein, Malcolm W. 1993. "Attempting Gang Control by Suppression: The Misuse of Deterrence Principles. Studies on Crime and Crime Prevention." *National Council for Crime Prevention* 2: 88–111.

———. 1995. *The American Street Gang: Its Nature, Prevalence, and Control.* New York: Oxford University Press.

Klein, Malcolm W., and Cheryl Lee Maxson. 1994. "Gangs and Crack Cocaine Trafficking." In *Drugs and Crime: Evaluating Public Policy Initiatives,* ed. Doris Layton MacKenzie and Craig D. Uchida. Thousand Oaks, CA: Sage Publications.

———. 1996. "Gang Structures, Crime Patterns, and Police Responses." Unpublished report. Los Angeles, CA: Social Science Research Institute, University of Southern California.

Klein, Malcolm W., C. L. Maxson, and L. C. Cunningham. 1991. "'Crack,' Street Gangs, and Violence." *Criminology* 29: 623–50.

Kriesberg, Louis, Terrell Northrup, and Stuart Thorson. 1989. *Intractable Conflicts and Their Transformation.* Syracuse, NY: Syracuse University Press.

Lakin, Martin. 1995. "Psychological Perspectives on Interracial and Interethnic Group Conflict and the Amelioration of Intergroup Tensions." In *Racial and Ethnic Conflict: Perspectives from the Social Disciplines,* ed. Joseph Gittler. Greenwich, CT: JAI Press.

Langan, Patrick A. 1991. "America's Soaring Prison Population." *Science* 251: 1568–73.

Langan, Patrick A., and David J. Levin. 2002. *Recidivism of Prisoners Released in 1994.* Special Report, Bureau of Justice Statistics. Washington, D.C.: U.S. Department of Justice.

Light, Donald, and John Speigel, eds. 1977. *The Dynamics of University Protest.* Chicago: Nelson-Hall.

Lipsky, Michael. 1980. *Street-Level Bureaucracy: Dilemmas of the Individual in Public Services.* New York: Russage Foundation.

Loftin, Colin. 1984. "Assaultive Violence as a Contagious Process." *Bulletin of the New York Academy of Medicine* 62: 550–55.

Los Angeles Police Department. 1989. *The Oakwood Plan.* Manuscript.

———. [1990?]. *Los Angeles Police Department Gang Awareness School Training Manual.* Mimeograph.

———. 1994. *Oakwood Community Safety Plan, Pacific Community Police Station, 1994 Update.* Manuscript.

———. n.d. *Violence, Money, and Street Gangs.* Manuscript issued by the Detective Support Division, Gang Information Section.

Mach, Zdzislaw. 1993. *Symbols, Conflict, and Identity: Essays in Political Anthropology.* New York: State University of New York Press.

March, James G., and Johan Olsen. 1984. "The New Institutionalism: Organizational Factors in Political Life." *American Political Science Review* 78 (3): 734–49.

Mauer, Marc, and Tracy Huling. 1995. *Young Black Americans and the Criminal Justice System: Five Years Later.* Washington, D.C.: The Sentencing Project.

Mauro, R., and M. Kubovy. 1992. "Caricature and Face Recognition." *Memory and Cognition* 20: 433–40.

Maxson, Cheryl. 1998. "Gang Homicide: A Review and Extension of the Literature." In *Homicide: A Sourcebook of Social Research,* ed. D. Smith and M. Zahn. Thousand Oaks, CA: Sage Publications.

McCarthy, Terry. 2001. "L.A. Gangs Are Back." *Time* 158(9): 46–50.

McCorkle, Richard C. 2002. *Panic: The Social Construction of the Street Gang Problem.* Upper Saddle River, NJ: Prentice Hall.

Melendez, Edwin. 1993. *Understanding Latino Poverty.* London: Sage Publications.

Meyer, Josh. 1994. "Pitchess on Front Line of Jail Race War." *The Los Angeles Times,* January 17.

Miller, Walter B. 1958. "Lower Class Culture as Generating Milieu of Gang Delinquency." *Journal of Social Issues* 24 (3): 5–19.

———. 1990. "Why the United States Has Failed to Solve its Youth Gang Problem." In *Gangs in America,* ed. C. Ronald Huff. Newbury Park, CA: Sage Publications.

Montgomery, Michael. 2005. "Locked Down: Gangs in the Supermax." American Public Media, American Radioworks. http://americanradioworks.publicradio.org/features/prisongangs/. Accessed 7 March 2005.

Moore, Joan W. 1978. *Homeboys: Gangs, Drugs, and Prison in the Barrios of Los Angeles.* Philadelphia: Temple University Press.

———. 1990. "Gangs, Drugs, and Violence." In *Drugs and Violence: Causes, Correlates, and Consequences,* ed. M. De La Rosa, E. Y. Lambert, and B. Gropper. Research Monograph No. 103. Rockville, MD: U.S. Department of Health and Human Services, National Institutes of Health, National Institute on Drug Abuse.

———. 1991. *Going Down to the Barrio: Homeboys and Homegirls in Change.* Philadelphia: Temple University Press.

———. 1993. "Gangs, Drugs, and Violence." In *Gangs: The Origins and Impact of Contemporary Youth Gangs in the United States,* ed. S. Cummings and D. J. Monti. Albany: State University of New York Press, 257–75.

———. 1996. "Bearing the Burden: How Incarceration Policies Weaken Inner-City Communities." In *The Unintended Consequences of Incarceration,* ed. K. Fulbright. New York: Vera Institute of Justice.

Moore, Joan W., and James Diego Vigil. 1989. "Chicano Gangs: Group Norms and Individual Factors Related to Adult Criminality." *Aztlán: A Journal of Chicano Studies* 18: 27–44.

Morain, Dan. 1996. "1 Inmate Killed, 13 Hurt in Prison Fight." *The Los Angeles Times,* September 28.

Murphy, Dean E. 1991. "Complaints against L.A. Police Set Record." *The Los Angeles Times,* October 17.

Nagel, Joane, and Susan Olzak. 1982. "Ethnic Mobilization in New and Old States: An Extension of the Competition Model." *Social Problems* 30: 127–43.

National Institute on Drug Abuse. 1991. *National Household Survey on Drug Abuse: Population Estimates 1990.* Washington, D.C.: U.S. Government Printing Office.

Needle, Jerome A., and William Vaughan Stapleton. 1983. *Police Handling of Youth Gangs.* Washington, D.C.: American Justice Institute.

Niblack, Preston, and Peter Stan. 1992. "Financing Public Services in Los Angeles." In *Urban America: Policy Choices for Los Angeles and the Nation*, ed. James B. Steinberg et al. Los Angeles: RAND.

Nielsen, F. 1985. "Ethnic Solidarity in Modern Societies." *American Sociological Review* 50: 133–45.

Northrup, Terrell A. 1989. "The Dynamic of Identity in Personal and Social Conflict." In *Intractable Conflicts and Their Transformation*, ed. Louis Kriesberg, Terrell Northrup, and Stuart Thorson. Syracuse, NY: Syracuse University Press.

Office of Juvenile Justice and Delinquency Prevention. 1991. *Children in Custody 1989 (NCJ-127189)*. Washington, D.C.: U.S. Department of Justice.

——. 1998. *OJJDP Annual Report*. Washington, D.C.: U.S. Department of Justice.

——. 2000a. *OJJDP Annual Report*. Washington, D.C.: U.S. Department of Justice.

——. 2000b. *State Custody Rates*. Washington, D.C.: U.S. Department of Justice.

Ogbu, John. 1990. "Minority Status and Literacy in Comparative Perspective." *Daedalus* 119: 141–68.

Okamura, Jonathan. 1981. "Situational Ethnicity." *Ethnic and Racial Studies* 4: 452–63.

Oliver, Melvin L., and James Johnson Jr. 1984. "Interethnic Conflict in an Urban Ghetto: The Case of Blacks and Latinos in Los Angeles." *Social Movements, Conflicts, and Change* 6: 57–94.

Oliver, Melvin L., and Thomas M. Shapiro. 1995. *Black Wealth/White Wealth: A New Perspective on Racial Inequality*. New York: Routledge.

Olzak, Susan. 1992. *The Dynamics of Ethnic Competition and Conflict*. Stanford: Stanford University Press.

Olzak, Susan, and Joan Nagel, eds. 1986. *Competitive Ethnic Relations*. Orlando: Academic Press.

Omi, Michael, and Howard Winant. 1994. *Racial Formation in the United States: From the 1960s to the 1990s*. New York: Routledge and Kegan Paul.

Ong, Paul. 1994. *The State of Asian Pacific America: Economic Diversity, Issues, and Policies*. Los Angeles: LEAP Asian Pacific Public Policy Institute and UCLA Asian American Studies Center.

Paden, John N. 1970. "Urban Pluralism, Integration and Adaptation of Communal Identity in Kano, Nigeria." In *From Tribe to Nation in Africa: Studies in Incorporation Processes*, ed. R. Cohen and J. Middleton. Scranton, NJ: Chandler Publishing.

Padilla, Felix M. 1992. *The Gang as an American Enterprise*. New Brunswick, NJ: Rutgers University Press.

Park, Hae Won. 1995. *The Harlins/Du Story: "Race" as Marker in the Rhetorical Construction of Reality*. Unpublished manuscript.

Park, Kyeyoung. 1996. "Use and Abuse of Race and Culture: Black-Korean Tension in America." *American Anthropologist* 98 (3): 492–99.

Park, Robert Ezra. 1950. *Race and Culture*. Glencoe, IL: Free Press.

Parsons, Talcott. 1951. *The Social System*. Glencoe, IL: Free Press.

Petersilia, Joan. 2000. *When Prisoners Return to the Community: Political, Economic, and Social Consequences. Sentencing and Corrections: Issues for the 21st Century*. Papers from the Executive Sessions on Sentencing and Corrections, Department of Justice, National Institute of Justice, Office of Justice Programs.

Pinderhughes, Howard. 1997. *Race in the Hood: Conflict and Violence among Urban Youth*. Minneapolis: University of Minnesota Press.

Ralph, P., R. J. Hunter, J. W. Marquart, S. J. Cuvelier, and D. Merlanos. 1996. "Exploring the Differences between Gang and Non-Gang Prisoners." In *Gangs in America*, ed. C. R. Huff. Newbury Park, CA: Sage.

Ramos, George. 1996. "U.S. Uses Racketeering Law to Fight Mexican Mafia." *The Los Angeles Times*, 2 December.

Redding, R. E. 1999. "Juvenile Offenders in Criminal Court and Adult Prison: Legal, Psychological, and Behavioral Outcomes." *Juvenile and Family Court Journal* 50 (1): 1–20.

Reinarman, Craig, and Harry G. Levine. 1997. "The Crack Attack: Politics and Media in the Crack Scare." In *Crack in America: Demon Drugs and Social Justice,* ed. Craig Reinarman and Harry G. Levine. Berkeley, CA: University of California Press.

Reiner, Ira. 1992. *Gangs, Crime, and Violence in Los Angeles: Findings and Proposals from the District Attorney's Office.* County of Los Angeles.

Rennison, Callie Marie, and Michael R. Rand. 2003. *Criminal Victimization, 2002.* Washington, D.C.: U.S. Department of Justice, Bureau of Justice Statistics. *NCJ* 199994.

Rhodes, G., S. Brennan, and S. Carey. 1987. "Identification and Ratings of Caricatures: Implications for Mental Representations of Faces." *Cognitive Psychology* 19: 473–97.

Robinson, W. W. 1939. *Ranchos Become Cities.* Pasadena, CA: San Pasqual Press.

Romer, Daniel, Kathleen H. Jamieson, Catharine Reigner, Mika Emori, and Brigette Rouson. 1997. "Blame Discourse versus Realistic Conflict as Explanations of Ethnic Tension in Urban Neighborhoods." *Political Communication* 14: 273–91.

Rothmiller, Mike, and Ivan G. Goldman. 1992. *L.A. Secret Police: Inside the Elite Spy Network.* New York: Pocket Books.

Ryan, Stephen. 1990. *Ethnic Conflict and International Relations.* Aldershot, England: Dartmouth.

Saito, Leland. 1993. "Asian Americans and Latinos in San Gabriel Valley, California: Interethnic Political Cooperation and Redistricting, 1990–92." *Amerasia Journal* 19 (2): 55–68.

Sanchez-Jankowski, Martin. 1991. *Islands in the Street: Gangs and American Urban Society.* Berkeley: University of California Press.

Schattschneider, E. E. 1960. *The Semisovereign People: A Realist's View of Democracy in America.* New York: Holt, Rinehart, and Winston.

Schindler, M., and J. A. Arditti. 2001. "The Increased Prosecution of Adolescents in the Adult Criminal Justice System: Impacts on Youth, Family, and Community." *Marriage and Family Review* 32 (3–4): 165–87.

Sekou, F., and R. Seltzer. "Conflicts in the Coalition: Challenges to Black and Latino Political Alliances." *Western Journal of Black Studies* 26 (2): 75–89.

Serrano, Richard A. 1992. "'They Hit Me, So I Hit Back'; The Christopher Commission Spoke of 44 'Problem Officers' in the LAPD." *The Los Angeles Times,* 4 October.

Shaw, David. 1992. "Media Failed to Examine Alleged LAPD Abuses." *The Los Angeles Times,* 26 May.

Shön, Donald A., and Martin Rein. 1994. *Frame Reflection: Toward the Resolution of Intractable Policy Controversies.* New York: Basic Books.

Shuster, Beth. 2000. "Sheriff's Department Seeks Solution to Race Riots in Jails." *The Los Angeles Times,* 9 May.

Sickmund, Melissa. 1997. "The Juvenile Delinquency Probation Caseload, 1985–1994." Fact Sheet #54, Office of Juvenile Justice and Delinquency Prevention. Washington, D.C.: U.S. Department of Justice.

Skiba, R. J., and R. L. Peterson. 2000. "School Discipline at a Crossroads: From Zero Tolerance to Early Response." *Exceptional Children* 66 (3): 335–46.

Skolnick, Jerome. 1990. "The Social Structure of Street Drug Dealing." *American Journal of Police* 9: 1–41.

Skolnick, J. H., T. Correl, E. Navarro, and R. Rabb. 1988. *The Social Structure of Street Drug Dealing.* Report to the Office of the Attorney General of the State of California. Sacramento, CA: California Department of Justice.

Smith, C. P., T. E. Black, and F. R. Campbell. 1979. *A National Assessment of Case Disposition and Classification in the Juvenile Justice System: Inconsistent Labeling, vol. 1.* Sacramento, CA: American Justice Institute.

Snell, Tracy L. 1995. "Correctional Populations in the United States, 1993." Washington, D.C.: U.S. Department of Justice, Bureau of Justice Statistics *NCJ* 156241:12.

Soja, Edward W. 1987. "Economic Restructuring and the Internationalization of the Los Angeles Region." In *The Capitalist City: Global Restructuring and Community Politics,* ed. Michael Peter Smith and Joe R. Feagin. New York: Basil Blackwell.

Spergel, Irving A. 1995. *The Youth Gang Problem: A Community Approach.* New York and Oxford: Oxford University Press.

Spergel, I. A., R. Chance, C. Ehrensaft, T. Regulus, C. Kane, R. Laseter, A. Alexander, and S. Oh. 1994. *Gang Suppression and Intervention: Community Models.* Washington, D.C.: U.S. Department of Justice, Office of Juvenile Justice and Delinquency Prevention.

Spergel, Irving A., and G. David Curry. 1990. "Strategies and Perceived Agency Effectiveness in Dealing with the Youth Gang Problem." In *Gangs in America,* ed. C. Ronald Huff. Newbury Park, CA: Sage.

——. 1993. "The National Youth Gang Survey: A Research and Development Process." In *Gang Intervention Handbook,* ed. Arnold Goldstein and C. Ronald Huff. Champaign, IL: Research Press, 359–400.

Spergel, I. A., G. D. Curry, C. Kane, R. Chance, R. Ross, A. Alexander, P. Rodriguez, D. Seed, and E. Simmons. 1989. *Youth Gangs: Problem and Response.* Draft report of the National Gang Suppression and Intervention Project. Chicago: University of Chicago, School of Social Service Administration.

Stapleton, W. V., and J. A. Needle. 1982. *Police Handling of Youth Gangs.* Sacramento, CA: American Justice Institute.

Starr, Kevin. 1994. "Violence in Utopia: What the Venice Gang Killings Mean to L.A." *The Los Angeles Times,* July 3.

Stone, Deborah. 1997. *Policy Paradox: The Art of Political Reason.* New York: W. W. Norton.

Tajfel, Henri. 1981. *Human Groups and Social Categories: Studies in Social Psychology.* Cambridge: Cambridge University Press.

——. 1982. "Social Psychology of Intergroup Relations." *Annual Review of Psychology* 33: 1–39.

Takaki, Ronald. 1993. *A Different Mirror: A History of Multicultural America.* Boston: Little, Brown.

Tamaki, Julie. 1996. "Changes in Jail System Underlie Pitchess Brawls." *The Los Angeles Times,* January 21.

Taylor, Carl. 1990. *Dangerous Society.* East Lansing: Michigan State University.

Thomas, Bernard. 1992. *The Cycle of Juvenile Justice.* New York: Oxford University Press.

Thornberry, Terence P., Marvin D. Krohn, Alan J. Lizoutte, Carolyn A. Smith, and Kimberly Tobin. 2003. *Gangs and Delinquency in Developmental Perspective.* Cambridge and New York: Cambridge University Press.

Thrasher, Frederic M. 1927. *The Gang: A Study of 1,313 Gangs in Chicago.* Chicago: University of Chicago Press.

Tonry, Michael. 1995. *Malign Neglect: Race, Crime, and Punishment in America.* New York: Oxford University Press.

——. 1999. "Why Are U.S. Incarceration Rates So High?" *Crime and Delinquency* 45 (4): 419–37.

Travis, Jeremy, and Michelle Waul. 2002. *Reflections on the Crime Decline: Lessons for the Future?* Proceedings from the Urban Institute Crime Decline Forum. Washington, D.C.: Urban Institute, Justice Policy Center.

Turner, John C. 1982. "Towards a Cognitive Redefinition of the Social Group." In *The Social Dimension: European Developments in Social Psychology,* ed. Henri Tajfel. Volume 2. Cambridge and Paris: Cambridge University Press and Editions de la Maison des Sciences de l'Homme.

——. 1984. "Social Categorization and the Self-Concept: A Social Cognitive Theory of

Group Behavior." In *Advances in Group Processes: Theory and Research*, ed. E. J. Lawler. Volume 2. Greenwich, CT: JAI.

Umemoto, Karen. 1994. "Blacks and Koreans in Los Angeles: The Case of LaTasha Harlins and Soon Ja Du." In *Blacks, Latinos, and Asians in Urban America: Status and Prospects for Politics and Activism*, ed. James Jennings. Westport, CT: Praeger.

Umemoto, Karen, and C. Kimi Mikami. 1999. "A Profile of Race-Bias Hate Crimes in Los Angeles County." *Western Criminology Review* 2(2). Available from wcr.Sonoma.edu/v2n2/v2n2.html.

U.S. Department of Justice. 1984. *Sourcebook of Criminal Justice Statistics*. Washington, D.C.: Bureau of Justice Statistics.

———. 1988. *Sourcebook of Criminal Justice Statistics*. Washington, D.C.: Bureau of Justice Statistics.

———. 1989a. *Children in Custody, 1975–1985: Census of Public and Private Juvenile Detention, Correctional, and Shelter Facilities (NCJ-114065)*. Washington, D.C.: Bureau of Justice Statistics.

———. 1989b. *Communitywide Responses Crucial for Dealing with Youth Gangs*. Washington, D.C.: Office of Juvenile Justice and Delinquency Prevention, U.S. Department of Justice.

———. 1992a. *Sourcebook of Criminal Justice Statistics*. Washington, D.C.: Bureau of Justice Statistics.

———. 1992b. *Statistical Report/U.S. Attorney's Office*. Washington, D.C.: Bureau of Justice Statistics.

———. 1994. *Violent Crime Control and Law Enforcement Act of 1994*. U.S. Department of Justice Fact Sheet. *NCJ* FS000067. http://www.ncjrs.org/txtfiles/billfs.txt. Accessed 31 January 2005.

———. 2004a. "Number of Sentenced Inmates Incarcerated under State and Federal Jurisdiction per 100,000 Population." http://www.ojp.usdoj.gov/bjs/glance/tables/incrttab.htm#top. Accessed 31 January 2005.

———. 2004b. "Number of Persons Under Correctional Supervision." http://www.ojp.usdoj.gov/bjs/glance/tables/corr2tab.htm. Accessed 31 January 2005.

———. 2004c. "Percent of Adults Under Correctional Supervision by Race, 1986–97." http://www.ojp.usdoj.gov/bjs/glance/tables/cpracepttab.htm.

———. 2004d. "Jail Incarceration Rates by Race and Ethnicity, 1990–2003." http://www.ojp.usdoj.gov/bjs/glance/jailrair.htm. Accessed 31 January 2005.

U.S. House of Representatives. 1992. *Bureau of Alcohol, Tobacco and Firearms' Proposal for a Gang Information Network*. Hearing before the Subcommittee on Civil and Constitutional Rights of the Committee of the Judiciary, House of Representatives, 102nd Congress, 26 June 1992. Washington, D.C.: U.S. Government Printing Office.

Venkatesh, Sudhir Alladi. 1996. "The Gang and the Community." In *Gangs in America*, 2d ed., ed. C. Ronald Huff. Thousand Oaks, CA: Sage.

———. 1997. "The Social Organization of Street Gang Activity in an Urban Ghetto." *American Journal of Sociology* 101: 82–111.

Verdugo, R. R. 2002. "Race-Ethnicity, Social Class, and Zero-Tolerance Policies: The Cultural and Structural Wars." *Education and Urban Society* 35 (1): 50–75.

Vigil, James Diego. 1988. *Barrio Gangs: Street Life and Identity in Southern California*. Austin: University of Texas Press.

———. 2003. "Urban Violence and Street Gangs." *Annual Review of Anthropology* 32: 225–42.

Vigil, James Diego, and John M. Long. 1990. "Emic and Etic Perspectives of Gang Culture: The Chicano Case." In *Gangs in America*, ed. C. Ronald Huff. Newbury Park, CA: Sage.

Walmsley, Roy. 1999. "World Prison Population List." Research Findings, No. 88. Canberra, Australia: Home Office Research, Development and Statistics Directorate, Australian Institute of Criminology. http://www.aic.gov.au/stats/international/wpl.html. Accessed 17 February 2005.

———. 2001. "World Prison Population List." Research Findings, No. 166. Canberra, Australia: Home Office Research, Development and Statistics Directorate, Australian Institute of Criminology. http://www.aic.gov.au/stats/international/wpl.html. Accessed 17 February 2005.

Wasserman, G. A., L. S. Miller, and L. Cothern. 2000. *Prevention of Serious and Violent Juvenile Offending*. SVJ Bulletin. Washington, D.C.: U.S. Department of Justice, Office of Justice Programs, Office of Juvenile Justice and Delinquency Prevention.

Waters, Anita M. 1985. *Race, Class, and Political Symbols*. New Brunswick, NJ: Transaction Books.

Waters, Mary C. 1992. "Ethnic and Racial Groups in the USA: Conflict and Cooperation." Paper presented at the International Conference on Ethnic Conflicts, Autonomy, and the Devolution of Power in Multi-ethnic States. Moscow, 2–5 March.

Wilson, James Q., and G. L. Kelling. 1982. "Broken Windows: The Police and Neighborhood Safety." *The Atlantic Monthly*, March.

Winton, Richard. 2003. "Crime Edges Up in State." *The Los Angeles Times*, 28 April.

Wolfgang, M. E., and F. Ferracuti. 1967. *The Subculture of Violence*. London: Tavistock.

Young, Iris Marion. 1995. "Difference as a Resource for Democratic Communication." In *Deliberative Democracy*, ed. James Bohman and William Rehg. Cambridge, MA: MIT Press.

———. 2000. *Inclusion and Democracy*. Oxford and New York: Oxford University Press.

Zimring, Franklin E. 1996. "Kids, Guns, and Homicide: Policy Notes on an Age-Specific Epidemic." *Law and Contemporary Problems* 59: 261–74.

Index